THE BIG BOOK OF
POTLUCK

THE BIG BOOK OF POTLUCK

maryana vollstedt

GOOD FOOD—AND LOTS OF IT—
FOR PARTIES, GATHERINGS, AND ALL OCCASIONS

CHRONICLE BOOKS
SAN FRANCISCO

TEXT COPYRIGHT © 2003 BY MARYANA VOLLSTEDT.
COVER PHOTOGRAPH COPYRIGHT © 2003 BY LEIGH BEISCH.
ILLUSTRATIONS COPYRIGHT © 2003 BY MICHAEL MANNING.
ALL RIGHTS RESERVED. NO PART OF THIS BOOK MAY BE
REPRODUCED IN ANY FORM WITHOUT WRITTEN PERMISSION
FROM THE PUBLISHER.

LIBRARY OF CONGRESS CATALOGING-IN-PUBLICATION DATA AVAILABLE.

ISBN 978-0-8118-3818-4

MANUFACTURED IN CANADA.

DESIGNED BY EUN YOUNG LEE
PROP STYLING BY SARA SLAVIN
FOOD STYLING BY KATRINA NORWOOD
TYPESETTING BY KRISTEN WURZ

10 9 8 7 6 5 4 3

CHRONICLE BOOKS LLC
680 SECOND STREET
SAN FRANCISCO, CALIFORNIA 94107

WWW.CHRONICLEBOOKS.COM

DEDICATION

Again, to my husband, Reed, who is my advisor, tester, shopper, computer person, confidant, manager, and best friend. He has encouraged and supported me throughout my years of writing cookbooks. My books are really a team effort, and I couldn't have written them without him. Thank you, Reed. Also to Julie, Scott, Gregg, and Jon, who, for about as long as they can remember, have been eating their mother's test recipes.

ACKNOWLEDGMENTS

Thanks again to Bill LeBlond, editorial director of cookbooks at Chronicle Books, who suggested the idea for my fourth "Big Book," *The Big Book of Potluck,* to follow on the heels of *The Big Book of Breakfast, The Big Book of Casseroles,* and *The Big Book of Soups and Stews*. To Amy Treadwell at Chronicle Books for her help and advice during the writing of the book; to Deborah J. Kops for her expert copyediting, additions, and suggestions for the book; and to the Chronicle Books staff.

Special thanks to Brian Crow for his computer consulting, and to Donna Addison and Len Heffel for their help with recipe testing. I'm also grateful to neighbors, friends, and family who came to my potluck dinners.

CONTENTS

:: PREFACE

My husband, Reed, and I belong to a gourmet group of five couples who have been "potlucking" together every New Year's Eve for over thirty-five years. It all started when a local restaurant offered an elegant and lavish Alexandre Dumas theme dinner that was featured in *Esquire* magazine. The cost was forty-five dollars per person, which, at that time, was very expensive. We all said, "We can do that ourselves," and so the tradition began. Since then, we've held New Year's Eve gourmet dinners in our homes, with each couple contributing one or two dishes for the six- to eight-course meal. If we have a theme, it is usually ethnic, and we try to make something we have never made before. We make the event very formal, with the hosts using their finest dinnerware, linens, and silver. The women dress up, and one year the men even wore tuxedos!

Each dinner begins late, with a long cocktail hour featuring drinks and fancy hors d'oeuvres. Then each course is served slowly and carefully timed so dessert is served just before we welcome in the New Year.

Maybe this book will help inspire you to start a tradition, too.

The Big Book of Potluck is a collection of more than 275 exciting recipes suitable for potlucks on all occasions. Rediscovering some of your old favorites will bring back fond memories and make you want to try them all over again. The book also includes ethnic-inspired dishes as well as new and creative recipes and ideas for contemporary potlucks.

Many of the recipes include suggestions for complementary side dishes to help you plan your potluck. Also included here are guidelines for a successful potluck: helpful tips for the host and guests; theme ideas; serving suggestions; appropriate dishes; picnic essentials; tips on transporting dishes; and important food safety tips.

The recipes that follow are easy and practical, with straightforward directions that will appeal to all cooks. Most of the ingredients are either conveniently on hand or are readily available. Enjoy!

THE ART OF POTLUCK

A potluck is a shared meal to which everyone brings a contribution. At one time, *potluck* meant taking the luck of the day's pot. The dictionary says a potluck is "whatever food happens to be available, especially when offered to a guest." Whatever the meaning, it is a time for camaraderie, fellowship, and great food.

TYPES OF POTLUCKS

Potlucks have been popular for church suppers, meetings, and reunions for many years. Today potlucks are part of a wide variety of social events, such as tailgate parties, dinner parties, gourmet clubs, card clubs, showers, barbecues, picnics, office parties, brunches, farewell parties, anniversaries, singles' parties, block parties, and holiday dinners. They are also popular at rallies (whether political or religious), fundraisers, and business meetings.

A potluck can be large or small, formal or informal and casual, planned or impromptu. They can be whatever you want them to be.

WHY HOLD A POTLUCK?

- They are relaxed, carefree, casual, and fun.
- Everyone has a good time.
- They save time, energy, and expense.
- They offer a variety of great food.
- They appeal to people of any age, gender, or background.
- They are an easy way to entertain.
- They're a convenient way to feed a crowd.
- There's minimal cleanup afterward.

PICK A THEME FOR YOUR POTLUCK

Themes for potlucks are fun and festive, but they are optional. They help you to determine the food, dress, décor, and music. Here are some theme suggestions to get you started:

- International potlucks: Mexican, Italian, Asian, Moroccan, French, Japanese, Hawaiian, all-American (or regional American), etc.
- Holidays or seasonal potlucks: Fourth of July, Harvest Party, Warm and Cozy Winter, Spring Fling.
- Wine and hors d'oeuvre potlucks: Guests bring a bottle of wine and hearty hors d' oeuvres to take the place of dinner.
- Soup and salad potlucks: Assign several people to bring different soups or salads. Others can bring assorted breads, wine, or other drinks.
- Era parties: The Roaring '20s, the Fabulous '50s, etc.
- All-dessert potlucks: Time to splurge with your most decadent treat.
- All-ages parties: Foods that appeal to both adults and kids. (Macaroni and cheese is a must.)
- New foods potlucks: Each guest uses a recipe or ingredient that he or she has never made or tasted before.
- Favorite recipe nights: Everyone brings their all-time favorite recipes, along with printed recipe cards to share.
- Teenage parties: Teenagers plan food and music.
- Sports: A Super Bowl potluck party can be fun and easily accommodate sports fans, food fanatics, and hungry kids. The host can provide a huge pot of chili and the guests bring accompaniments such as home-baked bread, salads, and scrumptious desserts.
- Progressive dinners: A sort of reverse potluck, where guests travel from home to home, enjoying a single course at each stop.

POTLUCK LOCATIONS

Potlucks can be held in churches, schools, public buildings, community halls, private clubs, homes, backyards, parks, or almost anywhere else people assemble to share food.

POTLUCK FOODS

In the past, our grandmothers and mothers made dishes from scratch to show off their prized recipes. Then they would hover over the serving table to see if everyone was eating their contribution, and worry if they weren't. Later, with the improved quality of deli food, take-out food became a popular trend for potlucks, especially at last-minute affairs. Today, potluck fare seems to be returning to homemade and satisfying comfort food made with fresh ingredients.

Variety is the key to a good potluck. At a small gathering, specific dishes can be assigned to round out the menu and avoid duplicate dishes. If the group is on the large side, the alphabet can be divided into sections, such as main courses, salads, side dishes, and desserts. Those whose last names begin with a letter in a designated section bring that assigned course.

Your potluck contribution should be appropriate for the occasion. Casseroles are a popular choice because they transport well and are easy to serve. For a general potluck, especially if you don't know the tastes of the other guests, stick to the basic and familiar dishes. Avoid rich, overly spicy, or exotic foods. But if the theme is gourmet, by all means bring a creative dish. Take along appropriate garnishes and serving pieces to go with your dish. Provide a small sign with the name of the recipe, and list the ingredients in case anyone has food allergies.

POTLUCK ACTIVITIES

Eating and conversation are the main activities at a potluck, but other activities can add to the fun, depending on the location.
- In the home: board games or other games, singing, and dancing.
- In a church or hall: speeches, singing, dancing, other entertainment, and programs.
- At a picnic: horseshoes, badminton, races, croquet, softball, contests, swimming, and boating.

GUIDELINES FOR POTLUCKS AT HOME

The smart host provides a clean house and lets the guests do the cooking!

TIPS FOR THE HOST

- Give yourself enough time to plan.
- Determine the number of guests, and plan accordingly. Be sure there will be enough food, but not too much.
- Invite guests by invitation or phone early so they have time to shop and to prepare their contributions.
- The host often provides the main course and assigns guests to bring complementary side dishes and dessert.
- There is more than one way to contribute to the party. Those guests who are too busy to cook (or are culinarily challenged) can bring drinks, fresh bread or rolls, condiments, or flowers.
- Vegetarians may need to be accommodated.

DUTIES OF THE POTLUCK HOST

- Carry out the theme, if your potluck has one, with appropriate decorations.
- Set the table (buffet style works well) with linens or mats, dishes, flatware, flowers, and candles. Extra tables may be set up around the house.
- Provide space for guests' coats and accessories.
- Provide nametags if there are strangers at the potluck or if the gathering is especially large.
- Make sure there is a cleared work area in the kitchen for dishes and last-minute preparation.
- Provide microwave, stovetop, oven, and refrigerator space, if needed for last minute preparations.
- Provide condiments, as well as extra serving utensils for those who forgot or didn't think to bring these items.
- Label the dishes as they arrive with their contents. It's always nice for the guests to know what they are eating
- Stock a bar with beverages, both alcoholic and nonalcoholic. Provide coffee, tea, punch, and bottled water.
- Set the mood with background music that fits the occasion.

TIPS FOR THE POTLUCK GUEST

- Keep your contribution simple and appropriate. Most dishes should require minimal last-minute preparation or warm-up. Do not add extra confusion in the kitchen.
- Choose a dish that is easily transported.
- Let the host know ahead of time if you need oven, microwave, or refrigerator space.
- Bring your contribution in the dish in which it is to be served, and don't forget serving utensils. Bring the recipe if it's requested.
- Keep in mind the number of guests you will be serving. For a large potluck, a dish that usually serves six will serve eight or ten. For small potlucks, keep in mind how many people are bringing the same course, and size yours accordingly.
- Make yourself available to help the host with last-minute preparation, and definitely help clean up.

GUIDELINES FOR POTLUCK PICNICS AND OTHER OUTINGS

- Find out ahead of time what facilities are available. Some picnic sites are equipped with electrical outlets, running water, barbecues, restrooms, garbage cans, and areas for games.
- Make a "plan B" for inclement weather.
- Keep perishable foods in insulated chests until you're ready to eat. Take along these essentials: coolers and ice, tables, folding chairs, blankets, an easy-care tablecloth, plates, cups, plastic glasses, flatware, servers, sharp knives, a corkscrew, a can opener, a cutting board, condiments, and drinks. Don't forget damp cloths or towelettes, extra towels, and cartons for leftovers. Take large garbage bags if trash cans are not available. You may need to bring water if you're eating in a remote location. Don't forget games and music.

GUIDELINES FOR POTLUCKS HELD IN PUBLIC BUILDINGS

If you are in charge of a large potluck held in a church, school, or community hall, check the facility for proper kitchen equipment: ensure the facility has a stove, refrigerator, coffeemakers, tables, chairs, table service, trays, towels, serving utensils, and, hopefully, a dishwasher. In some cases, paper goods can be used, or you can ask guests to bring their own table service. Be sure there is a cleanup crew who will leave the building in good condition.

TIPS FOR TRANSPORTING FOOD TO A POTLUCK

- To transport food a short distance, place the dish in a basket or box and pack towels or newspapers around the dish to prevent it from sliding or spilling. Quilted carriers are also available.
- If you are traveling more than a half an hour, pack hot food in an insulated chest, or wrap in foil and several layers of newspapers or a thermal blanket (food will stay hot for several hours).

FOOD SAFETY TIPS

Observe these food safety tips if you're traveling a long distance.

- Keep hot foods hot and cold foods cold. Keeping food at an unsafe temperature promotes the growth of bacteria that can cause food poisoning.
- Transport cold food in a cooler with ice or frozen gel packs, and hot food in an insulated chest.
- Use a separate cooler for drinks so the cooler holding food will not have to be opened often.
- Place the cooler in an air-conditioned car, not in the trunk. (Trunks can get very hot, especially in warm weather.)
- Refrigerate leftover food immediately.

Now that you are prepared, get ready for a great potluck and have fun!

Start the potluck out right with several savory hors d'oeuvres to serve with drinks as an introduction to dinner. The Cream Cheese–Stuffed Mushrooms (page 32) will melt in the mouth, and Hot Wings (page 30) are sure to be a hit. Country Chicken Pâté (page 39) can be made ahead, and so can Marinated Roasted Red Peppers on Crostini (page 37).

If you are planning a cocktail party, include a variety of contrasting flavors and textures, some hot and some cold. For a wine and hors d'oeuvres potluck, the hors d'oeuvres should be hearty and satisfying because they usually replace dinner.

HORS D'OEUVRES AND APPETIZERS

CHUTNEY CHEESE BALL

Chutney is an East Indian condiment containing fruit, vinegar, sugar, and spices. Here it is combined with cream cheese to add a spicy flavor to the cheese ball. Serve as an hors d'oeuvre, followed by Roasted Moroccan Chicken with Dates and Apricots (page 269).

1	package (8 ounces) cream cheese, cut into chunks
1	green onion, including some tender green tops, coarsely chopped
1	garlic clove, minced
1/4	cup chutney, preferably Major Grey's
1/4	teaspoon salt
1/4	cup finely chopped pecans
	Apple slices for serving
	Water wafers for serving

Put all ingredients, except pecans, apples, and wafers, in a food processor and process until well blended. Scrape down the sides of the bowl. Transfer to a piece of plastic wrap and refrigerate several hours. Form cheese mixture into a ball.

Put nuts on a piece of waxed paper and roll the cheese ball in the nuts. Place on a plate and arrange apple slices and wafers around the cheese ball. Provide a small knife for spreading.

MAKES ONE 3-INCH CHEESE BALL

DILLED CRAB SPREAD

For the best flavor, try to get fresh crab to make this popular spread. If it is unavailable, frozen crabmeat can be used. Serve this with assorted crackers or crudités.

1   cup crabmeat, flaked

1/2   cup mayonnaise

1/4   cup sour cream or plain nonfat yogurt

1   teaspoon dried dillweed

2   green onions, including some tender green tops, finely chopped

1   teaspoon fresh lemon juice

   Dash of Tabasco sauce

1/4   teaspoon salt

In a small bowl, mix together all ingredients. Cover and chill several hours before serving.

MAKES ABOUT 1 3/4 CUPS

ROASTED RED PEPPER SPREAD

For an elegant potluck buffet, serve this flavorful spread of roasted peppers, cream cheese, and herbs with a variety of crackers.

1   large red bell pepper, roasted (see Note) and cut into chunks

2   garlic cloves, coarsely chopped

3   ounces cream cheese at room temperature, cut into chunks

2   parsley sprigs

1/4   teaspoon dried oregano

1/4   teaspoon dried basil

1/4   teaspoon paprika

1/4   teaspoon salt

2   drops of Tabasco sauce

Put all ingredients in a food processor or blender and blend until smooth. Transfer to a bowl, cover, and refrigerate several hours until well chilled.

MAKES ABOUT 1 CUP

Note: To roast a bell pepper, halve it lengthwise and remove seeds and ribs. Preheat broiler. Make several 1-inch slits in each pepper half. Place, skin-side up, on an aluminum foil–lined baking sheet. Press pepper halves down with the palm of your hand to flatten. Broil 4 inches from the heat until skin is charred, about 10 minutes. Remove from broiler, fold foil tightly over pepper, and let it steam for 10 to 15 minutes. Unwrap pepper and peel off skin. A whole pepper can also be roasted over a gas flame by spearing it with a long-handled fork and turning as it becomes charred. Or place on a grill and turn with tongs.

SMOKED SALMON SPREAD

Smoked salmon blended with capers, dill, and cream cheese makes a tempting hors d'oeuvre. Prepare this ahead of time so the flavors can mingle, and serve with jicama slices or crackers.

4 ounces smoked salmon, flaked

3 ounces cream cheese, cut into chunks

2 tablespoons mayonnaise

1 teaspoon fresh lemon juice

1/2 teaspoon dried dillweed

1 tablespoon capers, drained

2 parsley sprigs

2 green onions, including some tender green tops, cut into chunks

Lettuce leaves for lining platter

Slices of jicama or crackers

Place all ingredients, except lettuce leaves and jicama, in food processor and blend until chunky. Transfer to a small bowl, cover, and refrigerate several hours.

To serve, arrange lettuce leaves on a platter and mound the salmon mixture in the center. Arrange jicama or crackers around the salmon. Serve immediately.

MAKES ABOUT 1 CUP

GREEK CHEESE SPREAD WITH ROASTED RED PEPPER ON TOASTED PITA WEDGES

This mellow blend of three cheeses and roasted red bell pepper is traditionally served on pita toasts. Make it ahead of time to blend the flavors.

1/2 cup ricotta cheese or cottage cheese

3 ounces light cream cheese, cut into chunks

1/2 cup crumbled feta cheese

1 tablespoon olive oil

2 teaspoons fresh lemon juice

2 garlic cloves, minced

2 green onions, including some tender green tops, coarsely chopped

2 parsley sprigs

1 red bell pepper, roasted (see Note on page 18) and chopped

Toasted Pita Wedges (recipe follows)

Combine all ingredients, except red bell pepper and pita, in a food processor and process until blended. Add pepper and process again until well blended. Transfer to a bowl, cover, and chill several hours. Bring to room temperature and serve on Toasted Pita Wedges.

MAKES ABOUT 1 1/4 CUPS

TOASTED PITA WEDGES

Pita, also called pocket bread, is a Middle Eastern flatbread made of white or whole wheat flour. When split, it can be used for a sandwich.

1/4 cup olive oil

2 garlic cloves, minced

3 pita pockets

In a small bowl, mix together olive oil and garlic and let stand 30 minutes.

Preheat oven to 300°F. Halve pitas and cut each half into 4 wedges. Open wedges, split them into triangles, and place, smooth-side down, on a baking sheet. Brush with garlic oil and bake until slightly browned, about 10 minutes. Cool on a rack.

MAKES 48 WEDGES

WHITE BEAN AND GARLIC PURÉE

This garlicky spread is a perfect appetizer for an Italian-theme potluck to introduce an Italian entrée, such as Cheese-Filled Manicotti with Rich Meat Sauce (page 216). Serve with crostini.

1	can (15 ounces) small white beans, drained and rinsed
1	large garlic clove, coarsely chopped
2 or 3	fresh basil leaves, torn, or 3/4 teaspoon dried basil
2	parsley sprigs
1/4	teaspoon coarse salt
	Freshly ground pepper
1	teaspoon balsamic vinegar
2	tablespoons olive oil
	Crostini (page 35)

Put all ingredients, except crostini, in a food processor or blender and blend until smooth. Transfer to a bowl, cover, and refrigerate several hours. Bring to room temperature and serve with crostini.

MAKES ABOUT 1 CUP

ARTICHOKE SPREAD

Serve this delicious spread on crackers or baguette slices at the beginning of a book club potluck. Make it ahead to develop the flavors.

4 ounces cream cheese, cut into chunks

2 to 3 tablespoons mayonnaise

1 garlic clove, coarsely chopped

1 jar (6 1/2 ounces) marinated artichoke hearts, drained, with 1 tablespoon marinade reserved

2 green onions, including some tender green tops, coarsely chopped

2 parsley sprigs

1/4 cup Parmesan cheese

In a food processor, blend cream cheese, mayonnaise, and garlic. Add artichoke hearts and reserved marinade, green onions, parsley, and Parmesan cheese and blend until chunky. Cover and refrigerate several hours. Serve at room temperature.

MAKES ABOUT I CUP

FRESH TUNA SPREAD

Grilled fresh tuna gives this spread a deep, smoky flavor, but canned or vacuum-packed tuna can be substituted. The most popular tunas are the albacore and the yellowfin, which are available from late spring to early fall.

Juice of 1 lime

1 teaspoon vegetable oil

1 small tuna steak (about 4 ounces)

1 teaspoon capers, drained

1/4 cup mayonnaise

Salt and freshly ground pepper

1 large hard-cooked egg, chopped

Prepare the grill for cooking over direct high heat. Combine lime juice and oil in a glass baking dish. Add tuna and marinate 10 minutes, turning once.

Remove tuna from marinade, drain, and grill until it flakes, about 4 minutes on each side. (Alternately, place tuna under a broiler.) Transfer to a plate and break up into pieces.

Put tuna in a food processor with capers, mayonnaise, and salt and pepper to taste and blend until chunky (or smooth, if desired). Scrape down the sides of the bowl with a spatula, as needed. Transfer to a bowl. Sprinkle with egg, cover, and refrigerate until serving time.

MAKES ABOUT 1 CUP

SHRIMP AND AVOCADO DIP

Shrimp, avocado, and cilantro, tossed with crumbled goat cheese, make a tangy dip. It is perfect to serve for an intimate potluck gathering. Bay shrimp, also called salad shrimp, are the small cooked shrimp that are available fresh or frozen year-round. Provide large tortilla chips for dipping.

1	pound cooked small bay shrimp
1	large avocado, peeled and diced
2	ounces crumbled goat cheese, such as Montrachet
1	cup thinly sliced green onions, including some tender green tops
1/4	cup chopped fresh cilantro or parsley
1	tablespoon fresh lemon juice
2	tablespoons olive oil
1/2	cup chili sauce
1/4	teaspoon salt
1/4	teaspoon freshly ground pepper
	Large tortilla chips

Put shrimp, avocado, cheese, green onions, and cilantro in a medium bowl. In a small bowl, whisk together lemon juice, olive oil, chili sauce, salt, and pepper. Add to shrimp mixture and toss lightly. Arrange chips around the dip.

SERVES 6 TO 8

CURRY DIP FOR VEGETABLES

Here is an easy dip that can be made ahead to take to a cocktail potluck. Serve with jicama strips, cauliflower florets, carrot and celery strips, and turnip chunks, or other vegetables of your choice.

4	ounces cream cheese, cut into chunks
1/4	cup plain nonfat yogurt
2	tablespoons mayonnaise
1	teaspoon fresh lemon juice
1	green onion, including some tender green tops, cut up
2	parsley sprigs
1/2	teaspoon Worcestershire sauce
1/2 to 1	teaspoon curry powder, or more to taste
1/4	teaspoon salt
1/4	teaspoon dried tarragon

Put all ingredients in a food processor and process until well blended. Transfer to a bowl or a decorative dish and refrigerate several hours.

MAKES ABOUT 1 1/2 CUPS

CRAB AND SHRIMP DIP

A creamy dip made with crabmeat and shrimp is a good hors d'oeuvre to take to a potluck wine party. Bring along several kinds of crackers and a plate of assorted vegetables.

1   package (8 ounces) cream cheese, cut into chunks

2   tablespoons grated Parmesan cheese

1   tablespoon mayonnaise

1 to 2   tablespoons milk

1   garlic clove, coarsely chopped

1   teaspoon Worcestershire sauce

1   tablespoon fresh lemon juice

3   ounces crabmeat, flaked

3   ounces cooked small bay shrimp, coarsely chopped

1/4   cup finely chopped celery

In a food processor, blend cheeses, mayonnaise, milk, garlic, Worcestershire, and lemon juice until smooth. Transfer to a bowl and fold in crab, shrimp, and celery. Cover and refrigerate several hours.

MAKES ABOUT 2 CUPS

FRESH HERBS AND WALNUT DIP

Serve this mild-flavored, crunchy dip with apple slices and celery sticks for an easy hors d'oeuvre.

4 ounces cream cheese, cut into chunks

3 ounces crumbled feta cheese

1/2 cup chopped walnuts

2 large fresh basil leaves, torn, or 1 teaspoon dried basil

2 large fresh mint leaves, torn

2 parsley sprigs

2 green onions, including some tender green tops, sliced

1/4 teaspoon freshly ground pepper

2 tablespoons olive oil

Apple slices for an accompaniment

Celery sticks for an accompaniment

Put all ingredients, except appple and celery, in a food processor and process until blended. Transfer to a bowl, cover, and chill several hours. Place bowl on a platter with apple slices and celery sticks.

MAKES ABOUT 1 CUP

A CROCK OF CHEESE

Four cheeses are blended into a mellow spread to serve on crackers or cocktail rye bread. Perfect for a potluck wine party, this can be made ahead and stored in the refrigerator for up to ten days. Keep it on hand for the holidays, too.

1	cup grated sharp Cheddar cheese
1	cup grated Monterey Jack cheese
3	ounces cream cheese, cut into chunks
2	tablespoons grated Parmesan cheese
1	garlic clove, minced
1/2	teaspoon dry mustard
1	teaspoon Worcestershire sauce
2	drops of Tabasco sauce
1/4 to 1/3	cup dry white wine

Put all ingredients, except wine, in a food processor and process for a few seconds. Slowly add wine and blend until it reaches a spreadable consistency. Transfer to a crock or small bowl. Cover and store in the refrigerator. Bring to room temperature and serve with a small knife for spreading on crackers.

MAKES ABOUT 1 1/2 CUPS

Variations: Spread on thick slices of French bread and bake 10 minutes at 350°F. Use pepper Jack cheese instead of Monterey Jack for a zippy taste.

BAKED BRIE AND BLUE CHEESE

Two favorite cheeses meld together for a quick and easy spread. Brie is one of the world's great cheeses, appreciated for its edible rind and buttery-soft interior. It can be served at room temperature or warmed, as in this recipe. Serve with apple wedges or crackers.

1 wedge (8 ounces) Brie cheese

1/4 cup crumbled blue cheese

3 apples cut into wedges for an accompaniment (see Note)

Preheat oven to 350°F. Cut Brie in half to make 2 layers and place one half in a baking dish, cut-side up. Sprinkle with blue cheese, gently pressing it down on the Brie. Place remaining half of Brie, cut-side down, on top of the blue cheese layer. Bake until slightly soft, but not runny, about 8 minutes. Serve immediately with the apples and provide a small knife for spreading.

SERVES 8 TO 10

Note: If preparing apples ahead, brush with lemon juice to prevent discoloration.

HOT WINGS

Serve these snappy wings at a cocktail party or a big family potluck—adults and children of all ages love them. Accompany them with Blue Cheese Dip, and before you know it, all you will have left on the plate is a pile of bones.

MARINADE

2   tablespoons vegetable oil

1   cup cider vinegar

2   tablespoons Worcestershire sauce

1   tablespoon chili powder

1   teaspoon crushed red pepper flakes

2   teaspoons Tabasco sauce

1   teaspoon salt

1/4   teaspoon freshly ground pepper

4   pounds chicken wings, halved at the joint to make drumettes, wing tips cut off and discarded

    Blue Cheese Dip (recipe follows)

    Carrot sticks for an accompaniment

    Celery sticks for an accompaniment

To make the marinade: Stir together all the ingredients in a medium bowl.

Place the chicken wings in a large resealable plastic bag and pour in the marinade. Press air out of bag and seal tightly. Shake bag gently to distribute marinade. Set in a large bowl and refrigerate 4 hours, turning the bag occasionally.

Prepare the grill for cooking over medium indirect heat. Remove wings from marinade and drain. Boil marinade in a small saucepan for 1 minute (to kill bacteria from raw chicken). Place wings on an oiled grill rack. Grill over indirect heat until cooked through and crispy, 25 to 30 minutes, brushing with marinade and turning frequently with tongs. Serve on a platter along with the Blue Cheese Dip, and accompany with carrot and celery sticks.

SERVES 6 TO 8

BLUE CHEESE DIP

3/4 cup sour cream

3/4 cup mayonnaise

2 to 3 tablespoons milk

1 large garlic clove, minced

1 teaspoon Worcestershire sauce

1 cup crumbled blue cheese

1/4 teaspoon salt

Freshly ground pepper

In a medium bowl, whisk together sour cream, mayonnaise, milk, garlic, Worcestershire sauce, and blue cheese. Add salt and pepper to taste. Cover and refrigerate several hours.

MAKES ABOUT 2 CUPS

CREAM CHEESE–STUFFED MUSHROOMS

Few guests can resist these mushrooms with a cheese filling that melts in the mouth. They can be made ahead, then baked at the potluck. This goes well with Baked Almond-Coated Chicken Breasts (page 264).

1 pound medium mushrooms of uniform size (18 to 20)

   Vegetable oil for brushing on mushrooms

3 ounces cream cheese

3 tablespoons fine dry bread crumbs

1 tablespoon finely chopped fresh parsley

1 garlic clove, minced

1/4 teaspoon salt

1/4 teaspoon paprika

Preheat oven to 350°F. Remove mushroom stems with a melon baller, or twist off. Discard or reserve for another purpose. Rub or brush mushroom caps all over with oil and place, gill-side up, on a baking sheet lightly sprayed with vegetable oil.

In a medium bowl, blend together cream cheese, bread crumbs, parsley, garlic, and salt. Fill each mushroom cap with an equal amount of cream cheese mixture. Sprinkle with paprika and bake until golden, 6 to 7 minutes. Serve immediately.

SERVES 18 TO 20

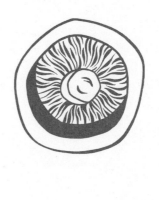

MUSHROOMS WITH PEPPER JACK–CHEESE FILLING

Prepare these mushrooms with a zippy cheese filling ahead of time, then bake at the potluck. They go well with a cooling drink of iced tea.

1   pound medium mushrooms
    (18 to 20)

    Vegetable oil for brushing on
    mushrooms

1   cup grated pepper Jack cheese

2   green onions, including some tender
    green tops, coarsely chopped

2   cilantro or parsley sprigs, coarsely
    chopped

1   garlic clove, sliced

1/4 cup light sour cream

Preheat oven to 350°F. Remove mushroom stems with a melon baller, or twist off. Discard or reserve for another purpose. Rub or brush mushroom caps all over with oil and place, gill-side up, on a baking sheet lightly sprayed with vegetable oil.

Put cheese, green onions, cilantro, garlic, and sour cream in a food processor and process until mixture is blended but still coarse. Fill each mushroom cap with about 1 tablespoon of cheese mixture. Bake until filling is bubbly, 6 to 7 minutes. Serve immediately.

SERVES 20

TRIPLE-OLIVE TAPENADE WITH CROSTINI

Tapenade originated in the Provence region of France. This thick, earthy paste made with olives, capers, anchovies, olive oil, and lemon juice is used as a condiment. Here three kinds of olives are blended into a great spread. Serve on crostini.

1/2 cup pitted kalamata olives, drained

1/2 cup pitted ripe black olives, drained

1/2 cup pimiento-stuffed green olives, drained

1 large garlic clove, coarsely chopped

1 anchovy fillet, coarsely chopped (optional)

1 teaspoon capers, drained

1 tablespoon fresh lemon juice

2 fresh basil leaves or 1/2 teaspoon dried basil

Freshly ground pepper

1 tablespoon olive oil

Crostini (recipe follows)

In a food processor, combine all ingredients except oil and crostini. With on/off pulses, process until coarsely chopped. Scrape down the sides of the bowl several times. Add oil and process again until smooth. Transfer to a small dish and serve immediately with crostini.

SERVES 10 TO 12

Variation: Crostini with Tapenade, Roasted Red Bell Peppers, and Feta Cheese: Spread the crostini with the tapenade, add some Marinated Roasted Red Bell Peppers (page 37), and sprinkle with crumbled feta cheese. Serve at room temperature.

CROSTINI

Crostini means "little toasts" in Italian. They serve as a base for a variety of savory appetizers, such as tapenade or Marinated Roasted Red Bell Peppers (page 37). They may be made ahead and stored for several days, wrapped in foil. You'll need to make the garlic oil 30 minutes before you broil the crostini.

1/4   cup olive oil

2   garlic cloves, sliced

1   large baguette, sliced 1/4 to 1/3 inch thick

In a small jar, combine oil and garlic. Let stand 30 minutes. Meanwhile, preheat broiler.

Arrange bread slices on a baking sheet and broil on one side until lightly browned, about 1 minute. Turn slices over and brush with garlic oil. Broil 1 minute longer. Alternately, arrange bread slices on baking sheet and place in a preheated 350°F oven. Bake 5 minutes, turn, and brush with garlic oil. Bake until lightly browned, about 5 minutes longer.

MAKES 35 TO 40 CROSTINI

BROILED ZUCCHINI TOASTS

These delicious little snacks can be assembled ahead of time and baked on arrival at the potluck. They go well with wine or iced tea.

2	cups unpeeled, grated zucchini (2 medium zucchini)
	Salt for sprinkling on zucchini
1/2	cup mayonnaise
1/2	cup plain nonfat yogurt
1/4	cup grated Parmesan cheese
4	green onions, including some tender green tops, thinly sliced
1	garlic clove, minced
1	teaspoon Worcestershire sauce
2	drops of Tabasco sauce
20 to 24	baguette slices

Preheat oven to 375°F. In a medium bowl, sprinkle zucchini with salt and let stand 1 hour. Drain and rinse well. Blot dry with a paper towel. Return zucchini to bowl and add remaining ingredients, except baguette slices.

Place bread on a baking sheet and spread about 1 tablespoon of zucchini mixture on each slice. Bake until mixture is bubbly, 10 to 12 minutes. Serve immediately.

MAKES 20 TO 24 TOASTS

MARINATED ROASTED RED BELL PEPPERS ON CROSTINI

Crostini topped with a colorful array of marinated, roasted red bell peppers make a festive introduction to a meal.

3   bell peppers (1 red, 1 green, and 1 yellow), roasted and peeled (see Note on page 18)

2   tablespoons olive oil

2   tablespoons balsamic vinegar or red wine vinegar

1   tablespoon chopped fresh basil or 1 teaspoon dried basil

1   large garlic clove, minced

    Crostini (page 35)

Chop roasted peppers into $3/8$-inch dice. In a medium bowl, stir together oil, vinegar, basil, and garlic. Add peppers and marinate several hours. Bring to room temperature, drain, and serve on crostini.

MAKES ABOUT 2 CUPS

CHILE CHEESE WHEELS

This is a great combination of Tex-Mex ingredients spread on flour tortillas, which are then rolled and sliced. They can be made ahead and warmed in the oven when the guests arrive.

4 ounces cream cheese, cut into chunks

1 cup grated Cheddar cheese

1 can (4 ounces) diced green chiles, drained

1/2 cup finely chopped green onions, including some tender green tops

1/2 cup finely chopped red bell pepper

1 can (2 1/4 ounces) chopped ripe black olives

4 eight-inch flour tortillas

Preheat oven to 350°F. In a medium bowl, mix together cheeses, chiles, green onions, bell pepper, and olives until well blended. Spread mixture evenly on the tortillas, almost to the edge. Roll up, wrap in plastic wrap, and refrigerate 1 hour or longer.

Cut rolled tortillas into ¾-inch slices and place on a baking sheet. Bake until warmed, about 10 minutes. Serve immediately.

MAKES ABOUT 2 DOZEN SLICES

Note: The cheese-filled tortillas freeze well. When partially thawed, they are easier to slice.

COUNTRY CHICKEN PÂTÉ

For those who don't like liver, here is a pâté made with a blend of savory meats and herbs, but no liver. It should be made several days in advance to allow the flavors to blend. Serve the pâté on baguette slices or crackers and accompany with Dijon-Basil Mayonnaise and sweet gherkin pickles. If there is any left over, it will make a great sandwich filling.

3	slices bacon, diced
1	cup finely chopped yellow onion
1	pound ground chicken
12	ounces ground veal
4	ounces pork sausage
1/2	cup dry bread crumbs
1	large egg
1	teaspoon dried basil
1/2	teaspoon dried thyme
1/4	teaspoon ground allspice
1/2	teaspoon herbes de Provence
1	teaspoon salt
3	garlic cloves, minced
1/4	cup brandy
	Fresh basil leaves for garnish
	Dijon-Basil Mayonnaise (page 63)
	Sweet gherkin pickles for an accompaniment

Preheat oven to 350°F. In a small skillet over medium heat, cook bacon until lightly browned. Remove bacon to a plate, leaving drippings in the pan. Add onion to skillet and sauté until tender, about 5 minutes. Transfer onion and bacon to a food processor and add remaining ingredients, except basil, mayonnaise, and pickles. Process in batches until well blended. Spoon mixture into a 9-by-5-by-3-inch loaf pan lightly coated with cooking spray or oil and pat down firmly. Cover with aluminum foil.

Bake 45 minutes. Remove foil and bake until pâté is cooked through and set, at least 30 minutes more. Remove pâté from oven and pour off any fat that has accumulated. Let cool completely. Run a knife around edges of pan to loosen pâté, then invert onto a plate. Wrap in foil and refrigerate at least 8 hours or overnight before serving. Slice and serve cold, garnished with basil leaves and accompanied with the Dijon-Basil Mayonnaise and pickles.

SERVES 10 TO 12

PARTY ON A PLATTER

At the beginning of an Italian-theme potluck, present an *antipasto* ("before the pasta") platter of assorted vegetables, meats, fish, and cheeses for guests to nibble and enjoy. Use the following suggestions to create your own combination. An antipasto often takes the place of a salad on the menu.

VEGETABLES

1   small head cauliflower, trimmed and broken into florets

8   ounces fresh green beans, trimmed

8   ounces medium mushrooms

2   red bell peppers, roasted (see Note on page 18) and cut into strips

    Italian Dressing (facing page)

    Greens for lining platter, such as Swiss chard, romaine, or leaf lettuce

MEATS AND FISH (CHOOSE 2 OR 3)

3   ounces dry salami, sliced

3   ounces pepperoni, sliced

3   ounces prosciutto, thinly sliced and rolled

1   cup cooked fresh tuna or 1 can (6 ounces) albacore tuna in water, drained

1   tin (2 ounces) anchovy fillets, drained

To prepare vegetables: Place cauliflower on a steamer rack over gently boiling water, cover, and steam 7 minutes. Lift rack out of water, cool cauliflower under cold running water, drain, and set aside. Steam green beans on steamer rack, 5 to 6 minutes. Cool under cold running water and drain. Marinate cauliflower, green beans, mushrooms, and bell peppers separately in small bowls with small amounts of the Italian Dressing for several hours in the refrigerator.

To assemble the antipasto: Line a large platter or tray with greens. With a slotted spoon, arrange drained vegetables in groups on leaves. Add your selection of meats, fish, and cheeses in groups. Add garbanzo beans and artichoke hearts. Garnish with eggs, olives, and onions and sprinkle with capers. Serve extra dressing on the side, if desired.

SERVES 8 TO 10

CHEESES (CHOOSE 2 OR 3)

4   ounces provolone cheese, thinly
    sliced and rolled

4   ounces mozzarella cheese, thinly
    sliced and rolled

4   ounces feta cheese, cut into
    1/2-inch dice

1   can (15 ounces) garbanzo or
    cannellini beans, drained, rinsed, and
    marinated in a small amount
    of Italian Dressing

1   jar (6 1/2 ounces) marinated artichoke
    hearts, drained

3   large hard-cooked eggs, quartered

1   cup pitted ripe black olives, drained

2   bunches green onions, trimmed

2   tablespoons capers, drained

ITALIAN DRESSING

1/2   cup olive oil

1/4   cup red wine vinegar

1   garlic clove, minced

1/2   teaspoon dried basil

1/2   teaspoon dried oregano

1/4   teaspoon dried thyme

1/4   teaspoon salt

   Freshly ground pepper

In a medium bowl, whisk together all ingredients. Cover
and refrigerate. Bring to room temperature before using.

MAKES 3/4 CUP

SPICY COCKTAIL MEATBALLS

These spicy meatballs are always the first to disappear at a cocktail party. Serve them in a chafing dish and provide toothpicks for spearing. Double the recipe for a large crowd.

SAUCE

1	can (8 ounces) tomato sauce
1/4	cup ketchup
3	tablespoons cider vinegar
1	tablespoon water
2	tablespoons packed brown sugar
1	garlic clove, minced
1	tablespoon minced yellow onion
1	tablespoon Worcestershire sauce
1	teaspoon dry mustard
1/8	teaspoon cayenne pepper
1 to 2	drops of Tabasco sauce

MEATBALLS

1	pound ground beef
1/2	cup fine dry bread crumbs
1	tablespoon flour
1/2	teaspoon salt
	Freshly ground pepper
2	tablespoons minced yellow onion
2	teaspoons prepared horseradish
1	large egg, lightly beaten

To make the sauce: In a large saucepan over medium heat, combine all ingredients. Bring to a simmer and continue simmering, uncovered, until flavors are blended, about 10 minutes.

To make the meatballs: Preheat the oven to 400°F. In a medium bowl, combine all ingredients and mix well, using your hands. Form into ½-inch balls and place on a baking sheet. Bake until browned, 10 to 12 minutes. Add meatballs to sauce and simmer 10 minutes. Transfer to a chafing dish to serve.

MAKES ABOUT 3 DOZEN MEATBALLS

PARTY DEVILED EGGS

If you want to be popular at a potluck, take deviled eggs—there can never be enough! Here, fresh mushrooms are added for variety. You could also add some chopped shrimp, salsa, diced celery, or chopped olives into the filling.

6 large hard-cooked eggs

1/4 cup mayonnaise

1 teaspoon Dijon mustard

Salt and freshly ground pepper

1/4 cup diced mushrooms

1 tablespoon finely chopped red bell pepper

2 green onions, including some tender green tops, minced

Paprika for sprinkling on top

Parsley sprigs for garnish

Peel and halve the eggs lengthwise. Scoop out the yolks, and put in a small bowl. Add the mayonnaise, mustard, and salt and pepper to taste. Mash with a fork until blended. Stir in mushrooms, bell pepper, and green onions. Spoon mixture into the depressions in egg white halves and arrange on a platter (see Notes). Sprinkle with paprika and garnish with parsley.

MAKES I DOZEN DEVILED EGG HALVES

Notes: Eggs will peel more easily when slightly warm. If they are already chilled, rinse under warm water before peeling.

A platter designed to hold deviled eggs is helpful for transporting.

CAPONATA

Caponata is a Sicilian dish served as an appetizer or a salad. It is a zesty combination of eggplant, onions, bell pepper, tomatoes, olives, pine nuts, and capers, braised in vinegar and the juice from the tomatoes. Serve the caponata on warmed baguette slices. This recipe is for a large group.

1	large eggplant, unpeeled, cut crosswise into 1-inch slices
4	tablespoons olive oil, plus extra for brushing on baguette slices
1	cup chopped yellow onion
1/2	cup chopped green bell pepper
1/2	cup diced celery
3	garlic cloves, minced
1	can (28 ounces) plum tomatoes with basil, with their juices, coarsely chopped
1/4	cup red wine vinegar
1/2	cup pitted ripe black olives
1	tablespoon capers, drained
2	teaspoons dried oregano
2	tablespoons chopped fresh basil, or 1 teaspoon dried basil
1	teaspoon salt
1/4	teaspoon freshly ground pepper
1/4	cup toasted pine nuts (see Note)
2	baguettes, sliced
	Grated Parmesan cheese for sprinkling on baguette slices

Preheat broiler. Place eggplant slices on a broiler pan and brush both sides generously with 2 tablespoons of the oil to coat. Broil 4 inches from heat until golden brown, 3 to 4 minutes on each side. Cool, cut into cubes, and set aside.

In a large saucepan over medium heat, warm 1 tablespoon of the oil. Add onion, bell pepper, celery, and garlic and sauté until soft, about 5 minutes, adding more oil, if needed. Stir in eggplant, tomatoes and juice, vinegar, olives, capers, oregano, basil, salt, and pepper. Bring to a simmer, reduce heat to low, and continue simmering, uncovered, stirring occasionally, until mixture is thick and juice is almost gone, about 1½ hours. Stir in pine nuts and let cool. Transfer to a bowl, cover, and refrigerate several hours. Bring to room temperature before serving.

Preheat oven to 350°F. Place baguette slices on a baking sheet, brush with olive oil, and sprinkle with Parmesan cheese. Bake 10 minutes. To serve, top each baguette slice with a spoonful of caponata.

MAKES ABOUT 4 CUPS

Note: To toast pine nuts, preheat oven to 350°F. Spread nuts on a baking sheet and bake until golden brown, 3 to 4 minutes. Watch carefully because they burn easily.

If you're asked to bring a salad to a picnic potluck, think about a fresh vegetable salad. Nothing compares to salads made with garden-ripe vegetables when they are at their peak, lightly dressed, and attractively arranged on a plate.

For a barbecue potluck, consider French Potato Salad with Mustard Vinaigrette (page 62) or Cabbage and Peanut Slaw (page 70). Marinated Summer Vegetables with Fresh Herb Dressing (page 56) would be perfect for a Fourth of July potluck. You can make Red and Green Salad (page 66), a colorful mix of beets and green beans, just about any time of the year. Turn the pages to find many other tempting combinations you will want to try.

When traveling with salads to a potluck, transport them in a cooler on ice.

VEGETABLE SALADS

LAYERED GARDEN SALAD

In this popular salad, layers of shredded lettuce and crunchy vegetables are topped with a creamy dressing, chopped eggs, and crisp bacon. This travels well and can be made a day before the potluck. For more color and crunch, see the variation below.

3 to 4	cups shredded lettuce
1/4	cup chopped fresh parsley
2	cups sliced mushrooms
1/2	red onion, chopped, or 6 green onions, including some tender green tops, sliced
1	package (10 ounces) frozen tiny peas, thawed
1 1/2	cups mayonnaise
1/4	cup sour cream
1	tablespoon Dijon mustard
1	garlic clove, minced
1	tablespoon sugar
2	cups (8 ounces) grated Cheddar cheese
3	large hard-cooked eggs, chopped
6	slices bacon, cooked, drained, and crumbled

In a 9-by-13-inch baking dish, layer the lettuce, parsley, mushrooms, onion, peas, and any variation ingredients you wish.

In a medium bowl, mix together mayonnaise, sour cream, mustard, garlic, and sugar. Spread over vegetables all the way to the edges of baking dish. Sprinkle with Cheddar cheese. Cover tightly with foil and refrigerate 8 hours or overnight. When ready to go to the potluck, sprinkle with eggs and bacon.

SERVES 6 TO 8

Variation: Add 1 cup chopped red bell pepper, 1 cup chopped broccoli or cauliflower, 1 cup sliced cucumber, 1 cup sliced celery, or any combination of these.

AVOCADO AND MUSHROOM SALAD

Serve this simple salad before a potluck dinner party to tease the palate. The Lemon Dressing adds a tart note to the avocados, marinated mushrooms, and cherry tomatoes. A sprinkling of blue cheese rounds out the flavor.

8	ounces mushrooms, sliced
	Lemon Dressing (recipe follows)
2	avocados, peeled and sliced
4	green onions, including some tender green tops, sliced
1	cup cherry tomatoes
1/2	cup crumbled blue cheese
	Parsley sprigs for garnish

Put mushrooms in a small bowl and toss with a little of the dressing. Cover and refrigerate several hours, stirring once.

Drain mushrooms and arrange on a large platter with a rim, along with the avocados. Scatter green onions on top. Add tomatoes around the outside. Drizzle dressing over all, sprinkle with blue cheese, and garnish with parsley.

SERVES 4

LEMON DRESSING

1/3	cup olive oil
	Juice of 1 lemon (about 3 tablespoons)
1	tablespoon dry white wine
1	tablespoon chopped fresh parsley
1	garlic clove, minced
1	teaspoon sugar
1/2	teaspoon salt
	Freshly ground pepper

In a medium bowl, whisk together all ingredients.

MAKES ABOUT 1/2 CUP

MUSHROOM AND RED BELL PEPPER SALAD WITH LEMON-DIJON-TARRAGON DRESSING

The mellow flavors of marinated mushrooms and red bell peppers complement the peppery bite of the watercress in this pretty salad. Serve with Shrimp and Chicken Casserole (page 280) and ask someone to bring Spiced Apple Crisp (page 306) for dessert.

1   pound mushrooms, sliced

1   red bell pepper, seeded and chopped

6   green onions, including some tender green tops, sliced

Lemon-Dijon-Tarragon Dressing (recipe follows)

1   bunch watercress, some stems removed

Put mushrooms, bell pepper, and green onions in a large bowl and toss with dressing to coat. Cover and marinate several hours in the refrigerator, stirring once. Place watercress on a large platter and pile the mushroom mixture on top.

SERVES 6

LEMON-DIJON-TARRAGON DRESSING

1   tablespoon Dijon mustard

1/4   cup olive oil

1/4   cup vegetable oil

2 1/2   tablespoons fresh lemon juice

1/4   teaspoon dried tarragon

1/4   teaspoon sugar

1/4   teaspoon salt

Freshly ground pepper

In a medium bowl, whisk together all ingredients.

MAKES ABOUT 3/4 CUP

HEARTS OF PALM AND ARTICHOKE SALAD

In winter, when garden-fresh vegetables are not available, this salad of hearts of palm, artichoke hearts, bell peppers, and onion, marinated in an Italian dressing, is a good substitute. It's very portable, too. Allow enough time to marinate the vegetables.

1   can (14 ounces) hearts of palm, drained and cut into bite-sized pieces

1   jar (6 1/2 ounces) marinated quartered artichoke hearts, drained

1   cup pitted black olives

1/4 red onion, sliced

1/4 red bell pepper, cut into strips

1/4 green bell pepper, cut into strips

     Italian Dressing (page 41)

3   cups red leaf lettuce, torn into large pieces

     Cherry tomatoes for garnish

In a medium bowl, stir together hearts of palm, artichoke hearts, olives, onion, and bell peppers and add enough of the dressing to coat. Cover and refrigerate several hours, stirring once or twice. Line a platter with lettuce, arrange the marinated vegetables on top, and garnish with cherry tomatoes. Drizzle with more dressing.

SERVES 4

GREEK FRESH VEGETABLE SALAD WITH FETA CHEESE

Feta cheese is the classic Greek cheese traditionally made with goat's milk, though it is often commercially made with cow's milk in this country. It has a rich, tangy flavor that adds zest to this salad. Serve with grilled lamb chops for a summer patio potluck.

3 to 4 tomatoes (about 1 1/2 pounds), seeded, chopped, and drained

1 large cucumber, peeled, halved lengthwise, seeded, and chopped

1/2 cup chopped red onion

1 cup diced red bell pepper

1/2 cup diced green bell pepper

3 tablespoons chopped fresh parsley

3 tablespoons olive oil

2 tablespoons red wine vinegar

1 teaspoon dried oregano

1/4 teaspoon salt

Freshly ground pepper

1/4 cup crumbled feta cheese

1/4 cup pitted kalamata olives

1/4 cup toasted pine nuts (see Note on page 44)

In a large bowl, combine tomatoes, cucumber, onion, bell peppers, and parsley. In a small bowl, whisk together oil, vinegar, oregano, salt, and pepper to taste. Pour over the vegetables and toss. Cover and refrigerate several hours. Before serving, gently stir in feta. Scatter olives on top and sprinkle with pine nuts.

SERVES 6

MARINATED TOMATOES WITH FRESH HERB DRESSING

Thick tomato slices are marinated in a vinaigrette made with fresh herbs and then sprinkled with tangy blue cheese or feta. Make this when garden tomatoes are at their peak. It's a great accompaniment for Grilled Beer Chicken (page 276) or other grilled meats at a summer barbecue potluck.

4	large tomatoes, thickly sliced
	Fresh Herb Dressing (recipe follows)
4	green onions, including some tender green tops, sliced
1/3	cup crumbled blue cheese or feta cheese
	Parsley sprigs for garnish

Place tomatoes in a shallow bowl or dish with a rim. Add dressing and turn tomato slices to coat. Cover and refrigerate several hours. Arrange tomatoes on a platter. Sprinkle with green onions and cheese and garnish with parsley.

SERVES 6 TO 8

FRESH HERB DRESSING

1/2	cup olive oil
3	tablespoons red wine vinegar
1	large garlic clove, coarsely chopped
2 or 3	parsley sprigs
1	teaspoon chopped fresh oregano or 1/4 teaspoon dried oregano
4 or 5	fresh basil leaves, torn, or 1/2 teaspoon dried basil
1	teaspoon snipped fresh rosemary leaves or 1/4 teaspoon dried rosemary
1/2	teaspoon salt
1/4	teaspoon freshly ground pepper

Combine all ingredients in a food processor or blender and blend until smooth.

MAKES ABOUT 2/3 CUP

MARINATED GREEN BEAN SALAD WITH HAZELNUTS AND BLUE CHEESE

Bring this summer salad of fresh garden beans, blue cheese, and toasted hazelnuts to a picnic or barbecue potluck. The beans should marinate in the dressing for several hours or overnight.

1 pound green beans, trimmed

1/2 cup diced red onion

Vinaigrette for Vegetables (recipe follows)

1/2 cup crumbled blue cheese

1/3 cup chopped toasted hazelnuts (see Note on page 89)

Tomato wedges for garnish

Fresh basil leaves for garnish

In a saucepan over medium heat, cook green beans in gently boiling salted water to cover until tender-crisp, 6 to 7 minutes. Cool under cold running water and drain. Put in a medium bowl, add onion and vinaigrette, and toss. Cover and refrigerate several hours or overnight.

To serve, drain bean mixture and place on a plate. (Reserve drained dressing for another use.) Sprinkle with blue cheese and nuts, and garnish with tomato wedges and basil leaves.

SERVES 4

VINAIGRETTE FOR VEGETABLES

1 tablespoon fresh lemon juice

1 tablespoon white wine vinegar

1 teaspoon Dijon mustard

1 tablespoon chopped fresh basil or 1/2 teaspoon dried basil

1/4 teaspoon sugar

1/2 teaspoon salt

Freshly ground pepper

1/3 cup vegetable oil

In a bowl, whisk together all ingredients.

MAKES ABOUT 1/2 CUP

SUGAR SNAP PEAS AND ARTICHOKE SALAD

Sugar snap peas are a cross between a common garden pea and a snow pea. Sweet, plump, and completely edible, they are served raw or cooked briefly. Here the raw peas are combined with artichokes and mushrooms in a crunchy salad.

8 ounces sugar snap peas, trimmed and halved

1 can (13¾ ounces) quartered artichoke hearts, drained

8 ounces mushrooms, sliced

½ cup chopped red bell pepper

Sour Cream Dressing (recipe follows)

¼ cup toasted almonds (see Note on page 108)

In a large bowl, combine peas, artichoke hearts, mushrooms, and bell pepper. Toss with dressing to coat. Add almonds just before serving.

SERVES 6

SOUR CREAM DRESSING

¼ cup red wine vinegar

2 tablespoons olive oil

¼ cup vegetable oil

2 garlic cloves, minced

2 teaspoons Dijon mustard

½ teaspoon salt

¼ teaspoon freshly ground pepper

½ cup sour cream

In a medium bowl, whisk together all ingredients. Cover and refrigerate until ready to use.

MAKES ABOUT ¾ CUP

CUCUMBERS IN SOUR CREAM

Cucumbers are available year-round, but they are crispest and most flavorful fresh from the garden. This makes a nice side dish for a seafood potluck.

3 garden cucumbers, halved length-wise, seeded, and thinly sliced (see Note)

1 teaspoon salt

1/4 cup chopped green onions, including some tender green tops

1/2 cup sour cream

1 tablespoon sugar

2 tablespoons cider vinegar

Freshly ground pepper

Arrange cucumber slices in 3 layers in a shallow bowl, sprinkling each layer lightly with some of the salt. Lay a paper towel on top of cucumbers and place another bowl on top to weight them down. Let stand 1 hour at room temperature.

Rinse cucumbers, pat dry with paper towels, and put in a clean medium bowl. In a small bowl, stir together green onions, sour cream, sugar, vinegar, and pepper to taste. Add to cucumbers and mix well. Cover and refrigerate several hours or overnight.

SERVES 4

Note: Garden cucumbers are not waxed and do not need peeling, unless desired.

JICAMA, RED BELL PEPPER, AND AVOCADO SALAD

The crunch in this salad comes from the jicama, a cool, juicy tuber native to Mexico that is often referred to as the Mexican potato. It has a white crunchy flesh and light-brown skin, which needs to be peeled off before use. Sweet and nutty, jicamas are good raw or cooked. This salad goes well with Chicken Enchiladas with Creamy Salsa Sauce (page 254).

1	jicama (1 to 1 1/2 pounds), peeled and cut into 1/2-inch strips
1	small red bell pepper, seeded and cut into 1/2-inch strips
	Citrus Dressing (recipe follows)
2	ripe avocados, peeled and cut into 1/2-inch dice
1	bunch watercress, some stems removed

Combine jicama and bell pepper in a bowl. Toss with 1/4 cup of the dressing. Cover and refrigerate several hours.

Just before serving, toss the avocado in a small bowl with remaining dressing. Arrange watercress around edge of a platter, and spoon jicama–bell pepper mixture in the center. Top with avocado.

SERVES 8

CITRUS DRESSING

3	tablespoons olive oil
2	tablespoons fresh lime or lemon juice
1	tablespoon fresh orange juice
1	tablespoon chopped fresh cilantro or parsley
1	teaspoon salt
1/4	teaspoon freshly ground pepper
1/2	teaspoon grated fresh ginger or 1/4 teaspoon ground ginger
1/2	teaspoon grated orange peel

In a small bowl, whisk together all ingredients.

MAKES ABOUT 1/2 CUP

MARINATED SUMMER VEGETABLES WITH FRESH HERB DRESSING

A walk through the vegetable stalls at our local farmers' market was the inspiration for this layered salad. Select seasonal vegetables of your choice and create your own market salad.

3   tomatoes, seeded, sliced, and drained

6   ounces mushrooms, sliced

1   cucumber, peeled, halved lengthwise, seeded, and sliced

6   radishes, sliced

1/2 green bell pepper, seeded and thinly sliced into rings

1/2 red onion, thinly sliced and separated into rings

Fresh Herb Dressing (page 51)

Salt and freshly ground pepper

1/2 cup cubed Monterey Jack cheese

2   large hard-cooked eggs, sliced

1   cup pitted ripe black olives

Parsley sprigs for garnish

In a medium glass salad bowl, arrange half of the sliced vegetables in 1 layer. Pour on half of the dressing and sprinkle lightly with salt and pepper to taste. Do not stir. Add the remaining vegetables in a second layer, pour on the remaining dressing, and season with salt and pepper to taste. Cover and refrigerate several hours.

Top with cheese cubes, egg slices, and olives before serving. Do not stir. Garnish with parsley.

SERVES 4

MARINATED WINTER VEGETABLE SALAD

For an easy winter salad, try this combination of canned vegetables and fresh carrots tossed with Italian Dressing. It travels well and will complement any meat dishes brought to a potluck. If you prefer, use fresh or frozen green beans and yellow beans instead of canned.

1 cup water

Pinch of salt

2 carrots, sliced diagonally into 1/4-inch slices

1/2 cup chopped yellow onion

1 can (15 ounces) mixed green beans and yellow beans, drained and rinsed

1 can (15 ounces) kidney beans, drained and rinsed

1 jar (6 1/2 ounces) marinated artichoke hearts, drained

1 cup pitted ripe black olives

1 tablespoon capers, drained

Italian Dressing (page 41)

In a medium saucepan over high heat, bring the water to a boil, add the salt and carrots, and cook 3 minutes. Drain, rinse under cold water, and put in a large bowl. Add onion, beans, artichoke hearts, olives, and capers. Pour dressing over all and mix well. Cover and marinate in the refrigerator overnight. Serve with a slotted spoon. This will keep, tightly covered, in the refrigerator for up to 1 week.

SERVES 8 TO 10

NEW POTATO AND BEET SALAD

In this composed salad, the vegetables are marinated in the dressing and then assembled just before serving for an impressive presentation. This travels well to a potluck.

4 cups water

1/4 teaspoon salt

5 large new potatoes (about 1 1/2 pounds), unpeeled, scrubbed, and halved

1 1/2 pounds beets, trimmed to 1 inch of greens and roots left attached, or 1 can (15 ounces) sliced beets, drained

1 medium cucumber, peeled, halved lengthwise, seeded, and diced

1/4 cup diced red onion

1/2 cup chopped celery

Fresh Dill Vinaigrette (facing page)

1/2 cup sour cream

1 tablespoon prepared horseradish

1 large hard-cooked egg, chopped

Dill sprigs for garnish

Bring 2 cups of the water to a boil in a medium saucepan, add salt, lower heat to medium, and cook potatoes, covered, until tender, about 20 minutes. Cool under cold running water and drain. Cut into bite-sized pieces.

In a large saucepan, bring remaining 2 cups water to a boil. Add beets, cover, reduce heat to medium-low, and cook until beets are tender, 30 to 40 minutes. Cool under cold running water and drain. Slip off skins and remove tops and roots. Slice beets crosswise and set aside.

In a medium bowl, toss warm potatoes, cucumber, onion, and celery with a few tablespoons of the dressing. In another medium bowl, toss beets with a few more table-spoons of dressing. Cover and refrigerate both bowls of vegetables 1 to 2 hours.

To assemble, arrange beet slices around the outside of a large plate. Add more dressing to the potato mixture, if needed. Mound the potato mixture in the center of the beets. In a small bowl, combine sour cream and horse-radish. Spoon mixture on top of the potatoes. Sprinkle with egg and garnish with dill sprigs.

SERVES 6 TO 8

FRESH DILL VINAIGRETTE

1/2 cup olive oil

3 tablespoons red wine vinegar

3 tablespoons chopped fresh dill
   or 1 teaspoon dried dillweed

1 tablespoon Dijon mustard

1/4 teaspoon salt

   Freshly ground pepper

In a bowl, whisk all together all ingredients.

MAKES ABOUT 3/4 CUP

LIGHT DILLED NEW POTATO SALAD

This potato salad is made with new potatoes and a light dill dressing. Fill a bowl with it and count on bringing the bowl home empty. It is perfect for warm-weather potlucks featuring grilled halibut or salmon.

2	cups water
1/4	teaspoon salt
6	large new red potatoes (about 2 1/2 pounds), unpeeled, scrubbed, and halved
1	tablespoon olive oil
1	tablespoon cider vinegar
1	cup diced red or yellow onion
4	large hard-cooked eggs, chopped
2 to 3	dill pickles, chopped
	Light Dill Dressing (recipe follows)

Bring water to a boil in a medium saucepan, add salt, lower heat to medium, and cook potatoes, covered, until tender, 15 to 20 minutes. Cool under cold running water and drain. Cut into bite-sized pieces and put in a large bowl.

In a small bowl, stir together olive oil and vinegar. Add to potatoes and toss gently to mix. Cover and chill 1 hour. Add onion, eggs, pickles, and dressing and toss lightly. Cover and refrigerate 4 to 6 hours before serving.

SERVES 8

LIGHT DILL DRESSING

3/4	cup light mayonnaise
1/2	cup plain nonfat yogurt
2	teaspoons Dijon mustard
2	teaspoons snipped fresh dill or 1 teaspoon dried dillweed
1	teaspoon salt
	Freshly ground pepper

In a small bowl, mix together all ingredients. Cover and refrigerate until ready to use.

MAKES ABOUT 1 1/4 CUPS

PICNIC POTATO SALAD

A potluck picnic is not complete without potato salad, and this is one of the best. A friend of mine says the secret to a good potato salad is to use as many eggs as potatoes, and she makes the best. The usual proportion is twice as many potatoes as eggs, but let your palate be your guide. See the variations below for ingredients you may wish to add to the salad.

2 cups water

1/4 teaspoon salt

8 medium russet potatoes (about 4 pounds), peeled and halved, or 4 pounds new red potatoes, unpeeled, scrubbed, and left whole

1 cup chopped yellow onion

1/2 cup chopped red bell pepper

4 sweet pickles, chopped

4 large hard-cooked eggs (or as many as desired), chopped

1/3 cup chopped fresh parsley, plus a few sprigs for garnish

Creamy Mustard Dressing (recipe follows)

Paprika for sprinkling on top

Bring water to a boil in a large saucepan, add salt, and lower heat to medium. Cook potatoes, covered, until tender, about 20 minutes. Do not overcook. Cool under cold running water and drain. Cut each half in half again and then slice.

Put potatoes, onion, bell pepper, pickles, eggs, and chopped parsley in a large bowl. Add dressing and stir gently to mix. Cover and refrigerate 4 to 6 hours before serving. Sprinkle with paprika and tuck in a few parsley sprigs around the edge of the bowl.

SERVES 6 TO 8

Variations: Add 1 cup chopped celery, 1 cup sliced radishes, 1 cup sliced olives (black or green stuffed with pimiento), or any combination of these. If you like, substitute dill pickles for sweet pickles and omit the 1 tablespoon of sweet pickle juice from dressing.

CREAMY MUSTARD DRESSING

1 cup mayonnaise

1/2 cup buttermilk

1 tablespoon yellow mustard

1 tablespoon Dijon mustard

1 tablespoon sweet pickle juice

1 teaspoon salt

Freshly ground pepper

In a medium bowl, whisk together all ingredients until smooth.

MAKES ABOUT 2 CUPS

FRENCH POTATO SALAD
WITH MUSTARD VINAIGRETTE

For a change from the traditional creamy potato salad, try this version. Tender new red potatoes are tossed with a tart vinaigrette and topped with a dollop of Dijon–Basil Mayonnaise.

2	cups water
1/4	teaspoon salt
6	new red potatoes (about 2 pounds), unpeeled, scrubbed, and halved
6	green onions, including some tender green tops, sliced
1/4	cup chopped fresh parsley
	Mustard Vinaigrette (facing page)
	Dijon-Basil Mayonnaise (facing page; optional)

Bring water to a boil in a medium saucepan, add salt, lower heat to medium, and cook potatoes, covered, until tender, about 20 minutes. Cool under cold running water and drain. Cut into bite-sized pieces.

Put potatoes, green onions, and parsley in a bowl. Add vinaigrette and toss lightly. Cover and refrigerate 6 to 8 hours. Accompany with a bowl of Dijon–Basil Mayonnaise, if desired, so guests can top their servings with a dollop.

SERVES 4 TO 6

MUSTARD VINAIGRETTE

- 1/3 cup olive oil
- 3 tablespoons white wine vinegar
- 1 teaspoon fresh lemon juice
- 1 garlic clove, minced
- 1 tablespoon Dijon mustard
- 1/4 teaspoon dried tarragon
- 1/4 teaspoon dried oregano
- 1/4 teaspoon salt
- 1/8 teaspoon freshly ground pepper

In a small bowl, whisk together all ingredients.

MAKES ABOUT 1/2 CUP

DIJON-BASIL MAYONNAISE

- 1/4 cup mayonnaise
- 1/4 cup plain nonfat yogurt
- 1 tablespoon Dijon mustard
- 1 teaspoon fresh lemon juice
- 1/2 teaspoon dried basil

In a small bowl, whisk together all ingredients until well blended. Cover and refrigerate until ready to use.

MAKES ABOUT 1/2 CUP

GERMAN POTATO SALAD

Take this traditional salad to a German-theme potluck to serve with an assortment of grilled sausages, rye bread, and spicy applesauce.

2 1/2   cups water

3/4   teaspoon salt

4   medium russet potatoes (about 2 pounds), peeled and halved lengthwise

3   thick slices bacon, diced

3/4   cup chopped yellow onion

1/2   cup chopped celery

1   tablespoon all-purpose flour

1   tablespoon sugar

1/4   teaspoon celery seed

  Freshly ground pepper

1/4   cup cider vinegar

3   tablespoons chopped fresh parsley

1   dill pickle, chopped

Bring 2 cups of water to a boil in a medium saucepan, add 1/4 teaspoon of the salt, lower heat to medium, and cook potatoes, covered, until tender, about 20 minutes. Cool under cold running water and drain. Cut into 1/4-inch slices and place in a bowl.

In a large skillet over medium heat, cook bacon until crisp. Drain on a paper towel, leaving 2 tablespoons bacon drippings in the skillet. Add onion and celery and sauté until tender, about 5 minutes. Stir in flour, sugar, celery seed, remaining 1/2 teaspoon salt, and pepper to taste and stir until bubbly. Add remaining 1/2 cup water and the vinegar and bring to a boil. Continue boiling, stirring constantly, until slightly thickened, 1 to 2 minutes. Remove from heat and add parsley, cooked bacon, and dill pickle. Pour over potatoes and mix gently until potatoes are coated with dressing. Serve in a large bowl warm or at room temperature.

SERVES 4 TO 6

GARDEN VEGETABLE SALAD

This combination of new potatoes, fresh beans, and peas captures the bounty of the growing season. It is an ideal salad to take to a summer church potluck. For added color, garnish with edible flowers, such as nasturtiums.

2 cups water

1¼ teaspoons salt

6 medium new red potatoes (about 2 pounds), unpeeled, scrubbed, and halved

¼ pound green beans, trimmed and halved crosswise

½ cup fresh peas or petite frozen peas, thawed

6 green onions, including some tender green tops, sliced

6 fresh basil leaves, slivered (see Note), plus whole leaves for garnish

½ cup mayonnaise

¼ cup sour cream or plain nonfat yogurt

2 tablespoons white wine vinegar

1 teaspoon Dijon mustard

Freshly ground pepper

Nasturtium flowers for garnish (optional)

Bring water to a boil in a medium saucepan, add ¼ teaspoon of the salt, and lower heat to medium. Cook potatoes, covered, until tender, about 20 minutes. Remove potatoes with a slotted spoon, cool under cold running water, and set aside. Add beans to cooking water and cook until tender-crisp, about 4 minutes. Add peas and cook 2 minutes longer. Cool vegetables under cold running water and drain.

Cut each potato half in half again and slice. Put potatoes, beans, peas, green onions, and slivered basil in a large bowl.

In a small bowl, stir together mayonnaise, sour cream, vinegar, mustard, remaining 1 teaspoon salt, and pepper to taste. Add to vegetables and stir until well combined. Cover and refrigerate several hours. Serve cold or at room temperature, garnished with whole basil leaves and nasturtium flowers, if desired.

SERVES 6

Note: To sliver basil (called a chiffonade), roll 4 or 5 leaves together tightly and thinly slice.

RED AND GREEN SALAD

This colorful composed salad of marinated red beets, bright-green beans, and earthy mushrooms always brings compliments. Two bold dressings are added for a zesty flavor. My husband, Reed, developed the Powerhouse Dressing. The more ingredients, the better he likes it! It is also good on tossed green salads.

8	ounces fresh mushrooms, quartered
1	cup Reed's Powerhouse Dressing (facing page)
1	pound green beans, trimmed
2	cups water
1	pound beets, trimmed to 1 inch of greens, roots left attached, well rinsed
	Romaine lettuce leaves for lining platter
	Radicchio or red cabbage leaves for lining platter
1	large red onion, sliced and separated into rings
8 to 10	cherry tomatoes for garnish
1	cup ripe black olives for garnish
1/4	cup Horseradish Cream (facing page)

In a medium bowl, toss mushrooms with enough dressing to coat. Cover and refrigerate several hours or overnight.

In a large saucepan over medium-high heat, cook beans in boiling salted water to cover until tender-crisp, 6 to 7 minutes. Cool under cold running water, drain, and put in a small bowl. Toss with just enough dressing to coat the beans. Cover and marinate several hours or overnight in refrigerator.

In a large saucepan over high heat, bring the 2 cups of water to a boil. Add beets, cover, reduce heat to medium-low, and cook until beets are tender, 30 to 40 minutes. Cool under cold running water and drain. Slip off skins and trim tops and roots. Slice beets crosswise and, in a small bowl, toss with enough dressing to coat. Cover and refrigerate several hours or overnight.

To assemble salad, place romaine leaves at one end of a large platter and radicchio leaves at opposite end. Arrange beans on radicchio leaves and beets on romaine leaves. Mound mushrooms in center, top with onion rings, and garnish with tomatoes and olives. Spread Horseradish Cream on beets, but do not cover entirely. Serve at once.

SERVES 6 TO 8

REED'S POWERHOUSE DRESSING

1/4   cup vegetable oil

1/4   cup olive oil

3   tablespoons red wine vinegar

2   garlic cloves, coarsely chopped

1   green onion, including some tender green tops, coarsely chopped

2   parsley sprigs, coarsely chopped

1/4   teaspoon salt

1/4   teaspoon dried thyme

1/4   teaspoon dried oregano

1/4   teaspoon dried basil

1/4   teaspoon celery salt

1/4   teaspoon freshly ground pepper

1/4   teaspoon paprika

1   tablespoon grated Parmesan cheese

1   teaspoon Dijon mustard

In a food processor or blender, combine all ingredients and process until well blended. Transfer to a jar with a tight-fitting lid and refrigerate until ready to use. Shake well before using.

MAKES ABOUT I CUP

HORSERADISH CREAM

Use freshly grated horseradish, if available, for a stronger flavor. Serve this zippy sauce with roast beef or on cooked beets, beans, or broccoli.

2/3   cup plain nonfat yogurt

1   tablespoon freshly grated horse-radish or prepared horseradish

1/4   teaspoon dry mustard

In a small bowl, stir together all ingredients until well mixed. Cover and refrigerate until ready to use.

MAKES ABOUT 3/4 CUP

COLESLAW WITH CREAMY CELERY SEED DRESSING

Coleslaw can be made any time of the year because cabbage is always available. Although it goes especially well with seafood, a good coleslaw is a welcome contribution to any potluck or backyard barbecue. Make this several hours ahead to allow the flavors to blend, and use a food processor for easy shredding.

1 medium head cabbage, cored and shredded (about 8 cups)

1 carrot, grated

6 green onions, including some tender green tops, sliced

1/4 cup sliced radishes (optional)

1/2 cup chopped green bell pepper (optional)

Creamy Celery Seed Dressing (recipe follows)

In a large bowl, combine cabbage, carrot, green onions, and radishes and bell pepper, if desired. Add dressing and stir to blend well. Cover and refrigerate 4 hours before serving.

SERVES 6

CREAMY CELERY SEED DRESSING

1/2 cup mayonnaise

1/4 cup plain nonfat yogurt

1 teaspoon Dijon mustard

2 tablespoons sugar

2 tablespoons cider vinegar

1/2 teaspoon celery seed

1/2 teaspoon salt

Freshly ground pepper

In a small bowl, stir together all ingredients until well blended.

MAKES ABOUT 1 CUP

Variation: Substitute dillweed for the celery seed.

TWENTY-FOUR-HOUR COLESLAW

Make this slaw a day ahead of the potluck picnic, and you'll be ready to go to the beach or mountains without any last-minute preparation. Tastes great with juicy grilled hamburgers. Serve cold with a slotted spoon.

1   medium head cabbage, cored and shredded (about 8 cups)

1/2   cup sugar

1   small green bell pepper, seeded and sliced

1   small yellow onion, sliced

    Hot Coleslaw Dressing (recipe follows)

Put cabbage in a large bowl and sprinkle with sugar. Add bell pepper and onion. Pour the hot dressing over all and mix well. Cover and refrigerate at least 8 hours, stirring occasionally. Serve with a slotted spoon.

SERVES 8

HOT COLESLAW DRESSING

1   cup white vinegar

1/2   cup vegetable oil

1   teaspoon salt

1   teaspoon celery seed

1   teaspoon dry mustard

In a small saucepan over high heat, combine all ingredients, bring to a boil, and continue boiling for 2 minutes. Pour dressing over coleslaw as directed.

MAKES ABOUT 1 1/2 CUPS

CABBAGE AND PEANUT SLAW

A hint of curry powder and roasted peanuts give this slaw an Asian accent. Bring it to a potluck, or enjoy it at home with Roasted Moroccan Chicken with Dates and Apricots (page 269).

1	medium head cabbage, cored and shredded (about 8 cups)
1/3	cup mayonnaise
1/4	cup sour cream
1	teaspoon white wine vinegar
1/2	teaspoon dry mustard
1/2	teaspoon curry powder
1/4	teaspoon salt
	Freshly ground pepper
1/2	cup roasted salted peanuts

Put cabbage in a large bowl. In a small bowl, mix together mayonnaise, sour cream, vinegar, mustard, curry powder, salt, and pepper to taste. Add dressing to cabbage and mix well. Cover and refrigerate several hours. Add peanuts and toss just before serving.

SERVES 4

SAUERKRAUT SALAD

Sauerkraut is German for "sour cabbage," but the fermented cabbage dish was originally adopted from Chinese cuisine. This salad with a sweet-and-sour flavor is a good accompaniment to serve with grilled sausage and German Potato Salad (page 64).

2	tablespoons vegetable oil
3/4	cup sugar
1/4	cup cider vinegar
1/2	cup chopped yellow onion
1/4	cup chopped celery
1/2	cup chopped red bell pepper
1/2 to 1	teaspoon celery seeds
1	jar (1 pint, 6 ounces) sauerkraut, rinsed and drained

In a bowl, mix together oil and sugar. Add remaining ingredients, except sauerkraut, and mix well. Stir in sauerkraut. Cover and refrigerate several hours or overnight. Serve with a slotted spoon.

SERVES 6

CHOPPED SALAD WITH BALSAMIC-GARLIC VINAIGRETTE

This colorful combination, which includes crispy bell peppers, tomatoes, and mozzarella cheese, should be made several hours ahead and chilled to allow the flavors to blend. A good "toteable" salad to take to a summer deck party or a beach potluck.

3 tomatoes, seeded, chopped, and drained

1 large cucumber, peeled, halved lengthwise, seeded, and chopped

1/2 green bell pepper, seeded and chopped

1/2 red bell pepper, seeded and chopped

4 ounces mushrooms, quartered

1/2 cup chopped red onion

Balsamic-Garlic Vinaigrette (facing page)

1 cup cubed mozzarella cheese

3/4 cup pitted black olives

In a large bowl, combine tomatoes, cucumber, bell peppers, mushrooms, and onion. Toss with enough dressing to coat. Cover and chill vegetables several hours in the refrigerator before taking to a potluck. Scatter cheese and olives on top before serving.

SERVES 4 TO 6

BALSAMIC-GARLIC VINAIGRETTE

2/3 cup olive oil

2 tablespoons balsamic vinegar

2 tablespoons red wine vinegar

2 garlic cloves, minced

1/4 teaspoon dried thyme

1/4 teaspoon dried oregano

1 tablespoon fresh lemon juice

1/2 teaspoon sugar

1/2 teaspoon salt

1/4 teaspoon freshly ground pepper

In a bowl, whisk together all ingredients.

MAKES ABOUT I CUP

FOUR-BEAN SALAD

This old salad standby appears at many picnics and is a great accompaniment for Baby Back Ribs with Tangy Barbecue Sauce (page 244). If you prefer, use cooked fresh green beans and yellow beans for an improved flavor.

1	can (15 ounces) red kidney beans, drained and rinsed
1	can (15 ounces) green beans, drained and rinsed
1	can (15 ounces) yellow beans, drained and rinsed
1	can (15 ounces) garbanzo beans, drained and rinsed
1	medium yellow onion, sliced
1/2	green bell pepper, sliced (optional)
1/2	cup cider vinegar
1/2	cup sugar
1/3	cup vegetable oil
1	teaspoon salt
	Freshly ground pepper

In a medium bowl, combine kidney beans, green beans, yellow beans, garbanzo beans, onion, and bell pepper, if using.

In a small bowl, whisk together vinegar, sugar, oil, salt, and pepper to taste and stir into bean mixture. Cover and marinate in refrigerator overnight. Serve with a slotted spoon. It will keep, tightly covered, in the refrigerator up to 1 week.

SERVES 6 TO 8

PICKLED BEETS

Just like grandmother used to make. They add great color and variety to a potluck picnic.

2 1/4	cups water
4 to 5	medium beets, trimmed to 1 inch of greens and roots left attached
1/2	cup sugar
1/2	cup cider vinegar
2	teaspoons dry mustard
1/2	teaspoon salt
	Prepared horseradish for topping (optional)

Bring 2 cups of the water to a boil in a large saucepan. Add beets, cover, reduce heat to medium-low, and cook beets until tender, 30 to 40 minutes. Cool slightly under cold running water and drain. Slip off skins and remove tops and roots. Slice beets crosswise.

In a large bowl, stir together sugar, vinegar, the 1/4 cup water, mustard, and salt until sugar is dissolved. Add beets and stir gently. Cover and refrigerate several hours or overnight, stirring several times. Drain before serving and add a touch of horseradish on top, if desired. Cover and store in the refrigerator up to 1 week.

SERVES 6

GAZPACHO SALAD IN AVOCADOS

Gazpacho soup is a combination of fresh tomatoes and other uncooked vegetables, served cold. Here the vegetables are presented in avocado halves for a refreshing salad to serve at a Mexican potluck.

1	tomato, seeded, chopped, and drained
1/2	cup chopped cucumber, drained
1/4	cup chopped green bell pepper
4	green onions, including some tender green tops, sliced
1/4	teaspoon dried oregano
1/4	teaspoon salt
1/8	teaspoon freshly ground pepper
	French Dressing (recipe follows)
2	avocados
2	cups shredded iceberg lettuce
2	large hard-cooked eggs, quartered

In a medium bowl, combine tomato, cucumber, bell pepper, green onions, oregano, salt, and pepper with ¼ to ⅓ cup dressing and mix lightly. Cover and refrigerate 1 hour. Just before serving, halve and peel avocados and fill each half with vegetable mixture. Serve on a bed of lettuce garnished with eggs. Pass remaining dressing in a small pitcher.

SERVES 4

FRENCH DRESSING

This dressing is also good on tossed green salads.

1/2	cup vegetable oil
1/2	cup ketchup
1/4	cup cider vinegar
1	tablespoon fresh lemon juice
1	tablespoon sugar
1/8	teaspoon paprika
1/2	teaspoon salt
	Freshly ground pepper

Whisk all ingredients together in a small bowl. Cover and refrigerate until ready to use. Whisk before using.

MAKES ABOUT 1¼ CUPS

Today's tossed salads go beyond chopped lettuce, tomatoes, and mayonnaise. Now, with the availability of new varieties of salad greens and a range of flavored oils and vinegars and cheeses, you can create some exciting salad combinations.

This salad chapter includes a wide selection of new and creative salads as well as traditional recipes along with favorite dressings. (Many of the salads and dressings are interchangeable.) Try a classic Caesar Salad (page 78), Spinach-Mushroom Salad with Creamy Balsamic Vinaigrette and Toasted Hazelnuts (page 81), Mesclun Salad Bowl with Blue Cheese Vinaigrette (page 91), and many more. Take them to potlucks or enjoy them at home.

All tossed salads should be kept cold in the refrigerator or a cooler chest and tossed with the dressing just before serving. To prevent the dressing from spilling, transport it in a jar with a tight-fitting lid. Shake well before using.

TOSSED GREEN SALADS

CAESAR SALAD

This popular salad was created in 1924 by an Italian chef, Caesar Cardini, who owned a restaurant in Tijuana, Mexico. It continues to be featured in many restaurants, but it can also easily be made at home. Crisp romaine and garlicky croutons mixed with a light anchovy dressing are the traditional ingredients. Have everything very cold and toss just before serving.

8	cups bite-sized pieces torn or sliced romaine lettuce (about 1 large head)
	Baked Garlic Croutons (recipe follows)
	Caesar Dressing (facing page)
	Parmesan cheese shaved with a vegetable peeler for topping

In a large bowl, toss lettuce and croutons with just enough dressing to coat. Top with Parmesan shavings.

SERVES 8

BAKED GARLIC CROUTONS

2 1/2	tablespoons olive oil
3	garlic cloves, coarsely chopped
1/4	teaspoon salt
2	cups 1/2-inch cubes of day-old French bread, such as a baguette
1	tablespoon grated Parmesan cheese (optional)

In a medium bowl, mix oil, garlic, and salt. Let stand 1 hour. In the meantime, preheat oven to 350°F. Discard garlic. Add bread cubes and toss to coat.

Spread cubes on a baking sheet and bake until golden, about 12 minutes. Put in a bowl and sprinkle with Parmesan cheese, if desired. Cool and store at room temperature in an airtight container for up to 24 hours.

MAKES ABOUT 2 CUPS

Variation: Sprinkle croutons with seasoned salt or mixed dried herbs for a more distinct flavor.

CAESAR DRESSING

Adjust the amount of anchovies or paste to your taste. Because salmonella, though rare, may be present in some eggs, mayonnaise is used in this dressing instead of a raw egg.

1/2 cup olive oil

3 or 4 anchovy fillets, coarsely chopped and drained, or 2 teaspoons anchovy paste or more to taste

3 tablespoons fresh lemon juice

2 garlic cloves, coarsely chopped

1 tablespoon mayonnaise

1 teaspoon Dijon mustard

1 teaspoon Worcestershire sauce

2 tablespoons freshly grated Parmesan cheese

Freshly ground pepper

Place all ingredients in a food processor or blender and process until smooth. Transfer to a bowl, cover, and refrigerate until ready to use.

MAKES ABOUT 1 CUP

ROMAINE SALAD
WITH MARINATED TOMATOES, BACON,
GREEN ONIONS, AND PARMESAN CHEESE

This salad is made in steps and finished just before serving. It is perfect for a potluck because it is made ahead, easy to tote, and delicious with any meal.

2	tablespoons olive oil
1	large garlic clove, minced
2	tomatoes, seeded, cut into eighths, and drained
1	large head romaine lettuce, torn into bite-sized pieces
6	green onions, including some tender green tops, sliced
1/4	cup grated Parmesan cheese
8	ounces bacon, diced, cooked, and drained
1/3	cup vegetable oil
	Juice of 1 lemon (about 3 tablespoons)
1/2	teaspoon dried oregano
1/4	teaspoon salt
	Freshly ground pepper

In a large salad bowl (preferably glass), stir together olive oil, garlic, and tomatoes. Add romaine on top. Add green onions, Parmesan cheese, and bacon. Do not stir. Cover and refrigerate several hours. In a small bowl, whisk together vegetable oil, lemon juice, oregano, salt, and pepper to taste. Pour dressing over salad and toss just before serving.

SERVES 6 TO 8

SPINACH-MUSHROOM SALAD WITH CREAMY BALSAMIC VINAIGRETTE AND TOASTED HAZELNUTS

Balsamic vinegar adds a sweet, pungent flavor to the dressing and complements this spinach and mushroom combination. Make in a large bowl for easy tossing.

1 bag (6 ounces) baby spinach, stems removed

6 green onions, including some tender green tops, sliced

6 ounces mushrooms, sliced

Creamy Balsamic Vinaigrette (recipe follows)

1/2 cup coarsely chopped toasted hazelnuts (see Note on page 89)

In a large bowl, combine spinach, green onions, and mushrooms. Add enough dressing to coat and toss. Sprinkle nuts on top.

SERVES 4 TO 6

CREAMY BALSAMIC VINAIGRETTE

2 tablespoons balsamic vinegar

2 tablespoons red wine vinegar

1 garlic clove, minced

1/4 teaspoon dried basil

1/4 teaspoon salt

Freshly ground pepper

1/2 cup olive oil

3 tablespoons mayonnaise

In a small bowl, whisk together all ingredients. Cover and refrigerate until ready to use.

MAKES ABOUT 3/4 CUP

ROMAINE, AVOCADO, AND MUSHROOM SALAD WITH GARLIC MAYONNAISE

This combination of avocados, crisp romaine, and mushrooms, tossed with a garlicky dressing, makes a good potluck salad. It travels well, can be assembled just before serving, and goes with most entrées.

1	bag (6 ounces) romaine hearts
2	avocados, sliced
6	ounces mushrooms, sliced
1/2	red onion, sliced and separated into rings
	Garlic Mayonnaise (recipe follows)

In a large bowl, combine the romaine hearts, avocados, mushrooms, and onion, and toss with enough dressing to coat.

SERVES 6

GARLIC MAYONNAISE

2	large garlic cloves, sliced
1/4	cup water
1	cup mayonnaise
1	tablespoon fresh lemon juice
1	teaspoon A.1. sauce
1/2	teaspoon Worcestershire sauce
1/4	teaspoon paprika

In a small saucepan over high heat, boil garlic in the water for 1 minute. Remove from heat and let stand for 10 minutes. In a medium bowl, stir together remaining ingredients. Strain garlic water into mayonnaise mixture and whisk until smooth. Discard garlic. Cover and refrigerate until ready to use.

MAKES ABOUT 1 1/4 CUPS

SPINACH SALAD WITH BACON, AVOCADOS, AND WARM DRESSING

Serve this outstanding salad of spinach, crisp bacon, and avocados at a summer potluck. This makes a tasty accompaniment for Grilled Chicken with Zesty Barbecue Sauce (page 275).

1 bag (6 ounces) baby spinach, stems removed if desired

8 slices bacon, diced

2 tablespoons pine nuts

1 avocado, peeled and sliced

3 slices red onion, separated into rings

Warm Dressing (recipe follows)

Put spinach in a large bowl and set aside. In a medium skillet over medium-high heat, sauté bacon until almost cooked. Add pine nuts and stir until bacon is crisp and nuts are lightly browned, about 2 minutes longer. Remove bacon and nuts to a plate lined with a paper towel. Discard drippings, but do not wash skillet. (Use same skillet for making Warm Dressing.)

Add bacon, pine nuts, avocado, and onion to the spinach in the bowl. Add the dressing and toss. Serve immediately.

SERVES 6

WARM DRESSING

Made in the same skillet as the sautéed bacon, this dressing has a bacon flavor without using the drippings.

2 1/2 tablespoons white wine vinegar

1 teaspoon Dijon mustard

1 teaspoon Worcestershire sauce

1/3 cup vegetable oil

1/4 teaspoon salt

Freshly ground pepper

In the same skillet in which you have sautéed the bacon, over low heat, add vinegar, mustard, and Worcestershire sauce. Whisk in oil until blended. Add salt and pepper to taste. Cool slightly.

MAKES ABOUT 1/2 CUP

SPINACH AND STRAWBERRIES WITH CANDIED PECANS AND RASPBERRY–POPPY SEED VINAIGRETTE

Make this special salad in early summer, when strawberries are in season. The contrasting flavors of spinach, fruit, and candied pecans complement Ham Loaf with Honey Mustard Sauce (page 240) and Orange-Glazed Sweet Potatoes (page 183) for an anniversary potluck.

8 to 10	cups baby spinach, stems removed if desired
1 1/2	cups sliced hulled strawberries
6	green onions, including some tender green tops, sliced
	Candied Pecans (recipe follows)
1/4	cup crumbled blue cheese
	Raspberry–Poppy Seed Vinaigrette (facing page)

In a large bowl, combine all ingredients and toss with enough dressing to coat.

SERVES 6 TO 8

CANDIED PECANS

1	tablespoon butter or margarine
1	tablespoon packed brown sugar
1/2	cup pecan or walnut halves

In a small skillet over medium heat, melt butter and stir in brown sugar. Add nuts and stir. Cook about 3 minutes, stirring occasionally. Dry on a piece of foil and separate the nuts so they won't stick together. Cool and store in a covered container.

MAKES ABOUT 1/2 CUP

Variations: For candied walnuts, substitute walnuts for pecans and proceed with recipe. For candied almonds, substitute sliced almonds for pecans, increase brown sugar to 2 tablespoons, and cook almonds for about 2 minutes.

RASPBERRY—POPPY SEED VINAIGRETTE

1/2 cup olive oil

1 tablespoon packed brown sugar

3 tablespoons raspberry vinegar

1/2 teaspoon Worcestershire sauce

2 teaspoons poppy seeds

1 garlic clove, minced

1/4 teaspoon salt

Freshly ground pepper

In a small bowl, whisk together all ingredients.

MAKES ABOUT 3/4 CUP

SPINACH, ARUGULA, MUSHROOM, AND RED ONION SALAD WITH ANCHOVY-GARLIC DRESSING

Arugula, also called rocket, is an aromatic salad green with an assertive, peppery taste. It should be mixed with other greens for a good balance of contrasting flavors. Tossed with Anchovy-Garlic Dressing, this bold salad goes well with Italian food.

1   bag (6 ounces) baby spinach, stems removed if desired

2   cups arugula, stems removed and torn into bite-sized pieces

4   ounces medium mushrooms, sliced

1/2   cup chopped red onion

Anchovy-Garlic Dressing (facing page)

In a large salad bowl, combine the spinach, arugula, mushrooms, and onion. Toss with enough dressing to coat.

SERVES 6 TO 8

ANCHOVY-GARLIC DRESSING

Anchovies are tiny fish that are salt cured and canned in oil. Used sparingly, they add a piquant note to dressings and sauces.

3 garlic cloves, coarsely chopped

1 green onion, including some tender green tops, coarsely chopped

1 or 2 anchovy fillets, cut up, or 1 to 2 teaspoons anchovy paste, to your taste

2 tablespoons red wine vinegar

1 tablespoon fresh lemon juice

1 teaspoon Dijon mustard

Salt and freshly ground pepper

1/2 cup olive oil

In a food processor or blender, process garlic, green onion, anchovies, red wine vinegar, lemon juice, mustard, and salt and pepper to taste. Add olive oil and process until blended.

MAKES ABOUT 2/3 CUP

MIXED GREEN SALAD WITH DRIED CRANBERRIES, CANDIED WALNUTS, AND CRANBERRY VINAIGRETTE

The deep-red dried cranberries, mixed greens, and crunchy walnuts, complemented with a cranberry dressing, suggest a salad for a holiday potluck. Dried cranberries are available at most supermarkets.

8 to 10	cups mixed greens
1/2	cup dried cranberries, reconstituted (see Note)
	Cranberry Vinaigrette (recipe follows)
1/2	red onion, thinly sliced and separated into rings
	Candied walnuts (see Variations on page 84) for garnish

Put greens in a large bowl. Add cranberries and toss with enough dressing to coat. Arrange onion slices on top and garnish with walnuts.

SERVES 6 TO 8

Note: To reconstitute dried cranberries, put them in a dish and soak in boiling water to cover for 10 minutes. Drain and dry.

CRANBERRY VINAIGRETTE

1/4	cup frozen cranberry juice concentrate, undiluted
1/4	cup white wine vinegar
2	teaspoons Dijon mustard
1/4	teaspoon salt
	Freshly ground pepper
1/2	cup vegetable oil

In a small bowl, combine cranberry juice concentrate, vinegar, mustard, salt, and pepper to taste. Slowly whisk in oil. Cover and refrigerate until ready to use.

MAKES ABOUT 1 CUP

MIXED GREENS WITH AVOCADO, BLUE CHEESE, AND HAZELNUTS

Toasted hazelnuts and blue cheese accent this salad, which will go with almost any main course—a perfect contribution to a potluck. Some of the popular blue cheeses include Danablu (Danish), Gorgonzola (Italian), Roquefort (French), and Stilton (English). Domestic blue cheese, crumbled or in blocks, is also available in most supermarkets.

8 to 10	cups mixed greens
2	avocados, peeled and cut into bite-sized pieces
1/2	cup coarsely chopped toasted hazelnuts (see Note)
1/3	cup crumbled blue cheese
	Dijon–Red Wine Vinaigrette (recipe follows)

In a large bowl, combine greens, avocados, nuts, and blue cheese and toss with enough dressing to coat.

SERVES 6 TO 8

Note: To toast hazelnuts, place nuts on a baking sheet in a 350°F oven and bake until lightly browned, 10 to 12 minutes. Wrap in a clean, rough towel and rub nuts together to remove most of the skins.

DIJON—RED WINE VINAIGRETTE

1/3	cup red wine vinegar
1/3	cup olive oil
1/3	cup vegetable oil
2	tablespoons Dijon mustard
1	garlic clove, minced
1/4	teaspoon salt
	Freshly ground pepper

In a small bowl, whisk together all ingredients.

MAKES ABOUT I CUP

SEASONAL TOSSED GREENS WITH VEGETABLES AND CREAMY BLUE CHEESE DRESSING

You can be as creative as you like with this salad by adding garden-fresh vegetables that are in season. For the greens, try a mix of butter lettuce, romaine, radicchio, and red leaf lettuce. This is a timely summer salad for a barbecue potluck.

8 to 10	cups mixed greens
6	mushrooms, sliced
4 to 6	green onions, including some tender green tops, sliced
2	ripe tomatoes, cut into wedges and drained
1	cucumber, peeled, halved lengthwise, seeded, and sliced
	Creamy Blue Cheese Dressing (recipe follows)

Combine all ingredients in a large bowl and toss with enough dressing to coat.

SERVES 6 TO 8

CREAMY BLUE CHEESE DRESSING

1/2	cup mayonnaise
1/4	cup buttermilk
1/4	cup sour cream
1	tablespoon red wine vinegar
1/4	teaspoon dry mustard
1/4	teaspoon salt
1/8	teaspoon white pepper
1/2	cup crumbled blue cheese

In a medium bowl, whisk together all ingredients, except blue cheese. Stir in cheese, cover, and refrigerate until ready to use.

MAKES ABOUT 1 1/2 CUPS

MESCLUN SALAD BOWL WITH BLUE CHEESE VINAIGRETTE

Mesclun, also called gourmet salad mix, is a combination of young, small greens, such as arugula, dandelion, frisée, mâche, and sorrel. In this salad, summer vegetables are added to the lettuces and tossed with a light dressing with bits of blue cheese for a pungent note. Feel free to vary the vegetables according to your taste and their availability.

8 to 10	cups mesclun
2	ripe tomatoes, cut into wedges and drained
1	cucumber, peeled, halved lengthwise, seeded, and sliced
1	cup fresh peas or sugar snap peas, halved
6	green onions, including some tender green tops, sliced
	Blue Cheese Vinaigrette (recipe follows)

In a large bowl, combine mesclun, tomatoes, cucumber, peas, and green onions. Toss with just enough dressing to coat.

SERVES 6 TO 8

BLUE CHEESE VINAIGRETTE

1/3	cup olive oil
2	tablespoons red wine vinegar
1	teaspoon sugar
1/4	teaspoon dried basil
1/4	teaspoon salt
	Freshly ground pepper
2	drops of Tabasco sauce
1/4	cup crumbled blue cheese

In a medium bowl, whisk together all ingredients, except blue cheese. Add cheese and stir. Cover and refrigerate until ready to use.

MAKES ABOUT 1/2 CUP

TOSSED GREEN SALAD WITH BERRIES AND POPPY SEED DRESSING

This is a variation of a salad we enjoyed at a joint birthday celebration with friends at a restaurant, where we also dined on Grilled Marinated Halibut Steaks with Sautéed Bell Peppers (page 296) and Carrot Cake (page 312).

8 to 10	cups mixed greens
	Poppy Seed Dressing (recipe follows)
1/2	cup crumbled Gorgonzola cheese
1/4	cup chopped pecans
1	fresh pear, peeled, cored, and thinly sliced
3/4	cup assorted fresh berries, such as strawberries, raspberries, and blackberries

In a large salad bowl, toss greens with just enough dressing to coat. Divide equally among 6 salad plates. Sprinkle with cheese and nuts. Arrange several pear slices on top and garnish with berries around the edge of each plate. For transporting to a potluck, arrange on a platter.

SERVES 6

POPPY SEED DRESSING

2	tablespoons honey
1/2	teaspoon dry mustard
1/2	teaspoon paprika
2	tablespoons fresh lemon juice
2	teaspoons white wine vinegar
1 1/2	teaspoons poppy seeds
1/2	cup vegetable oil

In a small bowl, mix together all ingredients, except poppy seeds and oil. Stir in poppy seeds and whisk in oil until well blended.

MAKES ABOUT 3/4 CUP

BIBB LETTUCE WITH GREEN GODDESS DRESSING

This famous creamy, tarragon-laced dressing was created during the 1920s at the Palace Hotel in San Francisco in honor of George Arliss, who was starring in the play *The Green Goddess*. Here it is tossed with light, tender Bibb lettuce leaves for a simple salad in which the dressing plays the starring role.

10 cups torn Bibb lettuce (1 large head)	Put lettuce in a large bowl and toss with dressing to coat.
Green Goddess Dressing (recipe follows)	SERVES 6 TO 8

GREEN GODDESS DRESSING

3/4 cup mayonnaise

1/4 cup plain nonfat yogurt or sour cream

1 green onion, including some tender green tops, coarsely chopped

1 garlic clove, coarsely chopped

2 parsley sprigs, coarsely chopped

2 tablespoons tarragon vinegar or 2 tablespoons white wine vinegar and 1/2 teaspoon dried tarragon

1 tablespoon anchovy paste (optional)

1 tablespoon fresh lemon juice

1/4 teaspoon salt

In a food processor or blender, combine all ingredients and process until well blended. Cover and refrigerate until ready to use.

MAKES ABOUT 1 CUP

MIXED GREENS WITH FRESH PEARS, BLUE CHEESE, AND RASPBERRY VINAIGRETTE

This is one of my favorite salads to make in the fall and winter, when fresh pears are in season. The best varieties to use are Comice, Anjou, and Bartlett. Buy the pears several days ahead to allow them to ripen. The Raspberry Vinaigrette adds a sweet, tart flavor.

8 to 10	cups mixed greens or baby spinach
2	ripe fresh pears, peeled, cored, and cut into bite-sized pieces
1/2	cup candied walnut or pecan halves (see Variations on page 84)
1/2	cup crumbled blue cheese
	Raspberry Vinaigrette (recipe follows)

In a large salad bowl, combine greens, pears, walnuts, and blue cheese and toss with enough vinaigrette to coat.

SERVES 6 TO 8

Variation: Substitute sliced fresh strawberries or whole raspberries for the pears for a summer salad.

RASPBERRY VINAIGRETTE

1/4	cup raspberry vinegar
1/4	cup olive oil
1/4	cup vegetable oil
2	garlic cloves, minced
1	teaspoon sugar
1/4	teaspoon salt
	Freshly ground pepper

In a small bowl, whisk together all ingredients.

MAKES ABOUT 3/4 CUP

HOLIDAY SALAD

Fresh Mandarin oranges, candied almonds, dried cranberries, and tender butter lettuce make a perfect salad for a holiday potluck. There are several varieties of Mandarin oranges. The most common one in the United States is the tangerine, available in the winter and early spring.

8	cups torn butter lettuce (1 head)
2	Mandarin oranges, peeled and separated into sections
1/2	small red onion, sliced and separated into rings
1/2	cup dried cranberries, reconstituted (see Note on page 88)
3	ounces Gorgonzola cheese
1/2	cup candied almonds (see Variations on page 84)
	Orange Dressing (recipe follows)

In a large bowl, combine lettuce, oranges, onion, cranberries, Gorgonzola, and almonds. Toss with enough dressing to coat.

SERVES 6 TO 8

ORANGE DRESSING

1/2	cup vegetable oil
1/4	cup red wine vinegar
2	tablespoons orange juice
4 or 5	fresh basil leaves, chopped, or 1 teaspoon dried basil
1	parsley sprig
2	garlic cloves, coarsely chopped
1/2	teaspoon salt
1/8	teaspoon pepper

Combine all ingredients in a food processor or blender and process until well blended. Cover and refrigerate until ready to use.

MAKES ABOUT 3/4 CUP

BUTTER LETTUCE, APPLE, WALNUT, AND BLUE CHEESE SALAD

This refreshing salad with a light dressing goes well with Beef and Vegetable Kabobs (page 246) for a late-summer barbecue potluck. The Granny Smith apple is crisp and juicy, with a sweet-tart flesh. It is a popular all-purpose green apple available year-round.

6 to 8	cups torn butter lettuce (1 head)
2	Granny Smith (or other tart green) apples, unpeeled, cored, and sliced
1/2	cup crumbled blue cheese
1/4	cup coarsely chopped toasted walnuts (see Note)
	Dijon Dressing (recipe follows)

In a salad bowl, combine lettuce, apples, blue cheese, and walnuts and toss with enough dressing to coat.

SERVES 4 TO 6

Note: To toast walnuts, preheat oven to 350°F. Place nuts on a baking sheet or piece of foil and toast 6 to 7 minutes, stirring once. Cool before using.

DIJON DRESSING

1	tablespoon Dijon mustard
3	tablespoons white wine vinegar
2	tablespoons fresh lemon juice
1/2	cup vegetable oil
1	garlic clove, minced
1/4	teaspoon salt
	Freshly ground pepper

In a small bowl, whisk together all ingredients until slightly thickened and creamy. Cover and refrigerate until ready to use.

MAKES ABOUT 3/4 CUP

CITRUS AND AVOCADO TOSS-UP

Here is a winning combination of juicy sweet oranges, buttery avocados, and crisp onion rings tossed with a tarragon-flavored dressing. It goes well with any entrée but is especially good with seafood.

8 to 10	cups torn red leaf lettuce
1	white sweet onion, thinly sliced and separated into rings
2	avocados, peeled and sliced
2	oranges, peeled (white pith removed), cut into bite-sized pieces, and drained
	Tarragon–Sesame Seed Dressing (recipe follows)

In a large salad bowl, combine lettuce, onion, avocados, and oranges and toss with enough dressing to coat. Serve immediately.

SERVES 6 TO 8

TARRAGON—SESAME SEED DRESSING

1/2	cup vegetable oil
3	tablespoons white wine vinegar
1/2	teaspoon dried tarragon
2	teaspoons sugar
1/4	teaspoon salt
1/2	teaspoon dry mustard
1/4	teaspoon paprika
1	tablespoon toasted sesame seeds (see Note)

In a small bowl, whisk together all ingredients.

MAKES ABOUT 1/2 CUP

Note: To toast sesame seeds, put them in a small nonstick skillet over medium-high heat and stir until golden, about 2 minutes.

WATERCRESS, SPINACH, BUTTER LETTUCE, AND MUSHROOM SALAD WITH CREAMY WATERCRESS DRESSING

Tossed together in one bowl, watercress, spinach, and butter lettuce make a great combination of tastes, textures, and colors. Watercress fans will really enjoy this salad because the peppery leaves are in the dressing, too.

1/2 cup watercress, coarse stems removed

2 cups baby spinach

8 cups torn butter lettuce (1 head)

2 cups sliced mushrooms

6 green onions, including some tender green tops, sliced

Creamy Watercress Dressing (recipe follows)

In a large bowl, combine watercress, spinach, lettuce, mushrooms, and green onions. Toss with enough dressing to coat.

SERVES 4 TO 6

Variation: For more texture and flavor, add avocado slices and 1 cup small shrimp.

CREAMY WATERCRESS DRESSING

3/4 cup mayonnaise

1/4 cup plain nonfat yogurt

1/2 cup watercress, coarse stems removed

2 green onions, including some tender green tops, coarsely chopped

2 parsley sprigs

1 garlic clove, coarsely chopped

1 teaspoon fresh lemon juice

1/4 teaspoon dried tarragon

1/4 teaspoon dried chervil

1/4 teaspoon salt

Freshly ground pepper

In a food processor, combine all ingredients and process until well blended. Cover and refrigerate until ready to use.

MAKES ABOUT 1 1/2 CUPS

TOSSED SALAD WITH GRAPEFRUIT, AVOCADO, AND GORGONZOLA WITH DIJON–RED WINE VINAIGRETTE

Add variety to the potluck with this interesting and tasty combination of mixed greens, tart grapefruit, mild avocados, and pungent Gorgonzola cheese, tossed with a flavorful dressing.

8 to 10	cups mixed greens
1/4	cup crumbled Gorgonzola cheese
1/2	cup toasted cashew nuts (see Note)
1/4	cup diced red onion
2	avocados, peeled and chopped
1	cup bite-sized grapefruit pieces, drained
	Dijon–Red Wine Vinaigrette (page 89)

In a large bowl, combine greens, Gorgonzola, cashews, onion, avocados, and grapefruit. Toss with enough dressing to coat.

SERVES 6 TO 8

Note: To toast cashews, preheat oven to 350°F. Place cashews on a piece of foil and bake until lightly browned, about 10 minutes.

ANTIPASTO TOSSED SALAD

For a fun spaghetti potluck, serve Big Meatballs in Herbed Tomato Sauce (page 228) with this salad and lots of garlic bread. Spumoni ice cream and purchased biscotti make an easy dessert.

1 cup garbanzo beans, drained and rinsed

1 jar (6 1/2 ounces) marinated halved artichoke hearts, plus marinade

4 ounces sliced salami, slivered

6 green onions, including some tender green tops, sliced

1 cup chopped celery

8 ounces mozzarella cheese, cubed

1 cup pitted black olives

1 cup cherry tomatoes, halved

10 cups red leaf lettuce, torn into bite-sized pieces

Italian Dressing (page 41)

1 can (2 ounces) anchovy fillets, drained

Freshly grated Parmesan cheese for topping

In a medium bowl, toss garbanzo beans with artichokes and marinade and let stand for 1 hour. Drain and discard marinade. Place beans and artichokes in a large bowl. Add salami, green onions, celery, mozzarella cheese, olives, and tomatoes. Add lettuce and toss with enough dressing to coat. Lay anchovy fillets on top of salad and sprinkle with Parmesan cheese.

SERVES 8

Pasta, grain, and legume salads are satisfying and healthful, as well as delicious. Meatless recipes, such as Couscous Salad (page 117) and Orzo and Sun-Dried Tomato Salad (page 113) make good side dishes. When meat, poultry, or fish is added, they serve as a main course. Tonnato Pasta with Broccoli (page 112) is elegant and satisfying, while the Chicken and Pasta Salad (page 108) is welcome at any potluck.

Since pasta and grains readily absorb the dressing, they should not be made too far in advance. If the salad seems dry, add more dressing before serving. Chill these salads thoroughly and transport in a cooler.

PASTA, GRAIN, AND LEGUME SALADS

CRAB AND PASTA SALAD

Fresh crab is the highlight of this luncheon salad, which also includes fresh vegetables, pasta, and a creamy dressing. Serve with a basket of warm croissants.

8	ounces (2 1/2 cups) rotini, cooked as directed on package and drained
4	green onions, including some tender green tops, thinly sliced
1/2	cup diced red bell pepper
1	cup peeled, seeded, and chopped cucumber
1	cup seeded and chopped tomato, drained
12	ounces crabmeat, flaked
	Creamy Dill Dressing (recipe follows)

In a large bowl, combine pasta, green onions, bell pepper, cucumber, tomato, and crab. Add the dressing, toss, cover, and refrigerate several hours.

SERVES 6 TO 8

Variation: Substitute 1 can (6 ounces) drained tuna for the crab.

Note: If salad seems dry, add more dressing or mayonnaise before serving.

CREAMY DILL DRESSING

3/4	cup mayonnaise
1/4	cup buttermilk
1	tablespoon fresh lemon juice
1	garlic clove, minced
2	tablespoons finely chopped fresh parsley
1	tablespoon snipped fresh dill or 1 teaspoon dried dillweed
	Salt and freshly ground pepper

In a medium bowl, whisk together mayonnaise, buttermilk, lemon juice, garlic, parsley, dill, and salt and pepper to taste.

MAKES ABOUT 1 CUP

SHRIMP, CRAB, AND PASTA SALAD

Shrimp, crab, and eggs mingle deliciously in this make-ahead salad for a beach potluck. To carry out the seafood theme, seashell pasta is used.

8	ounces (about 2½ cups) large shell pasta, cooked as directed on package and drained
1	tablespoon vegetable oil
8	ounces cooked small bay shrimp
4	ounces crabmeat, flaked
1	cup chopped celery
4	green onions, including some tender green tops, sliced
2	large hard-cooked eggs, chopped
	Parsley Dressing (recipe follows)
¼	cup sliced almonds

In a large bowl, mix pasta, oil, shrimp, crab, celery, green onions, and eggs with a small amount of dressing. Cover and refrigerate several hours. Add almonds and more dressing before serving.

SERVES 6

PARSLEY DRESSING

1	cup mayonnaise
1	tablespoon fresh lemon juice
1	cup coarsely chopped parsley sprigs
1	tablespoon chopped fresh chives
2	green onions, including some tender green tops, coarsely chopped
1	garlic clove, coarsely chopped
¼	teaspoon salt
	Freshly ground pepper

Place all ingredients in a food processor and blend. Cover and refrigerate until ready to use.

MAKES ABOUT 1½ CUPS

SALMON AND PASTA SALAD WITH PESTO MAYONNAISE

Flecks of fresh salmon tossed with pasta and a pesto dressing make an appetizing main course salad for a luncheon potluck. Prepare this several hours before serving to allow the flavors to blend. The Basil Pesto is also delicious when simply tossed with pasta, so make some extra in the summer, when basil is in season. The pesto freezes well.

8	ounces (2 1/2 cups) rotini, cooked as directed on package and drained
2	teaspoons vegetable oil
	Flaked Poached Salmon (facing page) or 1 can (7 3/4 ounces) salmon, drained, flaked, and dark skin removed
2	large hard-cooked eggs, chopped
2	celery stalks, chopped
1/4	cup chopped green onions, including some tender green tops
	Pesto Mayonnaise (recipe following)
	Basil leaves for garnish

In a large bowl, toss pasta with oil. Add salmon, eggs, celery, and green onions and stir gently to combine. Cover and refrigerate several hours. Toss with Pesto Mayonnaise 1/2 hour before serving. Serve cold, garnished with basil leaves.

SERVES 6

PESTO MAYONNAISE

1/2	cup mayonnaise
3	tablespoons Basil Pesto (recipe follows) or purchased pesto
1	tablespoon fresh lemon juice
1/4	teaspoon salt

To make the Pesto Mayonnaise: In a small bowl, mix together all ingredients. Cover and refrigerate until ready to use.

MAKES ABOUT 2/3 CUP

BASIL PESTO

2	cups firmly packed basil leaves, washed and dried
2	sprigs parsley
2	garlic cloves, coarsely chopped
1/4	cup chopped walnuts or pine nuts
1/4	cup finely grated Parmesan cheese
1/4	teaspoon salt
	Freshly ground pepper
3 to 4	tablespoons olive oil

Put all ingredients, except oil, in a food processor or blender. Process until minced. With motor running, slowly pour oil through feed tube and blend until paste forms. Scrape down sides of bowl with a spatula. Transfer to a bowl, cover, and refrigerate until ready to use, or freeze in an airtight container for up to 3 months.

MAKES ABOUT 1/2 CUP

FLAKED POACHED SALMON
POACHING LIQUID (COURT-BOUILLON)

2	cups water, or enough to cover the salmon steak
1/4	cup dry white wine
1/4	yellow onion, sliced
1/2	celery stalk, sliced
1	sprig parsley
4 or 5	whole black peppercorns
1	tablespoon fresh lemon juice
1	bay leaf
1/2	teaspoon salt
1	salmon steak (8 ounces)

To make the poaching liquid: In a medium saucepan over medium-high heat, combine all the ingredients, except salmon. Bring to a boil, reduce heat to low, and simmer, covered, 20 to 30 minutes. Strain and discard solids. Return liquid to pan, gently lower salmon into liquid, and simmer, uncovered, until salmon flakes, about 10 minutes. Remove from pan and cool. Remove the bones and flake salmon with a fork.

MAKES ABOUT 1 CUP

SEASHELL PASTA AND TUNA SALAD

For a last-minute potluck or for unexpected company, this is a convenient salad to make because most of the ingredients are usually on hand.

8 ounces (2 cups) small seashell pasta, cooked as directed on package and drained

1 cup cubed Cheddar cheese

1 can (6 ounces) albacore tuna in water, drained

1/4 cup diced dill pickle

1/2 cup diced yellow onion

1 cup mayonnaise

3/4 teaspoon salt

1/4 teaspoon freshly ground pepper

Chopped lettuce for lining platter

2 tomatoes, cut into wedges, for garnish

In a large bowl, mix together pasta, cheese, tuna, pickle, and onion. Add mayonnaise, salt, and pepper and mix well. Cover and refrigerate until chilled. Line a platter with lettuce, mound the salad on top, and garnish with tomato wedges.

SERVES 6 TO 8

PASTA SALAD WITH HAM

Easter dinner leftovers are the inspiration for this salad, but it can be made any time of the year with a few simple ingredients. The mustard dressing is wonderful with ham. If you are taking this to a big potluck, double the recipe.

8 ounces (2 1/2 cups) rotini, cooked as directed on package and drained

2 cups cubed cooked ham

1/2 cup chopped green or red bell pepper

1 cup chopped celery

1/4 cup sliced green onions, including some tender green tops

Creamy Mustard Dressing (page 61)

2 large hard-cooked eggs, sliced

1 plum tomato, sliced

Parsley sprigs for garnish

In a large bowl, combine pasta, ham, bell pepper, celery, and green onions. Add dressing and mix well. Cover and refrigerate several hours. Before serving, top with eggs and tomato slices and tuck in parsley sprigs around the edges.

SERVES 8

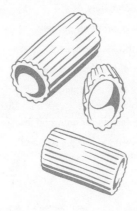

CHICKEN AND PASTA SALAD

This is a good way to use up leftover chicken or turkey for a delicious potluck luncheon salad. Jell-O Salad with Pineapple and Cottage Cheese (page 136) is a refreshing accompaniment.

8   ounces (2¹/₂ cups) rotini, cooked as directed on package and drained

1   tablespoon vegetable oil

3   cups cubed cooked chicken or turkey, preferably white meat

¹/₂ cup chopped red bell pepper

¹/₂ cup sliced green onions, including some tender green tops

¹/₂ cup sliced celery

¹/₄ cup chopped fresh parsley

¹/₂ cup pitted black olives

1   cup seedless green grapes

    Creamy Garlic Dressing (recipe follows)

    Lettuce leaves for lining platter

¹/₄ cup slivered almonds, toasted (see Note)

In a large bowl, toss pasta with oil and cool slightly. Add chicken, bell pepper, green onions, celery, parsley, olives, and grapes. Mix with enough dressing to coat. Cover and refrigerate 3 to 4 hours.

Serve on a lettuce-lined platter and sprinkle with a few nuts.

SERVES 6

Note: To toast almonds, put them on a small pan or piece of foil and bake at 350°F until lightly browned, about 5 minutes.

CREAMY GARLIC DRESSING

³/₄ cup mayonnaise

¹/₄ cup light sour cream or plain nonfat yogurt

1   large garlic clove, minced

2   teaspoons Dijon mustard

¹/₂ teaspoon dried oregano

¹/₂ teaspoon salt

¹/₈ teaspoon white pepper

In a small bowl, whisk together all ingredients until well combined. Cover and refrigerate until ready to use.

MAKES ABOUT 1 CUP

ASIAN NOODLE SALAD

Asian flavors dominate this colorful pasta salad with julienned vegetables and a spicy peanut butter sauce.

8	ounces angel hair pasta, cooked as directed on package and drained
1	red bell pepper, julienned (see Note)
1	green bell pepper, julienned
1	small zucchini, unpeeled, julienned
8	green onions, including some tender green tops, cut on the diagonal into 1/2-inch slices
1	cup chopped fresh cilantro or parsley
	Peanut Butter Sauce (recipe follows)

Put pasta in a large, shallow bowl (for easier tossing). Add vegetables to pasta and toss thoroughly with sauce. Cover and refrigerate 2 hours. Serve cold or at room temperature.

SERVES 6 TO 8

Note: To julienne vegetables, cut them into matchstick strips.

PEANUT BUTTER SAUCE

1/3	cup warm water
1/4	cup creamy peanut butter
2	garlic cloves, minced
1/4	cup soy sauce
1/4	cup vegetable oil
2	tablespoons white wine vinegar
1	teaspoon sugar
1/2	teaspoon salt
1/8	teaspoon cayenne pepper

Combine all ingredients in a food processor and blend until smooth.

MAKES ABOUT I CUP

GREEK PASTA SALAD
WITH LEMON-HERB DRESSING

This Greek-inspired salad goes well with grilled meats, especially lamb, and would be perfect for a Greek-theme potluck. It also makes a nice luncheon or picnic salad. Prepare several hours ahead and chill well. A kalamata olive is a Greek olive with a rich, fruity flavor. Be sure to buy the pitted ones, or pit them before serving.

8 ounces (2 1/2 cups) penne, cooked as directed on package, rinsed, and drained

1 small red bell pepper, seeded and cut into bite-sized pieces

1 large tomato, seeded, chopped, and drained

1 cucumber, peeled, halved lengthwise, seeded, and sliced

1/2 cup chopped red onion

4 ounces crumbled feta cheese

1/2 cup pitted kalamata olives or black olives

1/4 cup chopped fresh parsley

Lemon-Herb Dressing (facing page)

Tomato wedges for garnish

In a large bowl, combine pasta, bell pepper, tomato, cucumber, onion, feta cheese, olives, and parsley. Toss with enough dressing to coat. Cover and refrigerate 3 to 4 hours. Stir before serving and garnish with tomato wedges.

SERVES 4 TO 6

LEMON-HERB DRESSING

Juice of 1 lemon
(about 3 tablespoons)

2 or 3   garlic cloves, minced

1   teaspoon Dijon mustard

1/4   teaspoon dried thyme

1/2   teaspoon dried oregano

1/2   teaspoon sugar

1/4   teaspoon salt

Freshly ground pepper

1/3   cup olive oil

In a small bowl, stir together all ingredients, except olive oil. Slowly whisk in the olive oil.

MAKES ABOUT 2/3 CUP

TONNATO PASTA WITH BROCCOLI

Tonnato (from the Italian word *tonno,* which means "tuna") refers to dishes prepared with tuna. Here, the tonnato is a classy salad of pasta and broccoli tossed with a sauce made of tuna, anchovies, mayonnaise, capers, and lemon juice.

12	ounces (about 3 cups) corkscrew pasta, cooked as directed on package and drained
2	teaspoons olive oil
1	cup broccoli florets
1	can (6 ounces) albacore tuna in oil, drained
2 or 3	anchovies or 2 teaspoons anchovy paste
1	cup mayonnaise
2	tablespoons capers, drained
1	tablespoon fresh lemon juice

Put pasta in a large bowl and toss with oil. Cover and refrigerate until cool.

In a small saucepan over high heat, cook broccoli in gently boiling water to cover until tender-crisp, about 4 minutes. Cool under cold running water and drain. Chop broccoli and add to pasta.

In a food processor, combine tuna, anchovies, mayonnaise, capers, and lemon juice and blend until smooth. Toss with pasta and broccoli. Cover and refrigerate several hours.

SERVES 6

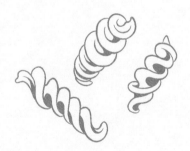

ORZO AND SUN-DRIED TOMATO SALAD

In this orzo salad, sun-dried tomatoes add a rich, intense flavor. Bring it to a potluck picnic or serve it at home as an accompaniment to a lamb or poultry dish.

8	ounces (1 cup) orzo, cooked as directed on package and drained
1/2	cup sun-dried tomatoes (not in oil), snipped into very small pieces with kitchen scissors (see Note)
1/2	cup chopped red bell pepper
1/2	cup pitted kalamata olives or ripe black olives, halved
1 1/2	cups seeded and chopped cucumber
	Red Wine Vinaigrette (recipe follows)

Put orzo in a large bowl and mix with sun-dried tomatoes, bell pepper, olives, and cucumber. Toss with enough dressing to coat and refrigerate several hours. Serve cold or at room temperature.

SERVES 6

Note: If tomatoes are very dry, place them in a small bowl, cover with boiling water, and let stand for 10 minutes to reconstitute. Drain and pat dry.

RED WINE VINAIGRETTE

1/2	cup vegetable oil
1/4	cup red wine vinegar
1	garlic clove, minced
1/2	teaspoon dried oregano
1/2	teaspoon dried basil
1/4	teaspoon dry mustard
1/4	teaspoon crushed red pepper flakes
1/4	teaspoon salt
	Freshly ground pepper

In a medium bowl, whisk together all ingredients.

MAKES ABOUT 3/4 CUP

CLASSIC MACARONI SALAD

This is one of those picnic salads you never get tired of. Make ahead to allow flavors to develop, and serve very cold. See the suggestions below for ways to vary the flavor.

8 ounces (2 cups) small salad macaroni, cooked as directed on package and drained

1 tablespoon vegetable oil

1 cup chopped yellow onion

4 large hard-cooked eggs, chopped

3 sweet pickles, chopped

Macaroni Dressing (recipe follows)

Put macaroni in a medium bowl and toss with oil. Add onion, eggs, and pickles and toss with dressing. Cover and refrigerate 4 hours or overnight. If the salad seems dry, add more mayonnaise.

SERVES 8

Variations: Add 1 1/2 cups cubed Cheddar cheese, 2 cups cooked small bay shrimp, 1 cup chopped fresh parsley, 1 cup chopped red bell pepper, 1 cup chopped celery, 1 cup sliced green stuffed olives, or 1 jar (3 ounces) pimientos, drained and chopped, or any combination of these.

MACARONI DRESSING

1/2 cup mayonnaise

1/2 cup plain nonfat yogurt

1/2 cup light sour cream

1 teaspoon dry mustard

1 tablespoon sweet pickle juice

1 teaspoon salt

1/4 teaspoon freshly ground pepper

1 teaspoon prepared mustard

In a medium bowl, whisk together all ingredients. Cover and refrigerate until ready to use.

MAKES ABOUT 1 1/2 CUPS

BLACK BEAN AND CORN SALAD

Here is a great salad to make for a patio potluck in the summer, when tomatoes and corn are at their peak. This goes well with Grilled Marinated Halibut Steaks with Sautéed Bell Peppers (page 296) and Chocolate-Apple-Spice Cake (page 310).

2	cans (15 ounces each) black beans, drained and rinsed
2	cups seeded, chopped, and drained tomatoes
1 1/2	cups freshly cooked corn kernels, scraped off the cob (3 or 4 ears), or frozen corn, thawed
2	jalapeño peppers, seeded and diced
1	cup diced red onion
1	cup chopped red bell pepper
1/2	cup chopped fresh cilantro or parsley
3	tablespoons vegetable oil
1/4	cup fresh lime juice
1/2	teaspoon dried cumin
1/4	teaspoon sugar
1/2	teaspoon salt
	Freshly ground pepper

In a large bowl, mix together beans, tomatoes, corn, jalapeño peppers, onion, bell pepper, and cilantro. In a small bowl, whisk together oil, lime juice, cumin, sugar, salt, and pepper to taste. Toss the salad with enough dressing to coat. Cover and refrigerate several hours or overnight. Serve at room temperature.

SERVES 6 TO 8

BLACK BEAN AND RICE SALAD

If you live near the ocean, summer is not complete without a beach potluck barbecue with grilled fish and this Cuban-inspired salad of beans and rice, flecked with red and green bell peppers.

1/2	cup olive oil
3	tablespoons orange juice
2	tablespoons red wine vinegar
1	garlic clove, minced
1/2	teaspoon ground cumin
1	teaspoon chili powder
2 to 3	drops of Tabasco sauce
3/4	teaspoon salt
	Freshly ground pepper
3	cups cooked long-grain white rice (1 cup raw)
2	cans (15 ounces each) black beans, drained and rinsed
1	cup chopped red bell pepper
1/2	cup chopped green bell pepper
1/2	cup chopped green onion, including some tender green tops
1/4	cup chopped fresh cilantro or parsley

In a medium bowl, whisk together oil, orange juice, vinegar, garlic, cumin, chili powder, Tabasco, salt, and pepper to taste.

In a large bowl, combine rice, beans, bell peppers, green onions, and cilantro. Toss lightly with about half of the dressing to coat, cover, and refrigerate. Add more dressing just before serving, as needed. Serve cold or at room temperature.

SERVES 8 TO 10

COUSCOUS SALAD

Couscous, a staple of North African cuisine, is available in most supermarkets. It is a popular grain because it takes just a few minutes to prepare. It can be served warm as a side dish or cold, with other ingredients added, as in this salad.

2	cups chicken broth or water
1¹/₂	cups couscous
1	cup chopped fresh parsley
¹/₂	cup chopped green onion, including some tender green tops
¹/₄	cup chopped fresh mint leaves, plus whole leaves for garnish
2	garlic cloves, minced
3 or 4	plum tomatoes, chopped (about 2 cups)
1	small cucumber, peeled, halved lengthwise, seeded, and diced
	Lemon-Herb Dressing (page 111)

In a medium saucepan over high heat, bring broth to a boil and stir in couscous. Remove from heat, cover, and let stand 5 minutes. Fluff couscous with a fork and cool slightly. Add parsley, green onions, chopped mint, garlic, tomatoes, and cucumber. Add enough dressing to coat and gently mix. Cover and refrigerate several hours before serving. Serve cold, garnished with whole mint leaves.

SERVES 6

ANTIPASTO PASTA SALAD

The Italian term *antipasto* refers to hot or cold hors d'oeuvres eaten before the pasta course. Here, some favorite antipasto ingredients are combined with pasta for an appealing picnic potluck dish.

8　ounces (about 2 1/2 cups) rotini, cooked as directed on package and drained

6　green onions, including some tender green tops, sliced

1/2　cup chopped green bell pepper

1/2　cup chopped red bell pepper

3　ounces mushrooms, sliced

1　cucumber, peeled, halved lengthwise, seeded, and sliced

1　can (15 ounces) garbanzo beans, rinsed and drained

4　ounces mozzarella cheese, cubed

4　ounces sliced salami, cut into strips

1/4　cup sliced black olives

2　tablespoons chopped fresh parsley

Italian Dressing (page 41)

In a large bowl, combine all the salad ingredients. Toss with 1/2 cup of dressing, cover, and refrigerate several hours. Add more dressing before serving.

SERVES 8

Fruit salads are so versatile, they can serve as a tempting first course, as an in-between course to clear the palate, as a complementary side dish, or as a refreshing dessert. Many of the salads made with fresh fruit are bursting with so much flavor, they do not need a dressing. A variety of fruit salads are presented here, including Tropical Fruit Salad (page 124); Orange Salad, Mexican Style (page 128); Fruit Bowl with Strawberry-Yogurt Dressing (page 129); and "New" Waldorf Salad (page 120).

Molded salads with Jell-O are old favorites that appeal to children as well as adults. With today's new flavors and combinations, they are more popular than ever. Included here are some savory gelatin salads, like Tomato Aspic with Shrimp (page 143) and Imperial Vegetable Jell-O Mold (page 140), along with some sweeter versions, such as Raspberry Jell-O Salad with Marshmallow Topping (page 134), Strawberry-Nut Jell-O (page 137), and for fun, Port Wine Jell-O Salad (page 138). All the molded salads can be made ahead and make fine side dishes for any potluck.

For all gelatin salads, use canned pineapple rather than fresh or frozen. Fresh pineapple contains an enzyme that inhibits the jelling; the canning process eliminates the chemical. For the same reason, avoid fresh papaya, guava, and ginger root.

FRUIT AND MOLDED SALADS

"NEW" WALDORF SALAD

Originally created at New York's Waldorf-Astoria Hotel in the 1890s, this crisp apple salad is still popular today. In this version, Cheddar cheese cubes and chopped dates add extra flavor.

3 large Red Delicious apples, unpeeled, cored, and cut into bite-sized pieces

1 cup Cheddar cheese cubes

1/2 cup chopped dates (use kitchen scissors for snipping)

1/4 cup chopped walnuts or pecans

1 celery stalk, chopped

About 1/4 cup mayonnaise

In a bowl, combine the salad ingredients and mix with enough mayonnaise to coat. Cover and refrigerate until ready to serve.

SERVES 6

TWENTY-FOUR-HOUR FRUIT SALAD

Everyone loves this familiar salad with a rich, sweet dressing combined with some popular fruit—pineapple, grapes, and bananas. It should be made one day ahead so the ingredients can blend together. It makes a very welcome side dish at a potluck.

2 large eggs

2 tablespoons sugar

Juice of 1 lemon
(about 3 tablespoons)

1/4 cup half-and-half

1 cup whipping cream, whipped until it holds stiff peaks

2 cups miniature marshmallows

2 cups pineapple chunks, fresh or canned, drained

1 cup seedless green grapes

1 banana

1/2 cup slivered almonds

In the top of a double boiler set over simmering water (but not touching it), combine eggs, sugar, lemon juice, and half-and-half and whisk constantly until thickened, about 5 minutes. Remove from heat and fold in whipped cream and marshmallows. Put pineapple and grapes in a large bowl. Add the warm dressing, cover, and refrigerate 24 hours. Before serving, slice the banana and fold in with the almonds.

SERVES 6

ORANGE, CUCUMBER, AND JICAMA SALAD

If you're organizing a Mexican-theme potluck, suggest this composed salad of sliced oranges, cucumber slices, and jicama strips, tossed with a tart dressing. Serve with Mexican Chicken (page 271) or Beef Enchiladas (page 214).

2	cups shredded lettuce
4	oranges, peeled, white pith removed, and sliced
1	cucumber, peeled, halved lengthwise, seeded, and sliced
1	small jicama, peeled and cut into thick strips (like French fries)
1/4	cup chopped white onion
1/4	cup chopped green bell pepper
	Lime Dressing (recipe follows)
	Parsley or cilantro sprigs for garnish

Line a platter with lettuce. Arrange oranges, cucumber, and jicama in groups on the lettuce. Sprinkle with onion and bell pepper. Drizzle about half of the dressing over the salad. Garnish with parsley or cilantro sprigs, cover, and chill several hours. Serve remaining dressing in a small pitcher or bowl.

SERVES 6

LIME DRESSING

	Juice of 2 limes
1	tablespoon white wine vinegar
1/2	cup vegetable oil
1	tablespoon honey
1/4	teaspoon dried oregano
1/4	teaspoon ground cumin
1/4	teaspoon dry mustard
1/4	teaspoon salt
1/4	teaspoon white pepper

In a bowl, mix together all ingredients. Cover and refrigerate until ready to use.

MAKES ABOUT 3/4 CUP

MELON AND GREEN GRAPE SALAD

This is a refreshing summer salad to serve for a bridal potluck shower or luncheon. A good entrée would be Ham Loaf with Honey Mustard Sauce (page 240). Choose melons that are heavy for their size, with a sweet fruity fragrance, and yield slightly to pressure at the blossom end. Store them in the refrigerator in a plastic bag because they absorb other odors.

1	small cantaloupe, cut into 1-inch cubes or balls
1	small honeydew melon, cut into 1-inch cubes or balls
1	cup watermelon cubes or balls
1	cup seedless green grapes
1	tablespoon chopped fresh mint leaves, plus some sprigs for garnish
	Juice of 1 lime
1	tablespoon honey
3 or 4	red lettuce leaves for lining salad bowl

In a medium bowl, toss together all ingredients, except the lettuce leaves and mint sprigs. Cover and refrigerate several hours.

In another large bowl, preferably glass, line lettuce leaves around the bottoms and sides. Mound the melon mixture in the center and garnish with mint sprigs.

SERVES 6 TO 8

TROPICAL FRUIT SALAD

Bring this light, refreshing salad of exotic fruit to a beach potluck or luau. Serve it with Chicken, Hawaiian Style (page 267).

1	honeydew melon, peeled
1	papaya, peeled and seeded
1	mango, peeled
1	avocado, peeled
1/2	cup salted cashews or peanuts
1/4	cup mayonnaise
1/4	cup sour cream
1	teaspoon fresh lemon juice
1/4	teaspoon curry powder, or to your taste
1	banana, sliced

Cut honeydew, papaya, mango, and avocado into large, bite-sized pieces. Put in a large bowl and add nuts.

In a small bowl, whisk together mayonnaise, sour cream, lemon juice, and curry powder and stir into the fruit mixture. Add banana just before serving. Let stand several hours to allow flavors to mellow.

SERVES 6

SUMMER FRUIT SALAD

Fruit salads are easy to make in the summer because so many delicious fruits are available at roadside stands and in the supermarket. Dressing is not needed for this salad, but if you wish, you can serve it topped with a fruit-flavored yogurt. We eat a lot of blueberries at our house because one of my sons has a large blueberry plant nursery that ships plants all over the world.

1 cup bite-sized cantaloupe cubes or balls

1 cup bite-sized honeydew melon cubes or balls

1 cup bite-sized watermelon cubes or balls

2 cups thinly sliced fresh peaches

Juice of 1 lime

1 tablespoon confectioners' sugar

1 cup blueberries

1/4 cup chopped walnuts

In a large bowl, combine cantaloupe, honeydew, watermelon, and peaches and stir in lime juice and sugar. Scatter blueberries on top and sprinkle with nuts. Serve cold.

SERVES 6

FRESH FRUIT PLATTER

The fresh flavors of summer star in this juicy combination, tossed with a simple Orange-Lime Dressing. Enjoy this salad at a neighborhood potluck when fresh fruit is available.

1 cantaloupe, cut into wedges, seeded, rind removed, and sliced

1 honeydew melon, cut into wedges, seeded, rind removed, and sliced

2 oranges, peeled, white pith removed, and sliced

1 cup seedless green grapes

1 cup strawberries, washed, hulled, and sliced

Mint leaves for garnish

Lime wedges for garnish

Orange-Lime Dressing (recipe follows)

Arrange fruit on a platter and garnish with mint leaves and lime wedges. Add a drizzle of dressing.

SERVES 6

ORANGE-LIME DRESSING

1/2 cup orange juice

2 tablespoons fresh lime juice

1 teaspoon sugar

In a small bowl, mix juices with sugar.

MAKES ABOUT 1/2 CUP

FRUIT SALAD WITH HONEY-CREAM-MINT DRESSING

There is a taste of the tropics in this exotic fruit salad, which includes kiwis. A kiwi is a fruit that looks like a brown egg with a hairy covering. Its bright-green flesh, sprinkled with tiny edible seeds, has a sweet-tart flavor. It is grown in New Zealand and California and is available year-round. The pear-shaped papaya has silky-smooth, golden flesh that is also both sweet and tart. Its cavity is filled with black seeds, which are usually discarded. Papayas are grown in semitropical climates. | Prepare the fruit ahead, then assemble the salad just before serving. Fresh mint adds a summery accent.

4	pineapple slices, fresh or canned, halved
2	kiwi, peeled and sliced
1	papaya, peeled, seeded, and cut into strips
2	bananas, sliced
1	orange, peeled, white pith removed, and sliced
	Honey-Cream-Mint Dressing (recipe follows)
	Mint leaves for garnish

Arrange fruit on a platter. Top with some dressing or serve alongside salad in a bowl. Garnish with mint leaves.

SERVES 6

HONEY-CREAM-MINT DRESSING

3/4	cup sour cream
2	tablespoons honey
1	teaspoon grated lemon zest
2	tablespoons finely chopped fresh mint leaves
	Dash of ground nutmeg

In a small bowl, mix together all ingredients, stirring until well blended.

MAKES ABOUT I CUP

ORANGE SALAD, MEXICAN STYLE

Make this appealing salad with layers of oranges, cucumber, and green bell pepper in a decorative glass bowl. The Cilantro Dressing gives the salad its south-of-the-border flavor. Cilantro leaves are the bright-green leaves of the coriander plant, also called Chinese parsley. The herb has a lively, pungent flavor and is used in Asian, Caribbean, and Latin American cuisine.

4 oranges, peeled, white pith removed, and sliced

1 large cucumber, peeled, halved lengthwise, seeded, and sliced

1 small green bell pepper, seeded and cut into bite-sized pieces

1/2 cup diced red onion

1 tablespoon chopped fresh cilantro or parsley, plus cilantro sprigs for garnish

Cilantro Dressing (recipe follows)

In a medium bowl, individually layer half the oranges, cucumber, bell pepper, onion, and cilantro, drizzling a little dressing between each layer. Repeat the layers, drizzling with more dressing in between. Garnish with cilantro sprigs.

SERVES 6

CILANTRO DRESSING

3 tablespoons red wine vinegar

1/2 cup vegetable oil

1 tablespoon chopped fresh cilantro

1/2 teaspoon salt

Freshly ground pepper

In a medium bowl, whisk together all ingredients.

MAKES ABOUT 2/3 CUP

FRUIT BOWL WITH STRAWBERRY-YOGURT DRESSING

This delightful dressing of strawberries and yogurt can be tossed with any combination of fruit, depending on choice and availability. Try seedless green grapes, pears, and figs, for example.

2	bananas, sliced
1 1/2	cups sliced strawberries
2	cups pineapple chunks, fresh or canned
1	Red Delicious apple, unpeeled, cored, and cut into bite-sized pieces
1	cup miniature marshmallows
	Strawberry-Yogurt Dressing (recipe follows)
1/4	cup coarsely chopped walnuts
	Mint leaves for garnish

In a large bowl, combine all the fruit and marshmallows. Toss lightly with enough dressing to coat and sprinkle the nuts on top. Garnish with mint leaves and serve immediately.

SERVES 6

STRAWBERRY-YOGURT DRESSING

1/2	cup plain nonfat yogurt
1/2	cup sliced strawberries
1	ripe banana, cut into chunks
1	teaspoon poppy seeds (optional)
1	teaspoon honey

Combine all ingredients in a food processor or blender and process until smooth.

MAKES ABOUT 1 1/3 CUPS

ORANGE, GRAPEFRUIT, AND AVOCADO SALAD WITH CITRUS DRESSING

For a refreshing taste at a winter potluck, juicy orange and grapefruit slices and buttery avocado slices are attractively arranged on a platter and drizzled with a tangy Citrus Dressing. The two most common avocado varieties are the almost black, pebbly-skinned Hass and the green, smooth-skinned Fuerte. Both are appreciated for their rich texture and mellow flavor. Ripe avocados are slightly soft to the touch.

1/2 head Bibb lettuce, leaves separated

3 oranges, peeled, white pith removed, and sliced crosswise

2 grapefruits, peeled, white pith removed, and sliced crosswise

2 avocados, peeled and sliced

Citrus Dressing (recipe follows)

Line a large platter with lettuce leaves. Arrange orange, grapefruit, and avocado slices in an alternating pattern. Drizzle the dressing over all and serve immediately.

SERVES 6 TO 8

CITRUS DRESSING

1/4 cup orange juice

2 tablespoons fresh lemon juice

2 tablespoons honey

2 teaspoons Dijon mustard

1/4 teaspoon ground cinnamon

1/4 teaspoon ground ginger

2/3 cup vegetable oil

In a small bowl, whisk together all ingredients. Cover and refrigerate until ready to use.

MAKES ABOUT 1 CUP

BLUEBERRY, AVOCADO, AND CANTALOUPE SALAD WITH LIME MAYONNAISE

Here is a refreshing summer salad to serve with Grilled Beer Chicken (page 276) at a potluck patio party. Include Easy Baked Beans (page 211) and cold beer. The Lime Mayonnaise is also good on asparagus and artichokes.

2	avocados, peeled and cubed
	Juice of 2 limes
1	kiwi, peeled, halved lengthwise, and sliced
3	cups cantaloupe cubes
2	bananas, sliced
1	cup blueberries
	Lime Mayonnaise (recipe follows)

In a medium bowl, toss avocado with lime juice. Stir in kiwi, cantaloupe, and bananas. Cover and refrigerate 1 hour. Just before serving, add blueberries and toss lightly. Serve the Lime Mayonnaise on the side.

SERVES 6

LIME MAYONNAISE

1/3	cup mayonnaise
1	tablespoon fresh lime juice
1	teaspoon sugar
1	teaspoon grated lime zest

In a small bowl, whisk together all ingredients. Cover and refrigerate until ready to use.

MAKES ABOUT 1/2 CUP

SUNBURST SALAD

If you are taking this composed salad of oranges, red onion, cucumber, and avocado to a potluck, arrange the ingredients on a platter just before serving. The Lime-Garlic Dressing adds a spicy, tart flavor.

3 or 4	red leaf lettuce leaves
3	oranges, peeled, white pith removed, and cut crosswise into 1/4-inch slices
1	red onion, thinly sliced
1	cucumber, peeled, halved lengthwise, and sliced
2	ripe avocados, diced
1/2	cup pitted black olives
	Lime-Garlic Dressing (recipe follows)

Line a platter with lettuce leaves. Arrange orange, onion, and cucumber slices in groups on the lettuce. Scatter avocado pieces and olives over the salad and drizzle lightly with the dressing. Serve the remaining dressing in a pitcher.

SERVES 6

LIME-GARLIC DRESSING

1/3	cup olive oil
	Juice of 1 lime
2	garlic cloves, minced
1/4	teaspoon ground cardamom
1/4	teaspoon ground cinnamon
1/4	teaspoon dried thyme
1/4	teaspoon salt
2	drops of Tabasco sauce

In a small bowl, whisk together all ingredients.

MAKES ABOUT 1/2 CUP

AMBROSIA FRUIT SALAD

Need a simple, easy salad to take to a potluck? This combination of fruit, coconut, sour cream, and marshmallows appeals to all ages. It should be made a day in advance, covered, and refrigerated until serving time.

1   cup pineapple chunks, fresh or canned, drained

1   can (11 ounces) Mandarin oranges, drained

1   cup sweetened shredded coconut

1   cup seedless green grapes

1   cup miniature marshmallows

1   cup sour cream

    Fresh mint leaves for garnish

In a large bowl, mix together all ingredients, except mint leaves. Cover and refrigerate overnight. Transfer to a glass bowl and garnish with mint leaves.

SERVES 4 TO 6

RASPBERRY JELL-O SALAD
WITH MARSHMALLOW TOPPING

This salad is a favorite for family dinners and potlucks. It serves as a salad or as a dessert and is especially popular with children.

1	large package (6 ounces) raspberry Jell-O
2	cups boiling water
1	bag (12 ounces) frozen raspberries
1 1/2	cups applesauce
1	cup sour cream
2	cups miniature marshmallows
3/4	cup chopped walnuts

In a medium heat-proof bowl, stir Jell-O into boiling water and continue stirring until dissolved. Cool slightly. Stir in raspberries and applesauce. Pour into a 9-by-13-inch glass baking dish. Refrigerate until firm, about 4 hours, or overnight.

In a medium bowl, mix sour cream and marshmallows. Cover and refrigerate several hours. Beat mixture with an electric mixer until fluffy and spread on top of the firm Jell-O. Sprinkle with walnuts and refrigerate until ready to serve.

SERVES 8

DOUBLE ORANGE JELL-O

Treat the kids to this tangy Jell-O salad with Mandarin oranges and mini marshmallows. My grandkids always requested it when they came to visit because they loved the "little" oranges.

1   large package (6 ounces) orange Jell-O

2   cups boiling water

1   can (12 ounces) ginger ale

1   cup frozen orange juice concentrate, undiluted

1   can (11 ounces) Mandarin oranges, drained

2   bananas, sliced

2   cups mini marshmallows

In a medium heat-proof bowl, stir Jell-O into boiling water and continue stirring until dissolved. Add ginger ale and orange juice concentrate. Pour into a 9-by-13-inch glass baking dish. Refrigerate until partially set, 1½ hours. Stir in oranges, bananas, and marshmallows. Refrigerate until firm, about 4 hours longer.

SERVES 8

JELL-O SALAD WITH PINEAPPLE AND COTTAGE CHEESE

Like all Jell-O salads, this one is conveniently made ahead and refrigerated, ready to take to a potluck. The cottage cheese and sour cream add a creamy texture.

1 package (3 ounces) lemon Jell-O

1 cup boiling water

1 can (8 ounces) crushed pineapple, with its juice

1/4 cup fresh lemon juice

1/3 cup sugar

1 cup cottage cheese

1/2 cup sour cream

In a medium heat-proof glass bowl, stir Jell-O into boiling water and continue stirring until dissolved. Add pineapple and juice, lemon juice, and sugar and mix well. Place in refrigerator until partially set, 1½ hours. Stir in cottage cheese and sour cream. Refrigerate until firm, about 4 hours longer.

SERVES 6

STRAWBERRY-NUT JELL-O

Some friends of ours have served this salad at every Christmas dinner, delighting three generations of their family. This tasty tradition is made in layers for a festive and attractive presentation.

1   large package (6 ounces) strawberry Jell-O

1   cup boiling water

2   packages (10 ounces each) frozen sliced strawberries, with their juice, thawed

1   can (8 ounces) crushed pineapple, with its juice

3   ripe bananas, mashed

1   cup coarsely chopped walnuts

1   pint sour cream

In a medium heat-proof bowl, stir Jell-O into boiling water and continue stirring until dissolved. Add strawberries and juice, pineapple and juice, bananas, and nuts. Place half of the Jell-O and fruit mixture in a 9-by-13-inch glass baking dish and set the remaining Jell-O mixture aside. Place baking dish in the refrigerator until the Jell-O is firm, about 4 hours. Spoon sour cream over the Jell-O layer and add remaining Jell-O and fruit mixture on top. Refrigerate until firm, about 4 hours, or overnight.

SERVES 8 TO 10

PORT WINE JELL-O SALAD

This festive salad made with cranberries and port wine is for grown-ups. At our house it makes a good holiday salad and conversation piece because Reed likes to brag about using some of his expensive port in this recipe. He now claims this dish as one of his specialties!

1   large package (6 ounces) Berry Blue Jell-O

1   cup boiling water

1   cup port wine

2   cans (8 ounces each) crushed pineapple, with its juice

1   can (16 ounces) whole berry cranberry sauce

1/2 cup slivered almonds

In a medium heat-proof bowl, stir Jell-O into boiling water and continue stirring until dissolved. Add wine, pineapple and juice, cranberry sauce, and almonds. Transfer to a 9-by-13-inch glass baking dish or 4-cup ring mold rinsed in cold water, and refrigerate until firm, about 4 hours. If using a ring mold, unmold onto a decorative plate (see Note).

SERVES 8 TO 10

Note: To unmold the salad, dip the ring mold into a large bowl of very hot water for a few seconds. Then invert it onto a plate.

LIME JELL-O WITH CABBAGE

Crunchy cabbage and crispy celery add texture to this combination of vegetables, fruit, and cottage cheese. This goes well with seafood dishes.

1	package (3 ounces) lime Jell-O
1	cup boiling water
1	cup chopped red or green cabbage
1/2	cup chopped celery
1	can (8 ounces) crushed pineapple, with its juice
1	cup mini marshmallows
1	cup cottage cheese
1/2	cup walnuts

In a medium heat-proof bowl, stir Jell-O into boiling water and continue stirring until dissolved. Add remaining ingredients and mix well. Pour into an 8-by-11¾-inch glass baking dish. Refrigerate until firm, about 4 hours, or overnight.

SERVES 6 TO 8

IMPERIAL VEGETABLE JELL-O MOLD

Not all molded salads have to be sweet and include fruit. This one is a rainbow of colors, with crispy vegetables and a creamy, tangy topping. Serve with a hearty meat dish, such as Big Meatballs in Herbed Tomato Sauce (page 228).

1	package (3 ounces) lemon Jell-O
1	cup boiling water
1	cup cold water
1	tablespoon fresh lemon juice
1/4	teaspoon seasoned salt
1	celery stalk, diced
3	green onions, including some tender green tops, sliced
1/3	cup diced red bell pepper
1	small cucumber, peeled, halved lengthwise, seeded, and diced
1/4	cup mayonnaise
1	teaspoon prepared horseradish sauce
2	tablespoons sour cream

In a medium heat-proof bowl, stir Jell-O into boiling water and continue stirring until dissolved. Add cold water, lemon juice, and seasoned salt. Cover and refrigerate until partially set, about 1½ hours. Add celery, green onions, bell pepper, and cucumber and mix well. Pour into a 3-cup mold rinsed in cold water. Refrigerate until firm, about 4 hours longer. In a small bowl, mix mayonnaise, horseradish sauce, and sour cream. Unmold Jell-O onto a decorative plate (see Note on page 138) and spread the mayonnaise mixture on top.

SERVES 4 TO 6

MOLDED CRANBERRY SALAD

A Thanksgiving potluck calls for a molded cranberry salad to go with all the trimmings. This one has a lovely cream cheese topping that makes it special.

1 envelope (1/4 ounce) unflavored gelatin

1/4 cup cold water

1/2 cup hot water

1/4 teaspoon salt

1 can (15 ounces) whole berry cranberry sauce

1 can (8 ounces) crushed pineapple, with its juice

1/2 cup chopped celery

1/4 cup chopped walnuts (optional)

Cream Cheese–Mayonnaise Topping (recipe follows)

Place gelatin in a medium bowl. Add cold water and stir until dissolved. Add hot water and salt and mix well. Add cranberry sauce to the gelatin and mix well. Stir in pineapple and juice, celery, and nuts. Transfer into a 4-cup mold rinsed in cold water. Refrigerate until firm, 3 to 4 hours. Unmold onto a decorative plate (see Note on page 138) and spread with topping.

SERVES 6 TO 8

CREAM CHEESE—MAYONNAISE TOPPING

3 ounces cream cheese at room temperature

2 tablespoons mayonnaise

1 to 2 tablespoons milk

In a small bowl, beat together cream cheese and mayonnaise. Add enough milk for a spreadable consistency.

MAKES 1/2 CUP

CREAMY CUCUMBER MOLD

This refreshing, dill-flavored salad with crisp cucumber and green onions complements seafood. Bring to a seaside or lakeside potluck, or enjoy it at home with your favorite shrimp dish.

1   cup beef, chicken, or vegetable broth

1   envelope (1/4 ounce) unflavored gelatin

2   tablespoons sugar

1   cup sour cream

1/2   teaspoon dry mustard

1/2   teaspoon dried dillweed

2   tablespoons tarragon vinegar or 2 teaspoons white wine vinegar and 1/4 teaspoon dried tarragon

1   large cucumber, peeled, halved lengthwise, seeded, grated, and drained

2   green onions, including some tender green tops, chopped

In a small saucepan over medium heat, warm broth. Add gelatin and sugar and stir until dissolved. Set aside.

In a medium bowl, combine sour cream, mustard, dill-weed, vinegar, cucumber, green onions, and gelatin mixture. Pour into a 3-cup mold rinsed in cold water and refrigerate until firm, 3 to 4 hours. To serve, unmold onto a decorative plate (see Note on page 138).

SERVES 6

TOMATO ASPIC WITH SHRIMP

For those who like a zippy aspic, this one with shrimp is a winner. Every spring I host a Friday Lunch Bunch potluck at our cabin on the McKenzie River, and this salad is always requested. The Egg Dressing adds extra flavor.

1	large package (6 ounces) lemon Jell-O
2	cups boiling water
1	large can (15 ounces) tomato sauce
2	teaspoons fresh lemon juice
2	teaspoons prepared horseradish sauce
1	teaspoon grated yellow onion
1	cup chopped celery
1	cup cooked small bay shrimp
	Egg Dressing (recipe follows; optional)

Put Jell-O in a 9-by-13-inch glass baking dish. Add water and stir until dissolved. Refrigerate until partially set, about 1½ hours. Stir in remaining ingredients and refrigerate until firm, about 4 hours. Serve with Egg Dressing, if desired.

SERVES 12

EGG DRESSING

2	large hard-cooked eggs, chopped
1	cup mayonnaise
2	tablespoons ketchup

In a small bowl, mix together all ingredients.

MAKES ABOUT 2 CUPS

CRABMEAT MOLD

Crab is costly, so serve this wonderful molded salad of crab, celery, onions, olives, and mayonnaise for a special potluck luncheon. Accompany it with a basket of warm croissants.

1	envelope (1/4 ounce) unflavored gelatin
1/4	cup cold water
1/4	cup hot water
1	cup mayonnaise
1	cup diced celery
2	tablespoons finely chopped green onions, including some tender green tops
1/2	cup sliced pimiento-stuffed green olives
8	ounces crabmeat, flaked
1/4	teaspoon dried dillweed
1/4	teaspoon paprika
1/4	teaspoon salt
	Watercress for garnish

Place gelatin in a medium bowl. Add cold water and stir until dissolved. Stir in hot water and mix well. Cool slightly. Whisk in mayonnaise, and continue whisking until smooth. Fold in celery, greens onions, olives, crab, dillweed, paprika, and salt and mix well. Pour into an 8-inch-square glass baking dish. Refrigerate until firm, about 3 hours. Cut into squares and garnish with watercress.

SERVES 6

If you are hosting a potluck luncheon for a bridal shower, book or bridge club, ladies' neighborhood get-
together, or a casual summer potluck supper on the
patio, main course salads are the perfect answer. You
will enjoy the classics, such as the famous Cobb Salad
(page 150), Chicken Caesar Salad (page 148), and
Classic Crab Louie (page 162), as well as Grilled
Flank Steak and Red Onions on Mixed Greens (page
170) and many other exciting combinations.

Most of the preparation for main course salads can be
done in advance and the ingredients then assembled at
serving time. Accompany these salads with an assortment
of breads and a seasonal dessert for a complete meal.
Enjoy!

BIG B SALAD

The "Bs" stand for the butter lettuce, bacon, blue cheese, black beans, Blackened Chicken Breasts, and Buttermilk Herb Dressing. Serve this hearty salad at a potluck luncheon if men are included. The dressing is similar to ranch and is good on tossed green salads.

	Blackened Chicken Breasts, sliced (facing page)
8 to 10	cups torn butter lettuce (1 medium to large head)
4	slices bacon, cooked, drained, and crumbled
1	cup crumbled blue cheese
1/2	cup black beans, drained and rinsed
	Buttermilk Herb Dressing (facing page)

Prepare the chicken breasts and set aside. In a large salad bowl, combine lettuce, bacon, blue cheese, and beans. Toss with enough dressing to coat and place on a large platter or divide equally among 6 plates. Top with chicken breast strips and pass extra dressing in a pitcher.

SERVES 6

BLACKENED CHICKEN BREASTS

These chicken breasts are highly seasoned and then cooked quickly in a heavy cast-iron skillet over high heat until well browned but not really blackened.

4 tablespoons butter or margarine, melted

4 boned and skinned chicken breast halves (about 2 pounds), flattened

2 tablespoons Cajun seasoning (see Note)

Pour butter into a shallow bowl. Dip chicken in butter and place on a plate. Sprinkle both sides with seasoning.

Preheat a cast-iron skillet over high heat until drops of water sizzle, about 5 minutes. Place chicken in skillet and cook until thoroughly browned on one side, about 4 minutes. Drizzle with remaining butter, turn with tongs, and cook about 5 minutes longer. Remove from pan and cool slightly, then cut into strips. Cover and refrigerate until ready to use.

SERVES 6 IN A SALAD

Note: Cajun seasoning can be purchased at most supermarkets.

BUTTERMILK HERB DRESSING

1/2 cup mayonnaise

1/3 cup buttermilk

2 garlic cloves, minced

1/4 teaspoon dried basil

1/4 teaspoon dried thyme

1/2 teaspoon salt

Freshly ground pepper

1 teaspoon Worcestershire sauce

1 tablespoon grated Parmesan cheese

1 tablespoon finely chopped parsley

In a small bowl, whisk together all ingredients. Cover and refrigerate until ready to use.

MAKES ABOUT 3/4 CUP

CHICKEN CAESAR SALAD

Strips of lightly browned chicken breast straight from the grill transform the classic Caesar Salad (page 78) into a light meal. Crisp romaine, garlicky croutons, and a mild anchovy dressing are the other traditional ingredients. Feature this salad at a graduation luncheon along with a basket of warm croissants.

3	boned and skinned chicken breast halves (about 1 1/2 pounds)
	Vegetable oil for brushing on chicken breasts
	Salt and freshly ground pepper
8 to 10	cups torn romaine lettuce (about 1 head)
1	cup Baked Garlic Croutons (page 78)
	Caesar Dressing (page 79)
12	cherry tomatoes for garnish
	Pitted black olives for garnish
	Anchovy fillets for garnish (optional)
	Parmesan cheese shaved with a vegetable peeler for topping

Preheat a grill or broiler. Brush chicken breasts with oil on both sides and season with salt and pepper to taste. Grill or broil until center is no longer pink, about 5 minutes on each side. Cool and cut into 1/2-inch slices.

In a large bowl, mix romaine and croutons with enough dressing to coat. Place on a large platter or divide evenly among 6 salad plates. Top with chicken slices and add cherry tomatoes and olives. Add anchovy fillets, if desired, and a few Parmesan shavings on top.

SERVES 6

Variation: For Shrimp Caesar Salad, omit chicken and add 12 to 14 large cooked shrimp.

CITRUS TURKEY SALAD WITH AVOCADOS

Here is a refreshing, eye-catching salad of orange, grapefruit, and avocado slices arranged around a mound of cubed turkey breast seasoned with a tangy dressing. This is a good way to use leftover turkey from the holidays.

4	cups cubed cooked turkey breast
2	tablespoons diced red onion
1/4	teaspoon salt
	Orange Mayonnaise (recipe follows)
	Romaine lettuce leaves for lining platter
1	grapefruit, peeled, white pith removed, and sliced
2 or 3	oranges, peeled, white pith removed, and sliced crosswise
2	avocados, peeled and sliced
1/4	cup slivered almonds
	Clusters of seedelss green grapes for garnish

In a medium bowl, mix turkey, onion, and salt with ½ cup Orange Mayonnaise. Cover and refrigerate 1 to 2 hours. Arrange romaine leaves on a rectangular platter, stalks pointing toward the center. Mound the turkey mixture in the middle. Arrange grapefruit slices on one end of the platter and orange slices on the other. Arrange avocado slices around the turkey. Sprinkle almonds on top and garnish with grapes. Serve remaining dressing in a bowl.

SERVES 6

ORANGE MAYONNAISE

This dressing is good on any fruit combination.

1	cup mayonnaise
2	tablespoons orange juice
2	tablespoons white wine vinegar
1	teaspoon grated orange zest
1/4	teaspoon salt

In a small bowl, whisk together all ingredients until smooth. Cover and refrigerate until ready to use.

MAKES ABOUT 1 1/4 CUPS

COBB SALAD

This famous "salad of the stars" originated at the Brown Derby Restaurant in Hollywood in 1930, and it is still popular today. In some versions, all of the ingredients are mixed together, but in this one, they are added in rows on top of the greens. You can make it the way you prefer.

8 cups mixed torn greens

Balsamic Vinaigrette (facing page) or Creamy Blue Cheese Dressing (page 90)

2 chicken breast halves (1 to 1 1/2 pounds), cooked (see Note) and diced

8 ounces bacon, diced, cooked, and drained

2 large tomatoes, seeded, chopped, and drained

2 avocados, peeled and chopped

6 green onions, including some tender green tops, sliced

2/3 cup crumbled blue cheese

3 large hard-cooked eggs, chopped

Toss greens lightly with some of the dressing and place in a large shallow salad bowl or on 6 individual plates. Arrange chicken, bacon, tomatoes, avocado, and green onions in rows on top of the greens. Sprinkle blue cheese and egg on top. Serve the remaining dressing in a small pitcher or bowl.

SERVES 6

Note: To cook chicken breasts, use either skinned and boned chicken breasts or breasts with bone in and skin on. (The bones and skin add extra flavor.) Put chicken breasts in a saucepan and add enough water or chicken stock to cover. For 2 chicken breast halves, add a pinch of salt, 1 parsley sprig, 1 small chunk of onion, and 2 or 3 black peppercorns. Bring to a boil over high heat, immediately reduce to low, and simmer (liquid should barely bubble), covered, until chicken turns white, about 15 minutes. Remove chicken to a plate to cool until ready to use, or cool in liquid if time allows. Remove any skin and bones, if necessary. The broth may be strained and refrigerated or frozen for other uses. One 1/2-pound chicken breast half will yield about 1 cup of diced cooked chicken.

BALSAMIC VINAIGRETTE

Balsamic vinegar is a sweet, aromatic vinegar. It may be new to you, but it has been used in Italy for years.

2/3   cup olive oil

3   tablespoons balsamic vinegar or red wine vinegar

2   teaspoons fresh lemon juice

1   garlic clove, minced

1   tablespoon chopped fresh basil or 1/4 teaspoon dried basil

1/2   teaspoon sugar

1/2   teaspoon salt

1/8   teaspoon freshly ground pepper

In a medium bowl, whisk together all ingredients.

MAKES ABOUT 1 CUP

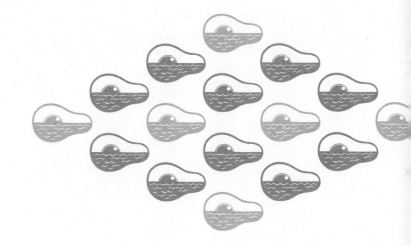

CONFERENCE SALAD

Caramelized almonds add a sweet, nutty taste and a crunchy texture to this combination salad, which will earn you raves. This was served to me at a potluck business meeting, and everyone wanted the recipe. Leftover chicken or turkey breast may be used.

5	cups torn green leaf lettuce (about 1/2 head)
5	cups torn romaine lettuce (about 1/2 head)
1	cup chopped celery
4	green onions, including some tender green tops, sliced
1	can (11 ounces) Mandarin oranges, drained
1	avocado, peeled and chopped
1	red apple, unpeeled, cored, and diced
1/2	cup crumbled blue cheese
3	cups cubed cooked chicken breast (see Note on page 150)
1/2	cup Caramelized Almonds (facing page)
	Sweet Wine Dressing (facing page)

In a large bowl, combine all ingredients, except dressing, cover, and refrigerate. Toss lightly with enough dressing to coat just before serving.

SERVES 6 TO 8

CARAMELIZED ALMONDS

3 tablespoons sugar

1/2 cup sliced almonds

In a small skillet over medium heat, combine sugar and almonds until sugar melts and nuts are coated, stirring constantly, about 3 minutes. Be careful not to burn. Spread nuts on a piece of foil to cool.

SWEET WINE DRESSING

1/4 cup vegetable oil

2 tablespoons sugar

2 tablespoons dry white wine

1/2 teaspoon salt

Freshly ground pepper

1 tablespoon chopped fresh parsley

In a small bowl, whisk together all ingredients.

MAKES ABOUT 1/2 CUP

CHICKEN AND FRESH PEAR SALAD

The ingredients for this salad can be made ahead and then assembled at serving time. Serve with freshly baked or purchased bread sticks. Good pears to use are Bartlett or Comice. They are mild and sweet with a creamy texture and are good eaten raw.

3 cups cubed cooked chicken breast (see Note on page 150)

2 fresh pears, peeled and cut into bite-sized pieces

1/3 cup chopped walnuts

1/4 cup chopped red onion

1/2 cup crumbled blue cheese

Herb Mayonnaise (recipe follows)

Romaine lettuce leaves for lining platter

In a large bowl, combine chicken, pears, nuts, onion, and blue cheese and mix with enough dressing to coat. Cover and refrigerate several hours. Line a platter with romaine leaves and mound the chicken mixture in the center.

SERVES 4

HERB MAYONNAISE

This dressing is also good on cooked, cold asparagus for a spring salad.

1/4 cup mayonnaise

3 tablespoons plain nonfat yogurt

1 tablespoon white wine vinegar

1/4 cup chopped fresh basil or 3/4 teaspoon dried basil

2 teaspoons snipped fresh rosemary or 3/4 teaspoon dried rosemary

1/4 teaspoon salt

Freshly ground pepper

In a small bowl, whisk together all ingredients. Cover and refrigerate until ready to use.

MAKES ABOUT 1/2 CUP

CHICKEN CURRY SALAD
WITH CHUTNEY DRESSING

For an informal summer potluck get-together, prepare this salad of cubed chicken, celery, and crisp green apples tossed with a mellow chutney dressing. Chutney is an East Indian condiment that contains vinegar, sugar, and spices. Serve with a tropical punch for a cooling drink.

3	cups cubed cooked chicken breast (see Note on page 150)
1	Granny Smith apple, unpeeled, cored, and chopped
1	cup seedless green grapes
1	cup chopped celery
1/4	cup diced red onion
1/4	cup raisins (optional)
	Chutney Dressing (recipe follows)
1/4	cup slivered almonds, toasted (see Note on page 108)

In a large bowl, combine chicken, apple, grapes, celery, onion, and raisins, if desired. Toss with enough dressing to coat and sprinkle with almonds. Serve immediately.

SERVES 4 TO 6

CHUTNEY DRESSING

3/4	cup mayonnaise
3	tablespoons chutney, preferably Major Grey's
1	teaspoon curry powder
2	tablespoons fresh lime juice
1	teaspoon grated lime zest
1/4	teaspoon salt

In a medium bowl, whisk together all ingredients until smooth. Cover and refrigerate until ready to use.

MAKES ABOUT 3/4 CUP

CURRIED CHICKEN, ARTICHOKE, AND RICE SALAD

Serve this salad to the book club while you discuss the latest best-seller. A light curry dressing binds together all the ingredients in this enticing salad. Serve with a fresh fruit platter.

1 1/2	cups cooked long-grain white rice (1/2 cup raw)
6	green onions, including some tender green tops, sliced
2	cups cubed cooked chicken or turkey breast (see Note on page 150)
1/4	cup diced red bell pepper
1/2	cup chopped celery
1	jar (6 1/2 ounces) marinated artichoke hearts, drained and coarsely chopped (reserve 1 tablespoon marinade for dressing)
1/2	cup sliced pimiento-stuffed green olives
	Curry Dressing (recipe follows)

In a medium bowl, combine rice, green onions, chicken, bell pepper, celery, artichoke hearts, and olives and mix with dressing.

SERVES 6

CURRY DRESSING

1/2	cup mayonnaise
2	tablespoons white wine vinegar
1	tablespoon marinade from marinated artichoke hearts
1	tablespoon vegetable oil
1 to 2	teaspoons curry powder, or to taste
1/2	teaspoon salt
1/8	teaspoon freshly ground pepper

In a small bowl, whisk together all ingredients until smooth. Cover and refrigerate until ready to use.

MAKES ABOUT 3/4 CUP

BRIDGE CLUB CHICKEN SALAD FOR "THE GIRLS"

My mother-in-law, who played bridge two or three times a week, always served this salad when it was her turn to host the bridge club potluck.

4   cups cubed cooked chicken breast
    (see Note on page 150)

1   cup diced celery

1/2 cup diced green bell pepper

1   cup seedless green grapes

1/2 cup slivered almonds

1/2 cup sliced pimiento-stuffed green
    olives (optional)

1   can (20 ounces) pineapple chunks,
    drained (reserve juice for dressing)

1   can (11 ounces) Mandarin oranges,
    drained

    Pineapple Salad Dressing
    (recipe follows)

    Lettuce leaves for lining plates

In a large bowl, combine all ingredients, except lettuce leaves, with enough dressing to coat and mix well. Cover and refrigerate several hours before serving. Mound on lettuce leaves on individual plates.

SERVES 8

PINEAPPLE SALAD DRESSING

1 to 1 1/2 cups salad dressing or mayonnaise

1   teaspoon Dijon mustard

1   teaspoon finely chopped yellow onion

3   tablespoons reserved pineapple juice

In a small bowl, whisk together all ingredients until smooth. Cover and refrigerate until ready to use.

MAKES ABOUT 1 1/2 CUPS

SALADE NIÇOISE

Salade Niçoise is a famous composed salad from the city of Nice, in southern France. The traditional ingredients are tuna, potatoes, green beans, onions, and tomatoes, arranged in groups on a platter and garnished with eggs, anchovies, and olives. It makes an elegant and appealing contribution to a potluck luncheon.

4 to 5   small new yellow potatoes (about 1 pound), unpeeled, scrubbed, and halved

      Lemon-Herb Dressing (page 111)

2   tablespoons chopped fresh parsley

8   ounces green beans, trimmed

6   cups (about 1/2 head) torn Bibb lettuce

1   large tuna steak (12 ounces), broiled and flaked (see Note), or 2 cans (6 ounces each) albacore tuna in oil, drained and flaked

2   plum tomatoes, quartered

1/2   red onion, thinly sliced

3   large hard-cooked eggs, quartered

1/2   cup pitted niçoise or kalamata olives

4 to 6   anchovy fillets, drained

1   tablespoon capers, drained

In a medium saucepan over medium heat, cook the potatoes in gently boiling salted water to cover until tender, 15 to 20 minutes. Drain and, while still warm, cut into 1/2-inch slices. Place in a medium bowl and toss with 3 tablespoons of the dressing and the parsley. Set aside.

In the same pan, cook beans over medium heat in gently boiling salted water to cover until tender-crisp, 7 to 8 minutes. Cool under cold running water and pat dry with a paper towel. Place in a medium bowl and toss with 3 tablespoons of the dressing. (The salad can be made up to this point several hours in advance. Cover vegetables and refrigerate.)

Serve on individual lettuce-lined plates or on a large platter. On top of the lettuce, arrange potatoes on one side, beans on the other side, and tuna in the middle. Add tomatoes, onion, eggs, and olives around the outside. Top with anchovy fillets and capers. Serve remaining dressing in a pitcher.

SERVES 4 TO 6

Note: To broil tuna, preheat broiler. Brush tuna with some olive oil and season with salt and pepper. Broil until fish flakes, 3 to 4 minutes on each side. (Tuna can also be grilled.)

TOMATOES STUFFED WITH TUNA SALAD

This classic summer luncheon salad is easy and inexpensive to make, and most of the ingredients are usually on hand. Buttery avocado cubes add a luscious texture to the filling.

6 medium firm tomatoes, unpeeled

2 cans (6 ounces each) albacore tuna in oil, drained (see Note)

1 tablespoon fresh lemon juice

3 hard-cooked eggs, chopped

1 cup diced celery

1 sweet pickle, chopped

2 green onions, including some tender green tops, chopped

2 avocados, peeled and cut into bite-sized pieces

1/2 cup mayonnaise

2 teaspoons Dijon mustard

1 teaspoon sweet pickle juice

Salt and freshly ground pepper

Lettuce leaves for lining the plate

With a sharp knife, cut stem-end out of each tomato and discard. Then quarter it about halfway down, keeping the tomato intact.

In a medium bowl, combine remaining ingredients and mix well. Cover and refrigerate 1 hour. Spread tomatoes open slightly and fill with equal amounts of filling mixture. Arrange on lettuce leaves.

SERVES 6

Note: To improve the taste and texture of canned tuna, rinse in a strainer under cold water and flake with your fingers, breaking up the chunks. Over a bowl, let tuna drain in the strainer, in the refrigerator, for 30 minutes.

CRAB, SHRIMP, AND AVOCADO SALAD WITH ARTICHOKE MAYONNAISE

Add style to the buffet table with this terrific composed salad of crab, shrimp, avocados, and onions, arranged on tender lettuce leaves and served with Artichoke Mayonnaise.

1 pound large shrimp (about 24), peeled, deveined, and cooked (see Note)

1 tablespoon fresh lemon juice

1 head Bibb lettuce, torn into large pieces

12 ounces crabmeat, flaked

2 avocados, sliced

1 medium red onion, sliced

2 tomatoes, cut into wedges, or 12 cherry tomatoes

Artichoke Mayonnaise (recipe follows)

Toss shrimp with lemon juice. On a platter lined with the lettuce, arrange shrimp, crab, avocados, and onion in groups. Add tomato wedges around the outside. Serve the mayonnaise in a bowl on the side.

SERVES 6

Note: To cook the shrimp, put them in gently boiling salted water to cover and continue boiling until they turn pink, 2 to 3 minutes. Cool under cold running water and drain.

ARTICHOKE MAYONNAISE

1 jar (6 1/2 ounces) marinated artichoke hearts, drained (reserve 2 table-spoons marinade)

1 cup mayonnaise

3 parsley sprigs

In a food processor or blender, combine artichoke hearts, reserved marinade, mayonnaise, and parsley and blend until smooth. Cover and chill until ready to use.

MAKES ABOUT 2 CUPS

TWELFTH-STREET BISTRO SALAD

This recipe was inspired by a dish served at a cozy restaurant in a nearby city. Freshly grilled salmon tops this salad of romaine, Belgian endive, bell pepper, tomatoes, and chunks of blue cheese. A great main course salad for a bridge club potluck.

	Juice of 1 lemon (about 3 tablespoons)
2	tablespoons olive oil
1/4	teaspoon salt
	Freshly ground pepper
1	tablespoon chopped fresh parsley
1 1/2 to 2	pounds salmon fillet (about 1 1/2 inches thick)
1	large head romaine lettuce, sliced (about 10 cups)
3	Belgian endives, cut into 1/4-inch slices
1	cup chopped red bell pepper
2	tomatoes, seeded, chopped, and drained
1	cup chunks of blue cheese
	Lemon Mayonnaise (recipe follows)
	Lemon wedges for garnish

Combine lemon juice, oil, salt, pepper to taste, and parsley in a shallow dish. Add salmon and turn to coat. Let stand 10 to 15 minutes at room temperature.

Prepare the grill for cooking over direct high heat. Remove fillet from marinade and place, skin-side down, on an oiled grill rack. Brush on remaining marinade. Grill until fish begins to flake when tested with a fork, 12 to 15 minutes. Do not turn. To serve, remove fish from its skin with a spatula and divide evenly into 6 pieces.

In a large bowl, place romaine, endive, bell pepper, tomatoes, and blue cheese. Toss with Lemon Mayonnaise until coated. Divide mixture evenly among 6 plates and top each with a piece of salmon. Garnish with lemon wedges.

SERVES 6

LEMON MAYONNAISE

1/2	cup mayonnaise
1/4	cup plain nonfat yogurt
1	teaspoon Dijon mustard
2	tablespoons fresh lemon juice
1/2	teaspoon grated lemon zest
1/2	teaspoon sugar
1/4	teaspoon salt
	Freshly grated pepper

In a small bowl, whisk together all ingredients. Cover and refrigerate until ready to use.

MAKES ABOUT 3/4 CUP

CLASSIC CRAB LOUIE

Crab Louie is an all-time favorite main course salad for a luncheon potluck. The Tangy Thousand Island Dressing is one of the best for seafood salads. All ingredients should be thoroughly chilled before assembling. Have someone bring assorted breads and a fancy dessert.

1   large head iceberg lettuce, shredded

1   pound crabmeat, flaked

3   tomatoes, seeded and cut into wedges

4   large hard-cooked eggs, quartered

2   avocados, peeled and sliced

1   tablespoon fresh lemon juice

Pitted black olives for garnish

Lemon wedges for garnish

Tangy Thousand Island Dressing (facing page)

Divide lettuce evenly among 4 dinner plates. Mound crabmeat on top of lettuce and arrange tomato wedges and egg quarters around the outside. Sprinkle avocado with lemon juice and add to each plate. Garnish with olives and lemon wedges. Pass the dressing in a bowl.

SERVES 4

TANGY THOUSAND ISLAND DRESSING

1	cup mayonnaise
1	tablespoon fresh lemon juice
1/4	cup chili sauce or ketchup
1	teaspoon prepared horseradish sauce
1	tablespoon sweet pickle relish or 1 sweet pickle, coarsely chopped
2	green onions, including some tender green tops, coarsely chopped
1	parsley sprig, torn up
1/2	teaspoon dry mustard
1	teaspoon Worcestershire sauce
1/2	teaspoon salt
2	drops of Tabasco sauce

In a food processor, combine all ingredients and process until well blended. Cover and refrigerate until ready to use.

MAKES ABOUT 1 1/3 CUPS

SHRIMP AND FRUIT SALAD WITH LIME DRESSING

Shrimp and exotic fruit complement each other in this main course salad drizzled with a sprightly lime dressing. Papayas are grown in semitropical regions. They are pear-shaped, with golden skin and a sweet-tart flesh. Ripe papayas are soft to the touch and can be purchased year-round.

Green leaf lettuce leaves for lining platter

1 pound large shrimp (about 24), peeled, deveined, and cooked (see Note on page 160)

1 cantaloupe, cut into wedges, seeded, rind removed, and wedges cut into spears

1 papaya, peeled, seeded, and sliced

1 fresh pineapple, peeled, cored, and sliced

1 cup seedless green grapes

Lime Dressing (page 122)

On a large plate or platter lined with lettuce leaves, arrange shrimp, cantaloupe, papaya, and pineapple slices. Scatter grapes on top. Serve the dressing on the side.

SERVES 6 TO 8

SHRIMP AND VEGETABLE SALAD

This composed salad of shrimp, cucumber, and tomatoes, attractively arranged on a platter, makes a refreshing, light main course for a summer potluck supper. Have all of the ingredients cold and assemble just before serving. Accompany with warm cheese bread.

1   **pound large shrimp (about 24), peeled, deveined, and cooked (see Note on page 160)**

¼   **cup diced red onion**

1   **cup diced celery**

     Tangy Thousand Island Dressing (page 163)

     Lettuce leaves for lining platter

2   **tomatoes, sliced**

1   **cucumber, peeled and sliced**

¼   **cup pitted black olives**

In a medium bowl, combine shrimp, onion, and celery with enough dressing to coat. Line a platter with lettuce and place shrimp in the middle. Arrange tomatoes on one side and cucumber slices on the other. Garnish with olives. Pass additional dressing in a bowl.

SERVES 4

COLD ROAST BEEF, GREEN BEANS, AND POTATO COMBO

Men will enjoy this hearty salad of chopped roast beef and vegetables with a zippy Horseradish Dressing for a summer-evening potluck. This is a good way to use up leftover roast beef. Serve with a good dry red wine and Walnut Brownies with Caramel Sauce and Ice Cream (page 317) for dessert.

2	cups water
1/4	teaspoon salt, plus more to taste
4	cups diced potatoes, preferably russet or Yukon Gold
8	ounces fresh green beans, trimmed and cut into thirds
4	cups cooked roast beef, cut into bite-sized pieces
2 1/2	cups halved cherry tomatoes, drained (see Note)
1/2	cup sliced green onions, including some tender green tops
1	cup sliced radishes
1	dill pickle, chopped
	Horseradish Dressing (facing page)
	Freshly ground pepper
2	tablespoons capers, drained

In a medium saucepan, bring water to a boil, add ¼ teaspoon salt, and lower heat to medium. Cook potatoes, covered, until tender, about 15 minutes. Cool under cold running water and drain.

In another medium saucepan over high heat, cook beans in boiling salted water to cover until tender-crisp, 6 to 7 minutes. Cool under cold running water and drain.

In a large bowl, combine beans, potatoes, beef, tomatoes, green onions, radishes, and pickle. Toss with enough dressing to coat. Add salt and pepper to taste. Cover and refrigerate several hours. Sprinkle with capers before serving.

SERVES 8

Note: Drain cherry tomatoes, cut-side down, on a paper towel for 5 minutes.

HORSERADISH DRESSING

1/2	cup mayonnaise
1/4	cup buttermilk
1 to 2	tablespoons prepared horseradish sauce, to your taste
1	teaspoon dry mustard
1/2	teaspoon salt
1/8	teaspoon freshly ground pepper

In a medium bowl, whisk together all ingredients. Cover and refrigerate until ready to use.

MAKES ABOUT 1 CUP

TACO SALAD

This lively combination of beef, tomatoes, beans, onions, and chopped lettuce, topped with a spicy dressing, is the next best thing to going to Mexico. The sour cream adds a cooling touch. Serve with a pitcher of ice-cold sangria.

1	pound ground beef
1	cup chopped yellow onion
2	garlic cloves, minced
1	teaspoon chili powder
1/4	teaspoon ground cumin
1/2	teaspoon salt
	Freshly ground pepper
3	tablespoons vegetable oil, as needed
1	can (15 ounces) red kidney beans, rinsed and drained
3/4	cup pitted and thinly sliced black olives
1	cup grated Cheddar cheese
4	medium tomatoes, seeded, chopped, and drained
2	avocados, peeled and cubed
4 to 5	cups chopped iceberg lettuce
	Spicy Mexican Dressing (facing page)
	Tortilla chips
	Sour cream as an accompaniment

In a large skillet over medium-high heat, sauté meat, onion, garlic, chili powder, cumin, salt, and pepper to taste, breaking up meat with a spoon, until meat is no longer pink, about 5 minutes. Add vegetable oil, if needed. Stir in beans, transfer mixture to a large bowl, and cool slightly. Add olives, cheese, tomatoes, avocados, and lettuce and toss with enough dressing to coat. Tuck a few chips around the edges of the bowl and accompany with a bowl of sour cream and additional chips.

SERVES 6

Note: If making ahead, do not add avocados, lettuce, dressing, or chips until serving time.

SPICY MEXICAN DRESSING

1/2   cup vegetable oil

1/4   cup sugar

1/4   cup cider vinegar

1   teaspoon salt

1/4   teaspoon dry mustard

1/2   teaspoon paprika

1   teaspoon chili powder

1/2   teaspoon ground cumin

1/4   teaspoon dried oregano

1/4   cup chili sauce

1   tablespoon fresh lemon juice

In a medium bowl, stir oil, sugar, and vinegar until sugar is dissolved. Whisk in remaining ingredients. Cover and refrigerate until ready to use. Whisk again before using.

MAKES ABOUT 3/4 CUP

GRILLED FLANK STEAK AND RED ONIONS ON MIXED GREENS

In the summer, when the barbecue is fired up, make this hearty salad of grilled beef strips and onions on a bed of crisp mixed greens and mushrooms, garnished with garden tomatoes. Serve with warm garlic bread for an informal supper. If you don't want to fire up the grill, you can broil the meat instead.

1	flank steak (about 1 1/2 pounds)
	Red Wine Vinaigrette (page 113)
1	red onion, thickly sliced (see Note)
10	cups mixed greens
8	ounces mushrooms, sliced
1	cup cherry tomatoes or 2 tomatoes, cut into wedges
1/2	cup pitted black olives for garnish

In an 8-by-10-inch glass baking dish, combine flank steak and 1/4 cup of the dressing and turn steak to coat. Cover and refrigerate several hours, turning several times.

Prepare the grill for cooking over medium indirect heat. Brush onion with some of the dressing on both sides. Grill steak until medium-rare, about 8 minutes on each side. When turning the steak, add onion slices to the grill and grill about 7 minutes, turning once.

Place steak on a flat surface and let stand 5 minutes. Cut diagonally across the grain into 3/8-inch slices.

In a large bowl, toss greens and mushrooms with enough of the remaining dressing to coat. Arrange greens on a large platter and top with meat and grilled onion slices. Garnish with tomatoes and olives.

SERVES 6 TO 8

Note: To hold onion together while grilling, place a toothpick through the onion slices. Remove toothpick before serving.

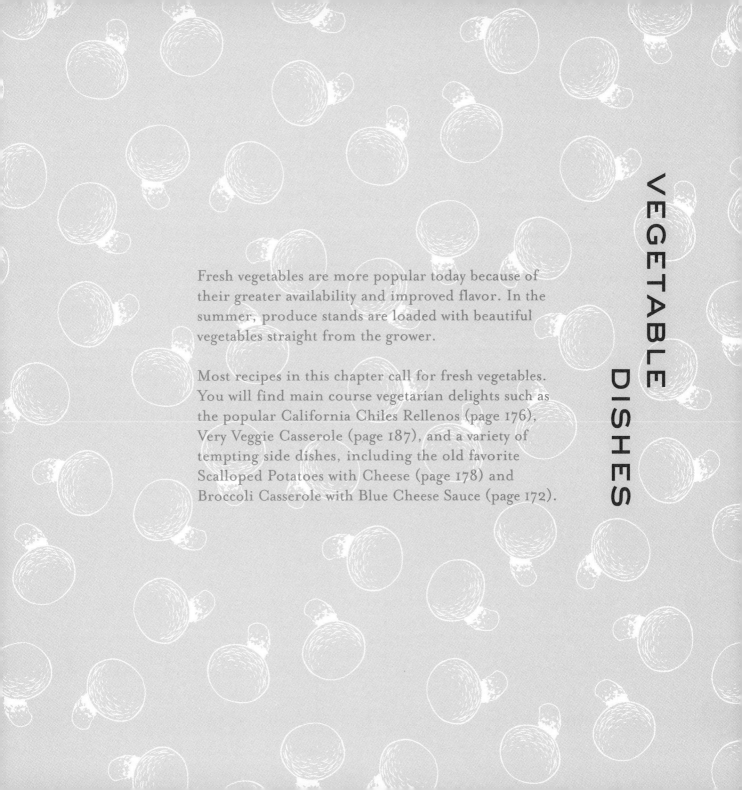

Fresh vegetables are more popular today because of their greater availability and improved flavor. In the summer, produce stands are loaded with beautiful vegetables straight from the grower.

Most recipes in this chapter call for fresh vegetables. You will find main course vegetarian delights such as the popular California Chiles Rellenos (page 176), Very Veggie Casserole (page 187), and a variety of tempting side dishes, including the old favorite Scalloped Potatoes with Cheese (page 178) and Broccoli Casserole with Blue Cheese Sauce (page 172).

VEGETABLE DISHES

BROCCOLI CASSEROLE WITH BLUE CHEESE SAUCE

If you are looking for a complementary side dish for a holiday potluck, try this broccoli casserole with a bold blue cheese sauce. This dish was popular at one of our family potlucks.

5 cups broccoli spears

4 tablespoons butter or margarine

2 tablespoons all-purpose flour

1/4 teaspoon salt

1/8 teaspoon white pepper

1 1/4 cups milk

4 ounces cream cheese, cut into chunks

2 tablespoons crumbled blue cheese

1 cup coarse dry bread crumbs, preferably sourdough

Preheat oven to 350°F. In a medium saucepan over high heat, cook broccoli in boiling salted water to cover for 3 minutes and drain thoroughly. In an 8-by-11¾-inch glass baking dish lightly coated with cooking spray or oil, place broccoli in a single layer.

In a saucepan over medium heat, melt 2 tablespoons of the butter. Add flour, salt, and pepper and stir until bubbly. Add milk and stir constantly until thickened, about 2 minutes. Add cream cheese and blue cheese and stir until cheeses are melted and sauce is well blended. Pour over broccoli.

In a small saucepan over medium heat, melt remaining 2 tablespoons butter. Stir in bread crumbs and mix well. Sprinkle mixture over the casserole. Bake, uncovered, until casserole is bubbly and top is golden, about 30 minutes.

SERVES 4 TO 6

COMPANY CAULIFLOWER

Vegetable casseroles are often overlooked as potluck contributions, but they are always welcome accompaniments. The bacon and cheese topping adds flavor and interest to this satisfying dish.

1	large head cauliflower, trimmed and broken up into florets
1/4	cup mayonnaise
1	tablespoon Dijon mustard
1/4	teaspoon salt
	Freshly ground pepper
4	slices bacon, cooked and crumbled
3/4	cup grated Cheddar cheese
	Paprika for sprinkling on top

Preheat oven to 350°F. In a medium saucepan over medium-high heat, cook cauliflower in boiling salted water to cover until tender-crisp, about 8 minutes. Cool under cold running water and drain. Place in an 8-inch-square baking dish lightly coated with cooking spray or oil.

In a small bowl, combine mayonnaise, mustard, salt, and pepper to taste. Spread evenly over cauliflower. Top with bacon and cheese. Sprinkle lightly with paprika. Bake, uncovered, until heated through and cheese is melted, about 15 minutes.

SERVES 6

CAULIFLOWER AND BROCCOLI GRATIN

This tasty casserole combines two winter vegetables with a cheese sauce and a crunchy crumb topping. Perfect for a small potluck gathering. For a variation, substitute Gruyère cheese for the Cheddar.

2	cups cauliflower florets
2	cups broccoli florets
2	tablespoons butter or margarine
2	tablespoons all-purpose flour
1	cup milk
1/2	teaspoon salt
	Freshly ground pepper
3/4	cup grated Cheddar cheese
2	tablespoons dry white wine
1/2	cup coarse dry bread crumbs
	Freshly grated Parmesan cheese for sprinkling on top

Preheat oven to 350°F. In a saucepan over medium-high heat, cook cauliflower in boiling salted water to cover for 4 minutes. Add broccoli to the cauliflower in the pan and cook 3 minutes longer. Cool vegetables under cold running water and drain. (Do not wash saucepan.) Put vegetables in a gratin dish or casserole lightly coated with cooking spray or oil and set aside.

In the same saucepan, over medium heat, melt butter. Add flour and stir until bubbly. Add milk, salt, and pepper to taste and stir until thickened, about 2 minutes. Add Cheddar cheese and stir until the cheese is melted. Stir in wine and mix well. Pour sauce over vegetables. Sprinkle with bread crumbs and Parmesan cheese. Bake, uncovered, until bubbly, about 25 minutes.

SERVES 4 TO 6

SWEET-AND-SOUR CABBAGE

This side dish can be served hot or at room temperature with a menu of grilled sausages, warm German Potato Salad (page 64), and a good dark beer for a typical German-theme potluck.

4 tablespoons butter or margarine

1 head red cabbage, cored and sliced (about 10 cups)

1/2 cup cider vinegar

1/3 cup sugar

1 teaspoon caraway seeds

1/2 teaspoon salt

Freshly ground pepper

In a large Dutch oven over medium-low heat, melt butter. Add cabbage, vinegar, sugar, and caraway seeds and mix well. Cover and cook, stirring occasionally, until cabbage is tender, about 45 minutes. Remove lid and cook 10 minutes longer. Season with salt and pepper to taste.

SERVES 8

CALIFORNIA CHILES RELLENOS

Don't forget this classic casserole of chiles in a cheesy custard sauce topped with fresh tomatoes or tomato sauce. Either way, it is delicious. Serve as a main course or side dish.

3	cans (7 ounces each) whole green chiles, drained
4	cups grated Cheddar cheese
4	cups grated Monterey Jack cheese
4	large eggs
2/3	cup milk
1	tablespoon all-purpose flour
1/2	teaspoon salt
	Freshly ground pepper
2	tomatoes, sliced and drained, or 1 can (8 ounces) tomato sauce

Preheat oven to 325°F. Split open chiles, rinse, and remove seeds. In a 9-by-13-inch baking dish lightly coated with cooking spray or oil, layer half the opened chiles, then half the cheeses, and repeat with remaining chiles and cheeses.

In a medium bowl, whisk together eggs, milk, flour, salt, and pepper to taste. Pour over chiles and cheese in the baking dish. Bake, uncovered, 25 minutes. Arrange tomatoes on top and bake 10 to 15 minutes longer. Let stand 5 to 10 minutes before serving.

SERVES 6

MUSHROOM AND CHEESE STRATA

Assemble this strata several hours ahead or the night before and bake it for a late-morning brunch potluck. Start the meal with Bloody Marys and include an assortment of breakfast pasteries.

2	tablespoons butter or margarine
1/2	cup chopped yellow onion
1/2	cup chopped celery
1	garlic clove, minced
6	ounces mushrooms, sliced
4	cups cubed day-old bread
2	cups grated Cheddar cheese
2	large eggs
2	cups milk
1	teaspoon dry mustard
1/2	teaspoon dried marjoram
1	teaspoon salt
	Freshly ground pepper

In a large skillet over medium heat, melt butter. Add onion, celery, garlic, and mushrooms and sauté until tender, about 5 minutes. In an 8-by-11¾-inch baking dish lightly coated with cooking spray or oil, layer half of the bread cubes, half of the vegetable mixture, and half of the cheese. Add remaining bread and vegetable mixture in layers.

In a medium bowl, whisk together eggs, milk, mustard, marjoram, salt, and pepper to taste. Pour mixture over all. Add remaining cheese on top. Cover and refrigerate.

Preheat oven to 350°F. Bring casserole to room temperature. Bake, uncovered, until bubbly, 45 to 50 minutes. Let stand 10 minutes before serving.

SERVES 6

SCALLOPED POTATOES WITH CHEESE

Scalloped potatoes are a longtime favorite potluck dish. Here the potatoes and onions are layered in a creamy cheese sauce and served piping hot from the oven. They go especially well with Grilled Pork Chops with Dijon Baste (page 247).

1/4 cup grated Parmesan cheese

2 cups (about 8 ounces) grated Monterey Jack cheese

1 cup milk

2 tablespoons all-purpose flour

1 teaspoon salt

1/8 teaspoon white pepper

2 drops of Tabasco sauce

4 large russet potatoes (about 2 1/2 pounds), peeled and sliced (see Note)

6 green onions, including some tender green tops, sliced

Paprika for sprinkling on top

Preheat oven to 350°F. Toss the Parmesan and Monterey Jack cheeses together in a small bowl. In a medium bowl, whisk together milk, flour, salt, pepper, and Tabasco.

In a 2-quart casserole lightly coated with cooking spray or oil, layer half of the potatoes, all of the green onions, and half of the cheeses. Do not stir. Add remaining potatoes. Pour milk mixture over the potatoes. Add remaining cheeses on top and sprinkle with paprika. Cover and bake 30 minutes. Uncover and bake until potatoes are tender and golden on top, 30 to 35 minutes longer. Let stand 5 minutes before serving.

SERVES 6

Note: Use a food processor for easy slicing. If you prepare potatoes ahead of time, cover with cold salted water to prevent discoloring. Drain and dry with a paper towel before assembling.

CHEESY POTATOES

To complement a beef dish, consider these luscious potatoes with sour cream and cheese. They are the ultimate comfort food, perfect for a cozy potluck with friends. If you like, substitute new potatoes for the russets.

2 cups water

3/4 teaspoon salt

4 large russet potatoes (about 2½ pounds), peeled and halved crosswise

2 tablespoons butter or margarine, melted

1 cup sour cream

Freshly ground pepper

½ cup sliced green onions, including some tender green tops

2 tablespoons chopped fresh parsley

1½ cups grated Cheddar cheese

Paprika for sprinkling on top

Bring water to a boil in a large saucepan, add ¼ teaspoon of the salt, and lower heat to medium. Cook potatoes, covered, until almost tender, 15 to 20 minutes. (Potatoes should be slightly undercooked.) Cool under cold running water and drain. Cut each half in half again and then slice.

Preheat oven to 350°F. In a 2-quart casserole lightly coated with cooking spray or oil, place half of the potatoes in a layer. In a medium bowl, mix together butter, sour cream, remaining ½ teaspoon salt, and pepper to taste. Spread half of this mixture over the potatoes. Sprinkle with green onions, parsley, and half of the cheese. Add the remaining potatoes, top with remaining sour cream mixture, and sprinkle with remaining cheese and the paprika. Bake, uncovered, until bubbly, about 35 minutes.

SERVES 4 TO 6

TWICE-BAKED POTATOES

Time to reintroduce this old standby, which has been a favorite for years. The potatoes can be prepared ahead and then baked the second time at the potluck. This is one of my grandson's favorite potato recipes, which I cook for him when he comes for dinner. He likes to add sour cream on top.

4	medium russet potatoes (about 2 pounds), unpeeled, scrubbed, dried, and rubbed with vegetable oil
3/4	cup grated Cheddar cheese
4	ounces cream cheese at room temperature, cut into chunks
1 to 2	tablespoons milk
1/2	teaspoon salt
	Freshly ground pepper
3	green onions, including some tender green tops, chopped
	Sour cream for topping (optional)

Preheat oven to 350°F. Bake potatoes until soft, about 1 hour. Remove from oven, split each potato lengthwise, and scoop out the pulp, leaving the skin intact. Put the pulp in a mixing bowl. With an electric mixer or a potato masher, beat or mash pulp. Add Cheddar cheese, cream cheese, milk, salt, and pepper to taste and beat until fluffy. Stir in green onions. Spoon potato mixture back into the skins. Place in an 8-inch-square glass baking dish lightly coated with cooking spray or oil. Bake, uncovered, until heated through and lightly browned, 25 to 30 minutes. Top with sour cream, if desired.

SERVES 4

DEVILED NEW POTATOES

This updated version of twice-baked potatoes is made with large new potatoes with a spicy cheese filling. Arrange the potatoes on a platter around Four-Peppercorn Pork Loin Roast (page 238) for a dinner club potluck.

6   large new potatoes (about 2 pounds), unpeeled and scrubbed

1   cup cottage cheese

1/2   cup light sour cream

2   tablespoons grated Parmesan cheese

1   cup grated Cheddar cheese

1/2   teaspoon dry mustard

1   teaspoon dried dillweed

1/4   teaspoon chili powder

1   teaspoon salt

Freshly ground pepper

Paprika for sprinkling on top

Preheat oven to 350°F. Bake potatoes until soft, about 1 hour. Remove from oven and cool slightly. Cut potatoes in half lengthwise. Carefully scoop out pulp and transfer to a mixing bowl, leaving potato skins intact. With an electric mixer, beat pulp with remaining ingredients, except paprika, until fluffy.

Spoon potato mixture back into skins and sprinkle with paprika. Place in a 9-by-13-inch glass baking dish lightly coated with cooking spray or oil. Bake until heated through and lightly browned, 25 to 30 minutes longer.

SERVES 6 TO 12

MAKE-AHEAD GARLIC MASHED POTATOES

Mashed potatoes never go out of style for a holiday dinner. Avoid that last-minute hassle on the big day by making these potatoes ahead. They keep well for up to 3 days in the refrigerator and taste great with a roasted bird or baked ham.

2 cups water

3/4 teaspoon salt

8 russet potatoes (4½ to 5 pounds), peeled and quartered

4 garlic cloves, halved

8 ounces cream cheese at room temperature, cut into chunks

1 cup light sour cream

Freshly ground pepper

2 tablespoons butter

Bring water to a boil in a large saucepan, add ¼ teaspoon of the salt, and lower heat to medium. Cook potatoes and garlic, covered, until tender, about 20 minutes. Drain well.

Preheat oven to 375°F. Using an electric mixer, beat potatoes and garlic until blended. Add cream cheese and sour cream and beat until fluffy. Season with remaining ½ teaspoon salt and pepper to taste. Transfer to a 3-quart casserole lightly coated with cooking spray or butter. Dot with butter. Cover and refrigerate until ready to use or bake, covered, until heated through, 50 to 55 minutes. (If refrigerated, bring the potatoes to room temperature before baking.)

SERVES 10

ORANGE-GLAZED SWEET POTATOES

Sweet potatoes are cut into spears and topped with an orange sauce for an attractive presentation. This is an easy, make-ahead dish to take to a holiday potluck. Use either the pale sweet potato or the darker-skinned variety, which Americans call a yam. (The true yam, however, is grown in South America and is not related to the sweet potato.)

2 cups water

3/4 teaspoon salt

6 large sweet potatoes or yams (about 3 pounds), unpeeled

4 tablespoons butter

3 tablespoons firmly packed brown sugar

2 teaspoons grated orange zest

1 cup orange juice

Preheat oven to 350°F. In a large saucepan, bring the water to a boil, add ¼ teaspoon of the salt, and lower heat to medium. Cook potatoes, covered, until almost tender, about 15 minutes. Drain and cool. Peel and quarter lengthwise.

Arrange potato spears in a 9-by-13-inch baking dish lightly coated with cooking spray or oil. In a small pan over medium heat, melt butter. Add sugar, remaining ½ teaspoon salt, orange zest, and juice and stir until sugar is dissolved and flavors are blended, about 1 minute. Pour orange sauce over potatoes and bake, uncovered, until potatoes are heated through, about 30 minutes.

SERVES 8 TO 10

END-OF-SUMMER VEGETABLE AND FRESH HERB CASSEROLE

Bring the garden to the potluck table with this healthful side dish of mixed vegetables with thyme, basil, and parsley. Herbs are easy to grow in pots and can be kept conveniently close by on the deck or patio. Fresh herbs add a lively flavor to many dishes.

4   new potatoes (about 1 1/2 pounds), unpeeled, scrubbed, and sliced with a food processor or by hand

    Salt and freshly ground pepper

2   tomatoes, sliced

1   large zucchini, unpeeled and sliced

8   ounces mushrooms, sliced

1   yellow onion, sliced and separated into rings

2   garlic cloves, minced

1   teaspoon snipped fresh thyme or 1/2 teaspoon dried thyme

1   tablespoon chopped fresh basil or 3/4 teaspoon dried basil

1/4   cup chopped fresh parsley

1/2   cup chicken broth

2   tablespoons butter or margarine, cut into pieces

2   tablespoons freshly grated Parmesan cheese

1   cup grated Cheddar cheese

Preheat oven to 350°F. In a 9-by-13-inch glass baking dish lightly coated with cooking spray or oil, arrange half of the potatoes in a layer. Season with salt and pepper to taste. Add in layers half of the tomatoes, zucchini, mushrooms, onion rings, garlic, and herbs. Repeat the layers. Pour broth evenly over vegetables. Dot with butter. Do not stir.

Bake, covered, about 1 hour. Sprinkle cheeses over the top and bake, uncovered, until the vegetables are tender-crisp and the cheeses are melted, about 10 minutes longer.

SERVES 8

WINTER VEGETABLE GRATIN

Enjoy this colorful casserole of tomatoes, corn, onions, and a cheesy crumb topping alongside a baked ham at a Christmas family potluck. Include a brioche and a complementary wine.

4	tablespoons butter or margarine
1/2	cup chopped red bell pepper
1/2	cup chopped green bell pepper
1	garlic clove, minced
1/4	cup all-purpose flour
1	cup milk
1/4	teaspoon dried basil
1/4	teaspoon dried oregano
1/2	teaspoon salt
	Freshly ground pepper
1	can (14 1/2 ounces) diced tomatoes, with their juices
2	cups frozen corn, thawed
1	can (14 1/2 ounces) small onions, drained
1	cup grated Cheddar cheese
1/2	cup coarse dry bread crumbs

Preheat oven to 350°F. In a medium saucepan over medium heat, melt butter. Add bell peppers and garlic and sauté until tender, about 5 minutes. Add flour and stir until bubbly. Add milk, basil, oregano, salt, and pepper to taste and stir until thickened, 1 to 2 minutes. Add tomatoes, corn, onions, and half of the cheese. Stir until cheese melts. Pour into a 2½-quart casserole lightly coated with cooking spray or oil. Sprinkle bread crumbs and remaining cheese on top. Bake, uncovered, until bubbly, 45 to 50 minutes.

SERVES 6 TO 8

HARVEST SQUASH AND CORN CASSEROLE

Here's a good fall casserole of zucchini and crookneck squash, corn, and mushrooms to bake along with Burgundy Pot Roast (236). Add a loaf of French bread, request a dessert, and you have an easy potluck dinner to share with friends or family.

3   medium zucchini squash, unpeeled, ends trimmed, and cut into 3/8-inch slices

1   medium crookneck squash, unpeeled, ends trimmed, and cut into 3/8-inch slices

6   green onions, including some tender green tops, sliced

1   garlic clove, minced

2   cups freshly cooked corn kernels, scraped off the cob (about 3 ears), or frozen corn, thawed

8   ounces mushrooms, sliced

2   tomatoes, seeded, chopped, and drained

2   tablespoons chopped fresh parsley

1/2 teaspoon dried marjoram

1   teaspoon salt

    Freshly ground pepper

2   tablespoons butter or margarine

1   cup grated Cheddar cheese

Preheat oven to 350°F. In a 3-quart casserole lightly coated with cooking spray or oil, combine zucchini, crookneck, green onions, garlic, corn, mushrooms, tomatoes, parsley, marjoram, salt, and pepper to taste and stir gently. Dot with butter, cover, and bake until vegetables are tender-crisp, about 40 minutes. Uncover, sprinkle with cheese, and bake until cheese melts, about 10 minutes longer.

SERVES 6 TO 8

VERY VEGGIE CASSEROLE

For a meatless main course dish, here is a delicious casserole with layered fresh vegetables and tomato sauce. Serve it with cornbread and Chocolate Pudding Cake (page 314).

1	bag (10 ounces) spinach
4	medium new potatoes, unpeeled and sliced
4	ounces mushrooms, sliced
1	cup cottage cheese
1	small yellow onion, sliced
2 1/2	cups grated Monterey Jack cheese
1	large can (15 ounces) tomato sauce
1/4	cup chopped fresh parsley
1/4	cup chopped fresh basil or 1 teaspoon dried basil
1/2	teaspoon salt
	Freshly ground pepper

Preheat oven to 350°F. In a large saucepan over medium heat, cook spinach, covered, in an inch or so of gently boiling water, tossing with a fork several times, until wilted, about 3 minutes. Drain well, squeeze dry, and chop.

In a 9-by-13-inch baking dish lightly coated with cooking spray or oil, layer potatoes, mushrooms, cottage cheese, onion slices, 1 cup of the Monterey Jack cheese, and spinach.

In a small saucepan over medium heat, combine tomato sauce, parsley, basil, salt, and pepper to taste and simmer until flavors are blended, about 2 minutes. Pour over casserole. Bake, covered, until potatoes are tender, about 45 minutes. Sprinkle with remaining 1 1/2 cups cheese and bake, uncovered, 10 minutes longer.

SERVES 6

ZUCCHINI AND RICE CASSEROLE

Layers of rice, zucchini, tomatoes, chiles, and cheese serve as a substantial and satisfying meatless dish. Bring this to an early-fall supper potluck, when evenings are cool.

4   medium zucchini, unpeeled and sliced

3   cups cooked long-grain white rice (1 cup raw)

1   can (4 ounces) diced green chiles, drained

4   cups Monterey Jack cheese

3   tomatoes, sliced and drained

4   green onions, including some tender green tops, sliced

2   cups sour cream

1   teaspoon dried oregano

1/2   teaspoon salt

    Freshly ground pepper

Preheat oven to 350°F. In a medium saucepan over medium heat, cook zucchini in gently boiling salted water to cover for 2 minutes. Drain and cool.

Spread rice in bottom of a 9-by-13-inch baking dish lightly coated with cooking spray or oil. Spread chiles on top and sprinkle with 1 cup of the cheese. In layers, add zucchini slices, tomato slices, and green onions.

In a bowl, stir together sour cream, oregano, salt, and pepper to taste and spread over the top. Add remaining 3 cups cheese. Bake, uncovered, until bubbly, about 30 minutes.

SERVES 8

ZUCCHINI POLENTA

Polenta (a staple of Northern Italy) is made from cornmeal. It can be served as mush with butter and cream, or it can be fried or baked and served as a side dish. Here it is combined with grated zucchini and cheese and baked in the oven.

1	cup yellow cornmeal
1	cup water
2	cups chicken broth
1/2	teaspoon salt
1	large zucchini, shredded and drained on a paper towel
3/4	cup grated Cheddar cheese
1	tablespoon butter or margarine
1	can (8 ounces) tomato sauce
1/4	cup grated Parmesan cheese

Preheat oven to 350°F. In a small bowl, mix cornmeal with water. In a saucepan over medium-high heat, bring broth and salt to a boil. Reduce heat to medium-low. Slowly add cornmeal and stir until polenta is smooth, about 2 minutes. (Use a long-handled spoon to stir polenta; it bubbles up and will burn.) Remove from heat. Add zucchini, Cheddar cheese, and butter and stir until well mixed and cheese is melted. Spread the mixture into an 8-inch-square glass baking dish lightly coated with cooking spray or oil. Spoon tomato sauce over the top and sprinkle with Parmesan cheese. Bake, uncovered, until heated through, about 30 minutes. Let stand 5 minutes, then cut into squares to serve.

SERVES 4

CHEESE-STUFFED ZUCCHINI

If you have an overload in the garden and are tired of plain old steamed zucchini, try this cheese-laced version baked in the oven or on the grill.

4   medium zucchini, unpeeled and ends trimmed

1/2   cup grated Monterey Jack cheese

3/4   cup small-curd cottage cheese

1   tablespoon mayonnaise

2   tablespoons sour cream

1   tablespoon chopped fresh parsley

2   tablespoons coarse dry bread crumbs

  Salt

2   tablespoons Parmesan cheese

  Paprika for sprinkling on top

In a medium saucepan over medium heat, cook zucchini in salted water to cover, about 7 minutes. Cool under cold running water and drain. Cut zucchini in half lengthwise. Using a small spoon, scoop out a small amount of pulp and seeds and discard. Place zucchini, cut-side down, on paper towels to drain for a few minutes more.

Preheat oven to 350°F. In a medium bowl, combine Monterey Jack cheese, cottage cheese, mayonnaise, sour cream, parsley, and bread crumbs and mix well. Arrange zucchini halves, hollow-side up, in a 9-by-13-inch glass baking dish lightly coated with cooking spray or oil. Season with salt to taste. Fill each half with an equal amount of cottage cheese mixture. Sprinkle with Parmesan cheese and paprika. Bake until zucchini is tender, 12 to 15 minutes. Alternately, prepare grill for cooking over medium indirect heat. Place zucchini in a foil pan and grill about 15 minutes. Serve immediately.

SERVES 8

The pasta, grain, and legume dishes in this chapter are healthful, satisfying, and compatible with other potluck fare. They include many creative vegetable dishes that will appeal to vegetarians, such as Baked Rice and Mushroom Casserole (page 206), Pasta with Summer Vegetables and Fresh Herbs (page 192), and Mushroom, Spinach, and Noodle Casserole (page 194). You will also recognize some old favorites, such as Baked Four-Cheese Macaroni (page 196), a variation on the classic dish, and Green Onion, Chile, and Rice Casserole (page 203).

These dishes can be conveniently made ahead and baked later and are usually served in the dish in which they are baked. Most of them can be doubled to feed a large potluck crowd. Cook pasta in lots of boiling water according to the package directions. For hot dishes, drain it but do not rinse (the starch helps thicken the sauces). Cooking directions for different types of rice and legumes vary, so again, follow the package directions. The recipes in this chapter are appropriate for a side dish or a main course.

PASTA WITH SUMMER VEGETABLES AND FRESH HERBS

Fresh flavor is assured in this dish if you use fresh vegetables and herbs straight from the garden or local farmers' market. Bring to a summer potluck barbecue along with a baguette.

2	tablespoons olive oil
1	cup chopped yellow onion
1	garlic clove, minced
1	cup chopped red bell pepper
1	large zucchini, unpeeled and sliced
2	tomatoes, seeded, chopped, and drained
1/2	cup chicken or vegetable broth
1/4	cup chopped fresh parsley
1/4	cup chopped fresh basil or 1 teaspoon dried basil
1	tablespoon chopped fresh oregano or 1/2 teaspoon dried oregano
1	tablespoon chopped fresh rosemary or 1/2 teaspoon dried rosemary
1/4	teaspoon salt
	Freshly ground pepper
6	ounces rotini or other pasta, cooked as directed on package and drained
	Crumb Topping (recipe follows)

In a large skillet over medium heat, warm oil. Add onion, garlic, bell pepper, and zucchini and sauté until tender, about 5 minutes. Add tomatoes, broth, herbs, salt, and pepper to taste and sauté 5 minutes longer. Put pasta in a 2-quart casserole lightly coated with cooking spray or oil, add the sauce, and mix well. Sprinkle with the topping and bake, uncovered, until bubbly and flavors are blended, about 30 minutes.

SERVES 4 TO 6

CRUMB TOPPING

3	tablespoons butter or margarine
1	cup coarse dry bread crumbs
1/4	cup freshly grated Parmesan cheese

In a small skillet over medium heat, melt butter. Add bread crumbs and cheese and toss until coated.

OVEN PASTA WITH MUSHROOMS AND CHEESE, ITALIAN STYLE

Creamy fontina cheese and seasoned tomatoes are combined with mushrooms and pasta in this robust side dish. Serve with Crispy Oven-Fried Chicken (page 266) and a tossed green salad with Italian Dressing (page 41).

2 tablespoons vegetable oil

1 cup chopped yellow onion

2 large garlic cloves, minced

8 ounces mushrooms, sliced

1 can (15 ounces) Italian seasoned tomatoes, with their juices, chopped

1/2 cup chopped fresh parsley

1 teaspoon dried basil

1 teaspoon dried oregano

1/4 teaspoon salt

Freshly ground pepper

6 ounces (about 2 1/2 cups) fusilli, cooked as directed on the package and drained

1 cup grated fontina cheese

1/2 cup grated Parmesan cheese

Preheat oven to 350°F. In a large skillet over medium heat, warm oil. Add onion, garlic, and mushrooms and sauté until tender, about 5 minutes. Add tomatoes, parsley, basil, oregano, salt, and pepper to taste and simmer about 5 minutes. Transfer mixture to a 2-quart casserole lightly coated with cooking spray or oil. Add fusilli and fontina and mix well. Sprinkle with Parmesan and bake, uncovered, until bubbly, about 40 minutes.

SERVES 6

MUSHROOM, SPINACH, AND NOODLE CASSEROLE

A creamy sauce adds extra richness to this tasty combination of spinach, mushrooms, and noodles. This goes well with most seafood, and like many pasta dishes, it can be made ahead and baked just before serving. Swiss chard can be substituted for the spinach.

2 cups cottage cheese

1 package (8 ounces) cream cheese, cut into chunks

1 cup milk

2 tablespoons butter or margarine

1/2 cup chopped yellow onion

1 garlic clove, minced

8 ounces mushrooms, sliced

1/4 cup dry white wine

1/2 teaspoon dried thyme

1/2 teaspoon salt

Freshly ground pepper

1 package (10 ounces) frozen spinach, thawed, drained, and squeezed dry, or 1 pound fresh spinach, cooked, drained, squeezed dry, and chopped

12 ounces egg noodles, cooked as directed on package and drained

1/2 cup grated Parmesan cheese

Preheat oven to 350°F. In a food processor, combine cottage cheese, cream cheese, and milk and blend until smooth. Set aside.

In a medium skillet over medium heat, melt butter. Add onion, garlic, and mushrooms and sauté until tender, about 5 minutes. Add wine, thyme, salt, and pepper to taste. Stir in spinach and remove from heat.

Put noodles in a 4-quart casserole lightly coated with cooking spray or oil. Add cheese mixture and spinach-mushroom mixture and toss lightly. Cover and bake until bubbly, about 35 minutes. Uncover, sprinkle with Parmesan cheese, and bake 5 minutes longer.

SERVES 8 TO 10

PASTA WITH FRESH TOMATO AND BASIL SAUCE

Garden tomatoes and basil add a fresh flavor to this tasty sauce, which is mixed with penne and topped with cheese. Make it when locally grown tomatoes and fresh basil are at their peak and freeze another batch for a taste of summer in the winter. The sauce is also good on chicken and meats.

8 ounces penne, cooked as directed on package and drained

Fresh Tomato and Basil Sauce (recipe follows)

1/4 cup freshly grated Parmesan cheese

Preheat oven to 350°F. Put pasta in a 3-quart casserole lightly coated with cooking spray or oil. Add sauce and mix well. Bake, covered, until bubbly, about 25 minutes. Sprinkle with Parmesan and bake 5 minutes longer.

SERVES 6 TO 8

FRESH TOMATO AND BASIL SAUCE

1 tablespoon olive oil

1/2 cup chopped yellow onion

2 garlic cloves, sliced

8 medium tomatoes, peeled, seeded, chopped, and drained (see Notes)

1/2 cup chicken or vegetable broth

2 tablespoons tomato paste (see Notes)

1/4 cup fresh basil leaves, torn

2 parsley sprigs, coarsely chopped

1/8 teaspoon sugar

1/2 teaspoon salt

Freshly ground pepper

In a large saucepan over medium heat, warm oil. Add onion and garlic and sauté until tender, about 5 minutes. Add tomatoes, broth, tomato paste, basil, parsley, sugar, salt, and pepper to taste. Reduce heat to medium-low and simmer, uncovered, 10 minutes. Transfer to a food processor and process until smooth.

MAKES ABOUT 3 CUPS

Notes: To peel tomatoes, drop into a large pot of boiling water for 30 seconds. With a slotted spoon, lift tomatoes out of water and peel when they are cool enough to handle.

Freeze leftover tomato paste.

BAKED FOUR-CHEESE MACARONI

Who doesn't have fond childhood memories of mac 'n' cheese? This creamy version with four cheeses will appeal to all ages, and it can be doubled for a crowd.

8 ounces elbow macaroni, cooked as directed on package and drained

3/4 cup small-curd cottage cheese

1/2 cup sour cream

2 tablespoons all-purpose flour

1/4 teaspoon dry mustard

1/4 teaspoon salt

1/8 teaspoon white pepper

1 cup grated sharp Cheddar cheese

1 cup grated Monterey Jack cheese

1/2 cup freshly grated Parmesan cheese

1/2 teaspoon paprika

Preheat oven to 350°F. Place macaroni in a 2-quart casserole lightly coated with cooking spray or oil. In a food processor or blender, blend cottage cheese, sour cream, flour, mustard, salt, and pepper. Add mixture to the macaroni and mix well. Stir in Cheddar and Monterey Jack cheeses. Top with Parmesan cheese and sprinkle with paprika. Bake, uncovered, until bubbly, about 35 minutes.

SERVES 6

SPINACH LASAGNA

In this outstanding lasagna, layers of noodles alternate with a rich tomato sauce and a creamy spinach filling. At a testing party of nine dishes, guys from the computer office voted this as one of the best.

1	tablespoon vegetable oil
1	cup chopped yellow onion
3	garlic cloves, minced
1	can (14 1/2 ounces) crushed tomatoes in thick purée
1	can (8 ounces) tomato sauce
1	tablespoon chopped fresh basil or 3/4 teaspoon dried basil
1	tablespoon chopped fresh oregano or 3/4 teaspoon dried oregano
1/4	teaspoon sugar
1/2	teaspoon salt
	Freshly ground pepper
1	bag (10 ounces) fresh spinach
2	cups ricotta or cottage cheese
3	cups (about 12 ounces) grated mozzarella cheese
1/2	cup sour cream
1	cup freshly grated Parmesan cheese
9	lasagna noodles, cooked as directed on package and drained

In a large skillet over medium heat, warm oil. Add onion and garlic and sauté until tender, about 5 minutes. Stir in tomatoes, tomato sauce, basil, oregano, sugar, salt, and pepper to taste. Bring to a boil, reduce temperature to low, and simmer, uncovered, 10 minutes. Remove from heat.

While the sauce is simmering, prepare spinach: In a large saucepan over medium heat, cook spinach, covered, in an inch or so of water, tossing with a fork several times, until wilted, about 3 minutes. Drain well, squeeze dry, and chop. In a medium bowl, mix together ricotta, 1 1/2 cups of the mozzarella, sour cream, cooked spinach, and 1/2 cup of the Parmesan.

In the bottom of a 9-by-13-inch baking dish lightly coated with cooking spray or oil, spread 1 cup of the tomato sauce. In layers, add 3 noodles, one third of spinach-cheese mixture (it will not completely cover), and one third of remaining tomato sauce. Repeat layers two more times, ending with tomato sauce. Sprinkle remaining 1 1/2 cups mozzarella and 1/2 cup Parmesan on top. Bake, uncovered, 45 minutes. Let stand 10 minutes, cut into squares, and serve.

SERVES 8 AS A MAIN COURSE

ZITI WITH TOMATOES, ARTICHOKES, BASIL, CHEESE, AND OLIVES

A savory sauce of tomatoes and seasonings is slowly simmered, then baked with pasta, artichokes, and cheese. A good side dish for any potluck occasion, such as a block party.

1	tablespoon olive oil
1	cup chopped yellow onion
2	garlic cloves, minced
1	can (28 ounces) whole tomatoes, with their juices, coarsely chopped
1	can (8 ounces) tomato sauce
1/4	cup chopped fresh parsley
1	tablespoon chopped fresh basil or 3/4 teaspoon dried basil
1	teaspoon dried oregano
1/2	teaspoon salt
	Freshly ground pepper
8	ounces (about 3 cups) ziti, cooked as directed on package and drained
1	can (13 3/4 ounces) quartered artichoke hearts, drained
1	cup grated mozzarella cheese
3/4	cup pitted kalamata olives or ripe black olives, halved
1/2	cup freshly grated Parmesan cheese, plus additional cheese for serving

Preheat oven to 350°F. In a large saucepan over medium heat, warm oil. Add onion and garlic and sauté until tender, about 5 minutes. Add tomatoes, tomato sauce, parsley, basil, oregano, salt, and pepper to taste and bring to a boil. Reduce heat to medium-low and simmer, uncovered, until slightly thickened, about 15 minutes, stirring occasionally. Add pasta, artichokes, mozzarella cheese, and olives and mix well.

Transfer to a 3-quart casserole lightly coated with cooking spray or oil. Cover and bake 30 minutes. Uncover and sprinkle with Parmesan cheese. Bake until bubbly, about 20 minutes longer. Serve additional Parmesan cheese in a bowl.

SERVES 6

BAKED ORZO AND PARMESAN CHEESE

In Italian, *orzo* means "barley," but it is really a small oval pasta, which is often served in place of rice. The addition of cheese gives the dish extra flavor and a creamy texture. It makes a good side dish for a grilled or broiled steak.

2	tablespoons butter or margarine
6	green onions, including some tender green tops, sliced
1	large garlic clove, minced
1	cup orzo
2 1/4	cups chicken broth or water
1/2	teaspoon salt
	Freshly ground pepper
1/2	cup freshly grated Parmesan cheese, preferably Parmigiano-Reggiano
1/4	cup chopped fresh parsley

Preheat oven to 350°F. In a medium saucepan over medium heat, melt butter. Add green onions and garlic and sauté until vegetables are soft, about 5 minutes. Stir in orzo and cook 1 minute longer. Add broth, salt, and pepper to taste and bring to a boil. Transfer to a 2-quart casserole lightly coated with cooking spray or oil. Stir in Parmesan and parsley. Bake, covered, until liquid is absorbed, 35 to 40 minutes.

SERVES 4

FAMILY NOODLE DISH

This is a popular side dish at our house when we bake turkey or salmon on our covered barbecue. It is easy to make and will feed the whole family. It also makes a good potluck dish because it is complementary to most other casseroles.

1	package (12 ounces) egg noodles, cooked as directed on package and drained
2	cups sour cream
2	cups cottage cheese
1	cup sliced green onions (optional)
1/2	cup chopped fresh parsley (optional)
1	teaspoon Worcestershire sauce
2 to 3	drops of Tabasco sauce
1/2	teaspoon salt
	Freshly ground pepper
1/3	cup freshly grated Parmesan cheese

Preheat oven to 350°F. Put noodles in a 3-quart casserole lightly coated with cooking spray or oil. In a medium bowl, stir together sour cream, cottage cheese, green onions and parsley, if using, Worcestershire, Tabasco, salt, and pepper to taste. Add to noodles and mix well. Sprinkle top with Parmesan cheese. Bake, uncovered, until heated through, about 30 minutes.

SERVES 8

SPINACH-FILLED MANICOTTI

This dish takes a little time to prepare, but it makes a very welcome potluck casserole that will appeal to all ages. Serve it with Italian olive bread.

1   package (10 ounces) frozen spinach, thawed, drained, and squeezed dry

2   cups cottage cheese or ricotta cheese

1/4   cup sour cream

1   large egg, beaten

2   cups grated mozzarella cheese

2   tablespoons chopped fresh parsley

1   tablespoon chopped fresh basil or 1/2 teaspoon dried basil

1/4   teaspoon salt

Freshly ground pepper

Dash of ground nutmeg

2   cups Quick Tomato Sauce (page 252)

12   manicotti shells, cooked as directed on package and drained

1/4   cup freshly grated Parmesan cheese

Preheat oven to 350°F. In a large bowl, combine spinach, cottage cheese, sour cream, egg, 1 cup of the mozzarella cheese, the parsley, basil, salt, and pepper and nutmeg to taste. In the bottom of a 9-by-13-inch glass baking dish lightly coated with cooking spray or oil, spread a thin layer of the tomato sauce. Put drained shells on a clean kitchen towel. Spoon some of the filling mixture into each shell and place on top of the sauce
in the dish. Pour the remaining tomato sauce over all, making sure the noodles are covered, and sprinkle with remaining 1 cup of mozzarella and the Parmesan. Bake, uncovered, until bubbly, about 35 minutes. Let stand 8 to 10 minutes before serving.

SERVES 6

CONFETTI RICE

If you are hosting or organizing a Mexican-theme potluck, serve this colorful rice dish flecked with red and green bell peppers along with Mexican Chicken (page 271) and Orange Salad, Mexican Style (page 128). Don't forget the sangria!

2 1/4	cups chicken broth or water
1/2	cup diced red bell pepper
1/2	cup diced green bell pepper
1/2	cup chopped yellow onion
1	cup long-grain white rice
1/4	teaspoon salt
	Freshly ground pepper
1/2	cup chopped fresh parsley
1	tablespoon butter (optional)

Preheat oven to 350°F. In a medium saucepan over high heat, bring broth, bell peppers, and onion to a boil. Stir in rice, salt, and pepper to taste. Transfer to a 2-quart casserole lightly coated with cooking spray or oil and bake, covered, until liquid is absorbed, about 40 minutes. Stir in parsley and butter, if using.

SERVES 4

GREEN ONION, CHILE, AND RICE CASSEROLE

Green onions and chiles add color and flavor to this creamy casserole—a great side dish to take to a potluck. Quick, easy, and delicious, it goes well with Marinated Pork Tenderloin (page 248).

3 cups cooked long-grain white rice (1 cup raw)

1 cup sliced green onions, including some tender green tops

1 can (4 ounces) diced chiles, drained

1 cup cottage cheese

1 cup sour cream

3 cups (about 12 ounces) grated Cheddar cheese

1/4 teaspoon salt

Freshly ground pepper

Fresh Tomato Salsa (page 255) or purchased salsa for serving

Preheat oven to 350°F. In a large bowl, mix together rice, green onions, chiles, cottage cheese, sour cream, 2 cups of the Cheddar cheese, salt, and pepper to taste. Transfer to a 2-quart casserole lightly coated with cooking spray or oil.

Bake casserole, covered, 35 minutes. Sprinkle remaining 1 cup Cheddar cheese on top and bake, uncovered, until bubbly and the cheese is melted, about 10 minutes longer. Serve with salsa

SERVES 6 TO 8

BROWN RICE, FRESH VEGETABLES, AND HERBS

This meatless rice dish is enhanced by an assortment of fresh vegetables and herbs. It bakes for over an hour, so be sure to allow enough time.

1 tablespoon butter or margarine

1 tablespoon vegetable oil

1 cup chopped yellow onion

1 cup chopped green bell pepper

4 ounces mushrooms, coarsely chopped

1 celery stalk, sliced

1 cup long-grain brown rice

1 tablespoon chopped fresh basil or 1/2 teaspoon dried basil

1 tablespoon chopped fresh thyme or 1/2 teaspoon dried thyme

1/2 teaspoon salt

1/8 teaspoon freshly ground pepper

21/4 cups vegetable broth or water

1 tablespoon red wine vinegar

1/4 cup chopped fresh parsley

Preheat oven to 350°F. In a large skillet over medium heat, melt butter with oil. Add onion, bell pepper, mushrooms, and celery and sauté until tender, about 5 minutes. Stir in rice, basil, thyme, salt, and pepper. Add broth and vinegar and mix well. Transfer to a 3-quart casserole lightly coated with cooking spray or oil. Cover and bake until liquid is absorbed and rice is tender, about 1¼ hours. Stir in parsley and serve.

SERVES 4 TO 6

RICE AND SUGAR SNAP PEAS

The water chestnuts add a crunchy texture to this complementary side dish to serve with Chicken, Hawaiian Style (page 267), and Tropical Fruit Salad (page 124).

1	tablespoon vegetable oil
1	cup sliced celery
1/2	cup chopped yellow onion
1	cup long-grain white rice
1	can (6 ounces) water chestnuts, drained and sliced
2 1/4	cups chicken broth
1 to 2	tablespoons soy sauce, to your taste
	Salt and freshly ground pepper
1	cup sugar snap peas, trimmed
3	green onions, including some tender green tops, sliced

Preheat oven to 350°F. In a medium saucepan over medium heat, warm oil. Add celery and onion and sauté until vegetables are soft, about 6 minutes. Stir in rice and chestnuts. Add broth, soy sauce, and salt and pepper to taste and bring to a boil. Transfer to a 2-quart casserole lightly coated with cooking spray or oil and bake, covered, until liquid is absorbed, about 40 minutes. After 25 minutes, stir in sugar snap peas. Top with green onions and serve.

SERVES 4

BAKED RICE AND MUSHROOM CASSEROLE

This versatile side dish is a natural for a potluck. It will complement almost any meat or poultry entrée, and it goes from the oven to the serving table in the same dish.

2 tablespoons butter or margarine

1/2 cup chopped yellow onion

1 garlic clove, minced

8 ounces mushrooms, sliced

3/4 cup chopped red bell pepper

1 cup long-grain white rice

2 1/4 cups chicken broth

1/4 teaspoon dried thyme

1/2 teaspoon salt

Freshly ground pepper

1/4 cup freshly grated Parmesan cheese

2 tablespoons chopped fresh parsley

Preheat oven to 350°F. In a medium saucepan over medium heat, melt butter. Add onion, garlic, mushrooms, and bell pepper and sauté until tender, about 5 minutes. Add rice and stir to coat. Add broth, thyme, salt, and pepper to taste and bring to a boil. Transfer mixture to a 2-quart casserole lightly coated with cooking spray or oil. Cover and bake until liquid is absorbed, about 40 minutes. Stir in cheese and parsley and bake, uncovered, 5 minutes longer.

SERVES 4 TO 6

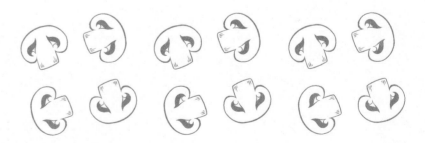

HAZELNUT–BROWN RICE CASSEROLE

Hazelnuts, also called filberts, are the world's most popular tree nut. Ninety-nine percent of the hazelnuts grown in the United States come from the Willamette Valley of Oregon. They add a subtle, nutty flavor and extra crunch to this savory rice dish.

1	cup long-grain brown rice
1 1/4	cups vegetable broth (see Note)
1	cup water
1	tablespoon soy sauce
2	teaspoons Worcestershire sauce
1	tablespoon butter or margarine, cut into pieces
1/4	teaspoon salt
1/8	teaspoon freshly ground pepper
1/4	cup chopped toasted hazelnuts (see Note on page 89)

Preheat oven to 350°F. In a medium saucepan over high heat, combine rice, broth, water, soy sauce, Worcestershire, butter, salt, and pepper. Bring to a boil and then transfer to a 2-quart casserole lightly coated with cooking spray or oil. Cover and bake until liquid is absorbed, about 1 hour. Stir in nuts just before serving.

SERVES 4

Note: If you prefer, omit the broth and use 2 1/4 cups water.

BASMATI RICE WITH NUTS AND SPICES

Grown in the foothills of the Himalaya mountains, basmati rice is appreciated for its fragrant aroma, nutlike flavor, and firm consistency. It can be served plain or with Indian spices and nuts, as in this recipe.

2	tablespoons butter or margarine
1/2	cup chopped yellow onion
2	garlic cloves, minced
1/4	cup slivered almonds
1/4	cup coarsely chopped unsalted cashews
1	cup basmati rice, rinsed
2	cups chicken broth or water
1/2	teaspoon curry powder
1/4	teaspoon ground cardamom
1/4	teaspoon ground coriander
1/2	cup chopped fresh parsley
1	tablespoon fresh lemon juice
1/4	cup golden raisins (optional)
1/4	teaspoon salt
	Freshly ground pepper

Preheat oven to 350°F. In a medium saucepan over medium heat, melt butter. Add onion and garlic and sauté until tender, about 5 minutes. Add nuts and rice and stir to coat. Stir in remaining ingredients and bring to a boil. Transfer to a 2-quart casserole lightly coated with cooking spray or oil and bake, covered, until liquid is absorbed, about 50 minutes.

SERVES 6

BARLEY AND MUSHROOM CASSEROLE

Barley is a hearty grain that dates back to the Stone Age. It has a chewy texture and nutty flavor and is often used in soups, casseroles, and cereals. To make pearl barley, the most common type in this country, the bran is removed and then the barley is steamed and polished. Here it is combined with mushrooms and nuts for a tasty potluck side dish.

4	tablespoons butter or margarine
1	cup chopped yellow onion
1	garlic clove, minced
1/2	cup chopped green bell pepper
4	ounces mushrooms, chopped
1/2	cup coarsely chopped walnuts or pecans
1	cup pearl barley, rinsed
3	cups chicken broth, warmed
1/4	teaspoon dried marjoram
1/4	teaspoon salt
	Freshly ground pepper

Preheat oven to 350°F. In a medium skillet over medium heat, melt butter. Add onion, garlic, bell pepper, and mushrooms and sauté until vegetables are tender, about 5 minutes. Stir in nuts and barley and cook 1 minute longer. Transfer to a 2-quart casserole lightly coated with cooking spray or oil. Add broth, marjoram, salt, and pepper to taste. Bake, covered, until tender, about 1 hour, stirring once.

SERVES 4 TO 6

BAKED BLACK BEANS WITH TOPPINGS

Black beans, also called turtle beans, are available dried or canned. Either may be used here, but canned beans are suggested for convenience. This is a tasty dish to serve with Mexican food. To make it more fun, take along small bowls of assorted toppings to offer with the beans at the potluck.

3	cans (15 ounces each) black beans, drained and rinsed
1/4	teaspoon dried oregano
1/4	teaspoon ground cumin
1/4	teaspoon salt
	Freshly ground pepper
1/4	cup chopped fresh cilantro or parsley
1/4	cup Fresh Tomato Salsa (page 255) or purchased salsa
1	tablespoon red wine vinegar
2	tablespoons water (optional)

Preheat oven to 350°F. In a 2-quart casserole lightly coated with cooking spray or oil, mix together all ingredients, except water and toppings. Cover and bake until heated through, about 30 minutes. Add water during last 10 minutes of cooking if beans seem dry. Serve with suggested toppings.

SERVES 6

TOPPINGS

Hard-cooked eggs, chopped

Tomatoes, seeded, chopped, and drained

Green onions, including some tender green tops, chopped

Sour cream

Grated Cheddar or Monterey Jack cheese

Avocado cubes

EASY BAKED BEANS

Canned beans are jazzed up here with brown sugar, vinegar, ketchup, and spices and baked in the oven until the flavors blend. Perfect for your potluck cookout. For a savory touch, add cooked crumbled bacon or diced cooked ham before baking.

1 cup chopped yellow onion

2 garlic cloves, minced

1 can (15 ounces) red kidney beans, drained and rinsed

1 can (15 ounces) black beans, drained and rinsed

1 can (15 ounces) baby lima beans, drained and rinsed; or 1 can (15 ounces) garbanzo beans, drained and rinsed; or 1 can (15 ounces) cannellini beans, drained and rinsed

1 can (28 ounces) baked pork and beans (do not drain)

2 tablespoons brown sugar

1 teaspoon Worcestershire sauce

2 tablespoons cider vinegar

1/4 cup ketchup

1 tablespoon prepared mustard

1 teaspoon chili powder

1 teaspoon salt

1/4 teaspoon freshly ground pepper

Preheat oven to 350°F. Stir together all ingredients in a 4-quart casserole lightly coated with cooking spray or oil. Bake, uncovered, until hot and bubbly, about 1 hour.

SERVES 10 TO 14

COUSCOUS WITH PINE NUTS

Couscous is a tiny, grainlike pasta made from semolina flour and is the basis of many North African dishes. It is popular because it has no fat, takes only minutes to prepare, and has an appealing texture. Here crunchy toasted pine nuts provide an interesting contrast to the tender couscous.

2 cups chicken broth or water

2 teaspoons olive oil

1 1/2 cups couscous

6 green onions, including some tender green tops, sliced

1/4 cup toasted pine nuts (see Note on page 44)

1/4 cup chopped fresh parsley

2 tablespoons chopped fresh mint leaves (optional)

1 tablespoon fresh lemon juice

2 to 3 tablespoons butter or margarine (optional)

Salt and freshly ground pepper

In a medium saucepan over high heat, bring broth and oil to a boil. Stir in couscous in a stream. Add green onions. Remove from heat, cover, and let stand about 5 minutes. Add pine nuts, parsley, mint, if using, lemon juice, and butter, if using. Season with salt and pepper to taste and fluff with a fork. Serve immediately or keep warm in the pan over hot water until ready to serve.

SERVES 4 TO 6

Meat dishes are considered the mainstay of many potlucks. They are hearty, filling, and full of flavor. A good source of protein, vitamins, and minerals, meat adds variety to our diet.

Included in this chapter are some old standbys like Tailgate Casserole (page 234), Beer Beef Stew (page 221), and Beef Enchiladas (page 214). You will want to try some of the new dishes, such as Tortilla Stack (page 223), Reuben Casserole (page 237), and Burgundy Pot Roast (page 236). For a barbecue potluck, consider Grilled Pork Chops with Dijon Baste (page 247) and Beef and Vegetable Kabobs (page 246).

MEAT DISHES

BEEF ENCHILADAS

Transport these popular enchiladas, along with a variety of toppings, to your next potluck. Don't expect to take home any leftovers! If you're short of time, make the Quick Enchilada Sauce.

MEAT FILLING

1 1/2	pounds ground beef
1	cup chopped yellow onion
1/2	teaspoon salt
	Freshly ground pepper
12	corn tortillas, softened (see Note)
	Homemade Enchilada Sauce or Quick Enchilada Sauce (facing page)
4	cups (about 16 ounces) grated Cheddar cheese
1/4	cup sour cream
1	cup pitted black olives (optional)

TOPPINGS

Green onions, including some tender green tops, sliced

Sour cream

Avocado chunks

To make the meat filling: In a large skillet over medium heat, cook beef, onion, salt, and pepper to taste, breaking up meat with a spoon, until meat is no longer pink and onion is tender, 6 to 7 minutes. Transfer to a bowl and set aside.

Preheat oven to 350°F. To assemble the enchiladas: Dip a tortilla in warm sauce to coat both sides and lay on a flat surface. Place 2 large spoonfuls of meat mixture in a strip down the center of the tortilla. Sprinkle about 1 tablespoon cheese and 1 teaspoon sour cream on top of meat mixture. Roll up and place, seam-side down, in a 9-by-13-inch glass baking dish lightly coated with cooking spray or oil. Repeat with remaining tortillas. Pour remaining sauce over all and sprinkle remaining cheese on top. Tuck in olives, if using, around the casserole. Bake, uncovered, until bubbly, about 35 minutes. Let stand 10 minutes before serving. Put toppings in bowls and serve.

SERVES 6 TO 8

Note: To soften tortillas, wrap in a small cloth towel and microwave for 1 minute on high. Alternately, wrap in foil and warm in a 325°F oven for a few minutes. Keep tortillas warm, wrapped in the towel or foil, until ready to use.

HOMEMADE ENCHILADA SAUCE

1	tablespoon vegetable oil
1	cup chopped yellow onion
2	garlic cloves, minced
1/4	cup diced green bell pepper
1	tablespoon chili powder
1/4	cup all-purpose flour
1/4	teaspoon dried oregano
1/4	teaspoon ground cumin
1/4	teaspoon salt
	Freshly ground pepper
1 1/2	cups beef broth
1	large can (15 ounces) tomato sauce
2 to 3	drops of Tabasco

In a large skillet over medium heat, warm oil and sauté onion, garlic, and bell pepper until tender, about 5 minutes. Add chili powder, flour, oregano, cumin, salt, and pepper to taste. Add broth and stir until thickened. Add tomato sauce and Tabasco. Reduce temperature to medium-low and simmer, uncovered, 10 minutes.

MAKES ABOUT 3 1/2 CUPS

QUICK ENCHILADA SAUCE

2	cans (10 ounces each) medium enchilada sauce
1	can (8 ounces) tomato sauce
1 1/4	cups beef broth

In a medium skillet over medium heat, combine enchilada sauce, tomato sauce, and broth and simmer until warmed, about 5 minutes.

MAKES ABOUT 3 1/2 CUPS

CHEESE-FILLED MANICOTTI WITH RICH MEAT SAUCE

This is a delicious Italian-style casserole to share with friends or family. For a vegetarian dish, omit the meat in the sauce and add mushrooms (see Variation on facing page). Either way, the sauce is great on spaghetti, too. Serve with garlic bread.

MEAT SAUCE

12	ounces ground beef
1/2	cup chopped yellow onion
1	garlic clove, minced
1	teaspoon vegetable oil, as needed
1	can (10 3/4 ounces) tomato purée
1	can (6 ounces) tomato paste
1	teaspoon brown sugar
1 1/2	cups water
3	tablespoons chopped fresh parsley
1/2	teaspoon dried basil
1/4	teaspoon dried oregano
1/4	teaspoon dried marjoram
3/4	teaspoon salt
	Freshly ground pepper
1/4	cup dry red wine

To make the meat sauce: In a large skillet over medium heat, brown beef with onions and garlic, breaking up meat with a spoon, until meat is no longer pink, and adding oil, if necessary, 6 to 7 minutes. Add tomato purée, tomato paste, sugar, water, parsley, basil, oregano, marjoram, salt, and pepper to taste. Reduce heat to low and simmer, uncovered, until thickened, about 15 minutes. Stir in wine.

To make the cheese filling: In a medium bowl, mix together ricotta cheese, half of the mozzarella cheese, the eggs, parsley, salt, and pepper to taste.

CHEESE FILLING

3	cups ricotta or cottage cheese, or a combination
2 1/2	cups grated mozzarella cheese
2	large eggs, beaten
1/4	cup chopped fresh parsley
1/2	teaspoon salt
	Freshly ground pepper
12	manicotti shells, cooked as directed on package, drained, and cooled
1/2	cup freshly grated Parmesan cheese

Preheat oven to 350°F. To assemble: Pour about one quarter of the meat sauce into a 9-by-13-inch glass baking dish lightly coated with cooking spray or oil. Spoon some of the filling into each shell and place on top of sauce in the dish. Pour remaining meat sauce over all, making sure all of the shells are covered. Sprinkle with Parmesan cheese and remaining mozzarella cheese. Bake, uncovered, until bubbly, 30 to 35 minutes. Let stand 8 to 10 minutes before serving.

SERVES 6 TO 8

Variation: For a vegetarian sauce, omit meat and add 1 cup sliced mushrooms with the onions and garlic. (You will need the oil.)

HUNGARIAN GOULASH

There are many versions of this famous dish, and all are delicious. Here beef cubes are baked in a tomato sauce seasoned with the traditional Hungarian spices of paprika and caraway seeds. Fold in the sour cream when the beef is done and serve it on noodles. This is a warming dish to take to a church potluck.

1 to 2	tablespoons vegetable oil
2 1/2	pounds top round steak, cut into 1-inch cubes
2	cups chopped yellow onion
2	garlic cloves, minced
2	tablespoons all-purpose flour
1	can (14 1/2 ounces) whole tomatoes, with their juices, coarsely chopped
1/2 to 1	cup beef broth, as needed
1/4	teaspoon dried thyme
1/4	teaspoon caraway seeds
1	teaspoon paprika
1	teaspoon salt
	Freshly ground pepper
1/2	cup sour cream
3	cups egg noodles, cooked as directed on package and drained

Preheat oven to 350°F. In a Dutch oven over medium-high heat, warm 1 tablespoon oil. Add meat and brown in batches, adding more oil, if needed, about 5 minutes per batch. Add onion and garlic to the meat and sauté until onion is tender, 5 to 10 minutes. Stir in flour and blend. Add tomatoes, 1/2 cup of the broth, thyme, caraway seeds, paprika, salt, and pepper to taste and stir until slightly thickened, about 2 minutes.

Cover and bake goulash until meat is tender, about 1 1/2 hours. If meat becomes dry during baking, add remaining 1/2 cup broth. Stir in sour cream and serve over noodles.

SERVES 6

OVEN STROGANOFF

This famous Russian dish of tender beef cubes and mushrooms in a flavorful gravy is served on noodles or rice. Add Mixed Greens with Avocado, Blue Cheese, and Hazelnuts (page 89) for a menu that is easy on the host.

1/4 cup plus 2 tablespoons all-purpose flour

1/2 teaspoon salt

Freshly ground pepper

2 pounds top round steak, cut into bite-sized pieces

4 tablespoons butter or margarine

4 ounces mushrooms, sliced

4 green onions, including some tender green tops, sliced

1 garlic clove, minced

1 cup beef broth

2 teaspoons Dijon mustard

1/2 cup dry white wine

1/2 cup sour cream

Preheat oven to 350°F. On a piece of waxed paper, combine flour, salt, and pepper to taste. Dredge meat in mixture and reserve leftover flour.

In a Dutch oven over medium heat, melt 2 tablespoons of the butter. Brown meat on all sides, 6 to 7 minutes. Transfer meat to a plate. Add mushrooms, green onions, and garlic to the pot and sauté until tender, about 5 minutes. Transfer vegetables to the plate holding meat. Melt remaining 2 tablespoons butter, add reserved flour, and stir until bubbly. Add broth, mustard, and wine and stir until well blended. Return meat and vegetables to Dutch oven and mix with gravy. Bake, covered, until meat is tender, about 1½ hours. Remove from oven and slowly stir in sour cream.

SERVES 6

ROUND STEAK WITH GREEN BELL PEPPER STRIPS

For those who like a meaty dish, this is a good choice. Serve these tender beef cubes and green peppers in a rich, flavorful sauce with rice or noodles for a satisfying entrée.

1   tablespoon butter or margarine

2   tablespoons vegetable oil, or
    as needed

2   pounds top round steak, 1 inch thick,
    cut into 1-inch strips

1   small green bell pepper, cut into
    1/2-inch strips

1   yellow onion, sliced

2   celery stalks, cut diagonally into
    1-inch slices

1   garlic clove, minced

1   can (14 1/2 ounces) whole tomatoes,
    with their juices, chopped

2   cups beef broth

1   teaspoon Worcestershire sauce

2   teaspoons soy sauce

1/2   teaspoon salt

    Freshly ground pepper

1   tablespoon cornstarch

2   tablespoons water

Preheat oven to 350°F. In a Dutch oven over medium-high heat, melt butter with 1 tablespoon of the oil. Add meat and brown on all sides, about 5 minutes. With a slotted spoon, remove meat to a plate. Reduce heat to medium. Add remaining 1 tablespoon oil, the bell pepper, onion, celery, and garlic and sauté until vegetables are tender, about 5 minutes. Add more oil if needed. Add tomatoes, broth, Worcestershire, soy sauce, salt, and pepper to taste. Return meat to Dutch oven and bake, covered, until meat is tender, about 1½ hours. To thicken gravy, in a small bowl, blend cornstarch with water. Stir into the liquid in the Dutch oven and bake, uncovered, until thickened, 5 minutes longer.

SERVES 6

BEER BEEF STEW

The next time you host a fall or winter potluck supper, serve this rich, flavorful stew with some small boiled new potatoes. Suggest that one guest bring Mixed Greens with Avocado, Blue Cheese, and Hazelnuts (page 89) and another might bake Chocolate-Apple-Spice Cake (page 310) for a wonderful meal.

1/2	cup all-purpose flour
4	pounds top round steak, cut into bite-sized pieces
1/4 to 1/2	cup vegetable oil, as needed
2	yellow onions, thickly sliced
4	garlic cloves, minced
2	tablespoons packed brown sugar
2	tablespoons red wine vinegar
1/2	cup chopped fresh parsley
2	bay leaves
2	teaspoons dried marjoram
2	teaspoons salt
	Freshly ground pepper
2	cans (10 1/2 ounces each) beef broth, undiluted
2	bottles (12 ounces each) flat beer
4	carrots, cut diagonally into 3/4-inch slices

Preheat oven to 325°F. Put flour on a piece of waxed paper. Thoroughly dredge beef pieces in flour, using all of the flour.

In a large Dutch oven over medium-high heat, warm 1/4 cup of the oil. Brown meat in batches, adding more oil as needed, about 5 minutes per batch. Return all the beef to the pot and add onions, garlic, sugar, vinegar, parsley, bay leaves, marjoram, salt, pepper to taste, broth, and beer. Stir to loosen browned bits.

Cover the casserole and bake 1 hour. Add carrots and bake, covered, until meat and carrots are tender, about 1 hour longer. Discard bay leaves before serving.

SERVES 12

OVEN BEEF BRISKET

Slices of tender brisket with assorted mustards and pumpernickel bread will make great sandwiches for your next potluck tailgate party. Have friends bring Picnic Potato Salad (page 61) and Crispy Hazelnut Cookies (page 322) to round out the meal.

1   beef brisket (4 to 5 pounds)

1   bottle (12 ounces) flat beer or
     1 1/2 cups beef broth

1   tablespoon pickling spices

1   teaspoon dry mustard

1/4 teaspoon salt

     Freshly ground pepper

2   garlic cloves, halved

6   parsley sprigs

1   carrot, cut into 1-inch pieces

1   yellow onion, cut into wedges

     Assorted breads for serving (optional)

     Flavored mustards for serving
     (optional)

Trim fat from brisket and place in a Dutch oven. Stir in beer, seasonings, garlic, parsley, and enough water, if needed, to cover the meat. Cover and marinate several hours in the refrigerator, turning once. Bring to room temperature before baking.

Preheat oven to 350°F. Add carrot and onion to the meat in Dutch oven. Cover and bake 2 1/2 hours, spooning liquid over meat several times. Uncover and bake until very tender, about 30 minutes longer. Add water as needed.

Drain meat and discard vegetables. Transfer meat to a platter and let stand 10 minutes. Slice diagonally and serve immediately, or refrigerate until cold if using for sandwiches, and serve with assorted breads and mustards, if desired.

SERVES 8 TO 10

TORTILLA STACK

You can be assured this casserole with a Mexican flavor will be popular at a potluck. The tortillas are stacked with layers of refried beans, spicy meat sauce, and cheese and are topped with a dollop of sour cream.

1	pound ground beef
1	cup chopped yellow onion
	Vegetable oil, as needed
1	can (15 ounces) whole tomatoes, with their juices, chopped
1	can (8 ounces) tomato sauce
1	can (4 ounces) diced green chiles, drained
1/2	teaspoon paprika
1/4	teaspoon dried oregano
1/4	teaspoon salt
	Freshly ground pepper
10	large corn tortillas, softened (see Note on page 214)
1	can (16 ounces) refried beans
3	cups (about 12 ounces) grated Cheddar cheese
	Sour cream for topping

Preheat oven to 350°F. In a large skillet over medium heat, cook beef and onion, breaking up meat with a spoon, until meat is no longer pink and onion is tender, about 5 minutes. Add oil if needed. Stir in tomatoes, tomato sauce, chiles, paprika, oregano, salt, and pepper to taste. Reduce heat to medium-low and simmer, uncovered, 10 minutes.

Spread ½ cup of the meat sauce in the bottom of a 9-by-13-inch glass baking dish lightly coated with cooking spray or oil. Place 2 tortillas side-by-side on top of sauce. Spread 2 to 3 tablespoons refried beans on top of each tortilla. Cover with some meat sauce. Sprinkle ¼ cup of the cheese on each tortilla. Repeat the layers until each stack contains 5 tortillas and all ingredients are used, ending with meat sauce and cheese. Bake, uncovered, until bubbly, about 40 minutes. Let stand 10 minutes before serving. Accompany with a bowl of sour cream for topping.

SERVES 6

HOT TAMALE PIE

At one of our potluck tasting parties, this lively tamale pie got unanimous approval. Serve with the Spicy Sauce for added flavor and plenty of cold Mexican beer or iced tea.

CORNMEAL TOPPING

1	cup yellow cornmeal
1	cup chicken broth
2 1/2	cups water
1	teaspoon salt

FILLING

1	pound ground beef
1	cup chopped yellow onion
1	cup chopped green bell pepper
2	teaspoons vegetable oil, as needed
1	teaspoon chili powder
1	teaspoon salt
	Freshly ground pepper
2	medium tomatoes, sliced
1/2	cup pitted black olives

SPICY SAUCE

1	can (10 ounces) medium enchilada sauce
1/2	cup chili sauce

Preheat oven to 350°F. To make topping: In a small bowl, mix cornmeal with broth. In a medium saucepan over medium-high heat, bring water and salt to a boil. Slowly stir in cornmeal mixture in a stream. Reduce heat to medium-low and simmer, uncovered, stirring constantly, until thickened, about 2 minutes.

To make filling: In a medium skillet over medium heat, combine beef, onion, and bell pepper and sauté until meat is no longer pink and vegetables are tender, 6 to 7 minutes. Add oil, if needed. Season with chili powder, salt, and pepper to taste and simmer a few minutes.

To assemble the dish: Spread half the cornmeal mixture in an 8-by-10-inch glass baking dish lightly coated with cooking spray or oil. Arrange half of the tomato slices on top of the cornmeal. Spoon meat mixture over tomatoes and cover with remaining cornmeal mixture. Arrange remaining tomato slices and olives on top. Bake, uncovered, until bubbly, about 30 minutes. Let stand 5 minutes before serving.

While the tamale is baking, make the sauce: Pour enchilada sauce and chili sauce into a medium saucepan and warm over medium heat. At serving time, pass the Spicy Sauce in a bowl to spoon on the pie.

SERVES 4

BEEF PICADILLO

Chicken, beef, or pork can be the main ingredient in this traditional Mexican "hash"—an exciting combination of beef, vegetables, apples, and spices. It is a fun casserole to serve for a Cinco de Mayo or Mexican-theme potluck. Your guests may want to wrap the mixture in a tortilla and eat it as finger food. Serve with black beans and Orange Salad, Mexican Style (page 128).

1	tablespoon vegetable oil
1	pound ground beef
1	yellow onion, chopped
2	garlic cloves, minced
1 to 2	jalapeño peppers, seeded and chopped (see Note)
1	can (15 ounces) crushed tomatoes in thick purée
1	cup raisins
2	apples, peeled, cored, and chopped
1	cup cashews
1	tablespoon brown sugar
1/2	teaspoon ground cinnamon
1/4	teaspoon ground cloves
1/2	teaspoon salt
	Freshly ground pepper
1	cup grated Cheddar cheese
2	limes, cut into wedges, for garnish
	Warm tortillas for serving

TOPPINGS

Green onions, including some tender green tops, sliced

Diced avocados

Sour cream

In a large skillet over medium heat, warm oil. Cook beef with onion, garlic, and jalapeño, breaking up meat with a spoon, until meat is no longer pink, about 5 minutes. Add tomatoes, raisins, apples, cashews, brown sugar, and seasonings and simmer 5 to 10 minutes.

Transfer the mixture to a 2-quart casserole lightly coated with cooking spray or oil and sprinkle with cheese. Bake, uncovered, until bubbly, 35 to 40 minutes. Garnish with lime wedges and add a squeeze of juice to the mixture, if desired. Serve with warm tortillas and toppings.

SERVES 4 TO 6

Note: Wash hands thoroughly and do not touch your eyes after working with chiles.

SHREDDED BEEF FOR SANDWICHES

Slowly cooked beef in a spicy barbecue sauce makes a hearty filling for small hamburger buns. We served these tasty sandwiches for a going-away party for good friends who were moving to Texas. The potluck had a cowboy theme, with everyone dressed in Western garb and the house decorated ranch style, with everything but the horse.

BARBECUE SAUCE

1	cup ketchup
1	cup water
1	yellow onion, chopped
3 or 4	garlic cloves, minced
2 1/2	tablespoons cider vinegar
1/2	cup purchased good-quality barbecue sauce
1 1/2	tablespoons Worcestershire sauce
2	teaspoons salt
1/4	teaspoon freshly ground pepper
1 or 2	drops of Tabasco sauce
1	bottom round or chuck roast (4 to 5 pounds)
	Small hamburger buns, halved (see Note), or other small rolls
	Horseradish Sauce (optional; facing page)

Preheat oven to 300°F. To make the sauce: In a medium saucepan over medium heat, combine the ingredients. Simmer, uncovered, until flavors are blended, 10 minutes.

Place roast in a large nonreactive roasting pan. Pour sauce over the roast. Cover and bake until well done and meat begins falling apart, about 5 hours. Baste with sauce frequently (at least once every hour).

To serve, remove meat from sauce and pull apart with a fork or fingers to shred. Return meat to sauce. Serve warm in a decorative bowl alongside the buns, and allow the guests to make their own sandwiches. Accompany with Horseradish Sauce in a bowl, if desired.

SERVES 16 TO 20

Note: Small (2 1/2-inch) buns may be special-ordered from a specialty bakery.

HORSERADISH SAUCE

- ¹/₂   cup sour cream
- 1   tablespoon purchased horseradish sauce
- 1   garlic clove, minced
- ¹/₄   teaspoon dry mustard

In a small bowl, mix together all ingredients.

MAKES ABOUT ¹/₂ CUP

BIG MEATBALLS IN HERBED TOMATO SAUCE

These light, fluffy meatballs are browned in the oven, then simmered in a rich tomato sauce and served on pasta. If there are any leftover meatballs, they will make great sandwiches the next day. The Herbed Tomato Sauce is also good on poultry and meat dishes.

2   large bread slices, crusts trimmed, torn into pieces

1/2 cup milk

2   pounds ground beef

1   pound ground pork sausage

1   large egg, beaten

1/2 cup diced yellow onion

2   garlic cloves, minced

1/2 cup chopped fresh parsley

1/2 cup grated Parmesan cheese

1   teaspoon salt

    Herbed Tomato Sauce, at a simmer (facing page)

1   pound spaghetti or angel hair pasta, cooked as directed on package and drained

    Freshly grated Parmesan cheese for topping

Preheat oven to 400°F. In a small bowl, combine bread and milk and soak 10 minutes. Squeeze bread to remove excess milk. In a large bowl, place beef, sausage, egg, onion, garlic, parsley, cheese, salt, and soaked bread. With moistened hands, combine meat mixture and shape into 1½-inch balls.

Place meatballs on a rimmed baking sheet and bake until browned, about 12 minutes. Remove from oven and add to the sauce. Simmer in the sauce, uncovered, 30 minutes longer. Serve on pasta, sprinkled with Parmesan cheese.

MAKES 30 MEATBALLS

HERBED TOMATO SAUCE

1 tablespoon vegetable oil

1 cup chopped yellow onion

2 garlic cloves, chopped

1 carrot, grated

1 celery stalk, diced

1 can (15 ounces) tomatoes, with their juices, chopped

1 can (10 3/4 ounces) tomato purée

1 can (8 ounces) tomato sauce

1/2 cup dry red wine or water or chicken broth

1 teaspoon Worcestershire sauce

2 or 3 drops of Tabasco sauce

1 bay leaf

1 tablespoon chopped fresh basil or 1 teaspoon dried basil

1 teaspoon chopped fresh oregano or 1/2 teaspoon dried oregano

1/2 teaspoon dried thyme

3/4 teaspoon salt

Freshly ground pepper

In a large saucepan over medium heat, warm oil. Add onion, garlic, carrot, and celery and sauté until tender, about 5 minutes. Stir in tomatoes and juice, tomato purée, tomato sauce, wine, Worcestershire, Tabasco, herbs, salt, and pepper to taste. Reduce heat to medium-low and simmer, uncovered, until flavors are blended, about 30 minutes. Discard bay leaf. For a smooth sauce, purée in batches in a food processor, return sauce to the pan, and bring to a simmer.

MAKES ABOUT 4 CUPS

MEATBALLS IN SPICY SPAGHETTI SAUCE

This piquant version of spaghetti and meatballs works well for a casual potluck spaghetti feed. It can be made ahead and will serve at least eight. Ask your guests to bring Antipasto Tossed Salad (page 100), garlic bread, and Pineapple Upside-Down Cake (page 309) for a fun evening.

SPICY SPAGHETTI SAUCE

1	can (46 ounces) tomato juice
1	can (6 ounces) tomato paste
1	can (14 1/2 ounces) crushed tomatoes in thick purée
1	cup beef broth
1/2	teaspoon celery seed
1/4	teaspoon dry mustard
1/4	teaspoon dried basil
1/4	teaspoon dried oregano
1/2	teaspoon chili powder
1/2	teaspoon salt
	Freshly ground pepper
1	teaspoon sugar
2	garlic cloves, minced
1	small yellow onion, chopped
1/2	cup diced celery
4	ounces mushrooms, chopped
1	tablespoon olive oil
2	teaspoons pickling spices, enclosed in tea infuser or tied in a cheesecloth sack
	Meatballs (facing page)
12	ounces spaghetti, cooked as directed on package and drained
	Freshly grated Parmesan cheese for topping

To make the sauce: In a large pot over medium-high heat, combine all ingredients. Cook, uncovered, 15 minutes. Remove pickling spices and discard. Reduce heat to medium-low or low and simmer, covered, 30 minutes. Add meatballs and simmer, uncovered, 30 minutes longer. Serve sauce and cooked spaghetti in separate bowls. Pass a bowl of Parmesan cheese for sprinkling on top.

SERVES 8 TO 10

MEATBALLS

2 pounds ground beef

1/4 cup diced yellow onion

1/2 teaspoon poultry seasoning

1/2 teaspoon salt

Freshly ground pepper

2 tablespoons grated Parmesan cheese

1/2 cup milk

Preheat oven to 400°F. In a bowl, combine all ingredients and mix well. Form into 1-inch balls. Place meatballs on a baking sheet and bake until browned, about 10 minutes. Add to sauce as directed.

MAKES ABOUT 50 MEATBALLS

GROUND BEEF AND ZUCCHINI CASSEROLE

This tasty, one-dish meal is wholesome and filling and is a good casserole to take to your next church supper or family get-together. Serve with garlic bread. This recipe can easily be doubled.

2   medium zucchini, unpeeled, ends trimmed, and cut into 3/8-inch slices

1   pound ground beef

1/2   cup chopped yellow onion

1   garlic clove, minced

Vegetable oil, as needed

1   cup cooked long-grain white rice (1/3 cup raw)

1   can (8 ounces) tomato sauce

1/2   teaspoon dried oregano

1/4   teaspoon salt

Freshly ground pepper

1   large egg, beaten

1   cup cottage cheese

1   cup grated Cheddar cheese

1/4   cup grated Parmesan cheese

In a medium saucepan over medium-high heat, cook zucchini in salted water to cover, 2 minutes. Cool under cold running water, drain, and set aside.

In a medium skillet over medium heat, sauté beef with onion and garlic, breaking up meat with a spoon, until it is no longer pink and vegetables are tender, 5 to 6 minutes. Add oil, if needed. Stir in rice, tomato sauce, oregano, salt, and pepper to taste and mix well.

Preheat oven to 350°F. In a small bowl, combine egg and cottage cheese. In a 2-quart casserole lightly coated with cooking spray or oil, arrange half the zucchini in a layer. Add half the meat mixture and then all the cottage cheese mixture in layers. Add remaining zucchini and meat mixture. Sprinkle Cheddar and Parmesan cheeses on top. Bake, uncovered, until bubbly, about 30 minutes.

SERVES 4 TO 6

SUPER CHILI FOR A CROWD

What fun it is to watch a football game or other sporting event on TV with friends while enjoying a bowl of chili with assorted toppings. Let your friends bring the side dishes, such as Coleslaw with Creamy Celery Seed Dressing (page 68), garlic bread, chips, and relishes, for a great potluck.

2	pounds lean ground beef
2	cups chopped yellow onion
1	can (28 ounces) whole tomatoes, with their juices, chopped
1	large can (15 ounces) tomato sauce
1	cup flat beer
1	cup beef broth
1	can (4 ounces) diced green chiles
1 1/2	tablespoons chili powder, or more to taste
1/2	teaspoon ground cumin
1/4	teaspoon ground cloves
2	teaspoons salt
1/4	teaspoon freshly ground pepper
4	cans (15 ounces each) red kidney beans, drained and rinsed

In a large pot over medium heat, brown meat and onion, breaking up meat with a spoon, until meat is no longer pink and onion is tender, 6 to 7 minutes. Reduce heat to medium-low. Add remaining ingredients, except toppings, and simmer, uncovered, 30 to 40 minutes. Serve in bowls and pass the toppings.

SERVES 8 TO 10

TOPPINGS

Grated Cheddar cheese

Chopped green onions

Sour cream

Plain nonfat yogurt

TAILGATE CASSEROLE

This popular dish of hamburger, mushrooms, tomato sauce, and cheesy noodles is an old standby at many of our tailgate parties. Caesar Salad (page 78), Party Deviled Eggs (page 43), and Butterscotch–Chocolate Chip Bars (page 321) complete the menu.

1¼	pounds lean ground beef
½	cup chopped green bell pepper
4	ounces mushrooms, sliced
	Vegetable oil, as needed
1	large can (15 ounces) tomato sauce
¾	teaspoon salt
	Freshly ground pepper
½	cup sour cream
4	ounces cream cheese at room temperature, cut into chunks
1½	cups cottage cheese
6	green onions, including some tender green tops, sliced
8	ounces egg noodles, cooked as directed on package and drained
2	cups grated Cheddar cheese

Preheat oven to 350°F. In a large skillet over medium heat, sauté beef, bell pepper, and mushrooms, breaking up meat with a spoon, until meat is no longer pink, 6 to 7 minutes. Add oil, if needed. Add tomato sauce, salt, and pepper to taste and simmer 5 minutes.

In a medium bowl, beat sour cream, cream cheese, and cottage cheese with an electric mixer until smooth. Fold in green onions and mix well.

In a 9-by-13-inch glass baking dish lightly coated with cooking spray or oil, layer half the noodles, half the cheese mixture, and half the meat mixture, and repeat the layers, ending with meat mixture. Top with Cheddar cheese. Bake, covered, until bubbling and top is golden brown, about 30 minutes. Uncover and cook 10 minutes longer. Let stand 5 to 10 minutes before serving.

SERVES 8 TO 10

GOOD OL' MEAT LOAF

Bake this moist, flavorful meat loaf with Twice-Baked Potatoes (page 180) for a homey potluck or family dinner. Double the recipe to make two loaves for a crowd. Leftovers make good sandwiches.

1¼	pounds lean ground beef
4	ounces bulk mild Italian sausage
½	cup crushed saltines
1	large egg, beaten
½	cup finely chopped yellow onion
½	cup finely chopped red or green bell pepper
¼	cup chopped fresh parsley
2	garlic cloves, minced
¼	cup milk
1	teaspoon Worcestershire sauce
2	drops of Tabasco sauce
½	teaspoon salt
	Freshly ground pepper

Preheat oven to 350°F. In a large bowl, combine all ingredients and mix well. Turn into a 9-by-5-by-3-inch loaf pan lightly coated with cooking spray or oil and bake about 1 hour. Let stand 10 minutes. Then remove from pan, slice, and serve.

SERVES 4 TO 6

BURGUNDY POT ROAST

It was a hot summer day (92°F) when I tested this recipe, but this winter meal tasted great as a change from a barbecue. The roast bakes slowly in the oven for several hours in a savory sauce until very tender and is served with juicy roasted vegetables. Sour Cream Pumpkin Pie with Pecan Topping (page 304) also passed the test.

1/2 cup all-purpose flour

1 tablespoon paprika

1/2 teaspoon dried thyme

1/2 teaspoon salt

Freshly ground pepper

1 chuck or rump roast
(4 1/2 to 5 pounds)

3 garlic cloves, sliced

2 tablespoons vegetable oil

1 cup Burgundy wine

1 cup beef broth

2 tablespoons ketchup

1 yellow onion, sliced

1 bay leaf

6 new potatoes, halved

4 carrots, cut diagonally into
1-inch slices

Preheat oven to 325°F. On a piece of waxed paper, combine flour, paprika, thyme, salt, and pepper to taste and set aside 1/4 cup of mixture for gravy, if desired (see Note). Roll meat in remaining mixture to coat and pat so it sticks to the meat. With a sharp knife, make 1/2-inch slits in meat and insert garlic slices.

In a large Dutch oven over medium-high heat, warm oil. Brown the roast on all sides, about 10 minutes. Transfer roast to a plate. Add wine, broth, and ketchup to the pan and stir to loosen browned bits. Add onion and bay leaf and bring to a boil. Return the roast to the pan and bake, covered, 2 1/4 hours. Add potatoes and carrots and cook, covered, until meat and vegetables are tender, about 45 minutes longer. Let roast stand 10 minutes and then slice. On a platter, arrange beef slices in the center and surround with vegetables. Serve with gravy, if desired.

SERVES 6 TO 8

Note: To make gravy, mix the 1/4 cup of reserved flour mixture with 1/2 cup water and whisk into juices until thickened. Add more water if too thick.

REUBEN CASSEROLE

Enjoy all the flavors of a Reuben sandwich in this casserole layered with sauerkraut, corned beef, cheese, and rye bread crumbs. Serve with cold beer for a summer potluck.

1 jar (32 ounces) sauerkraut, drained and rinsed

1/4 cup plus 2 tablespoons Tangy Thousand Island Dressing (page 163)

2 tablespoons butter or margarine, plus extra for serving

1/2 teaspoon caraway seeds

8 ounces corned beef, thinly sliced

2 cups grated Swiss cheese

2 1/2 cups dry rye bread crumbs

Sliced rye bread for serving

Preheat oven to 350°F. Spread sauerkraut in the bottom of a 9-by-13-inch glass baking dish lightly coated with cooking spray or oil. Spread dressing evenly on top. Dot with 1 tablespoon butter and sprinkle with the caraway seeds. Layer with corned beef and then cheese on top. Sprinkle with bread crumbs and dot with remaining 1 tablespoon butter. Bake, uncovered, until bubbly, 35 to 40 minutes. Serve with rye bread and butter.

SERVES 8

FOUR-PEPPERCORN PORK LOIN ROAST

For a wonderful potluck, impress your guests with this outstanding peppery pork loin roast. Complete the meal with Deviled New Potatoes (page 181); a vegetable dish; a salad of Mixed Greens with Fresh Pears, Blue Cheese, and Raspberry Vinaigrette (page 94); and Chocolate, Cranberry, and Ginger Trifle (page 318) to complete the menu.

3	tablespoons mixed peppercorns
1	pork loin roast (5 to 6 pounds)
	Salt
3	tablespoons butter at room temperature
1/3	cup, plus 2 tablespoons all-purpose flour
2	cups chicken broth
1	cup water
2	tablespoons red wine vinegar
	Rosemary sprigs for garnish

Preheat oven to 475°F. Crush peppercorns lightly with a mortar and pestle or place between sheets of waxed paper and roll with a rolling pin. Wash pork, pat dry, and season with salt. In a small bowl, combine butter and 2 tablespoons of flour to make a paste. Add the crushed peppercorns.

Place pork on a rack in a roasting pan. Spread peppercorn paste on top of roast and press in lightly with the back of a spoon. Roast 30 minutes, then reduce heat to 325°F and roast 45 minutes to 1 hour longer, or until a meat thermometer registers 150°F. Transfer the roast to a cutting board and let rest 10 minutes before carving.

While roast cools, make the gravy: Pour off most of the drippings, leaving 1/3 cup in the pan. Place pan on medium heat. Add remaining 1/3 cup flour and whisk until lightly browned, about 2 minutes. Add broth and water and bring mixture to a boil. Stir in vinegar and salt to taste. Reduce heat to medium-low and simmer until thickened, stirring constantly, about 5 minutes.

Cut pork into 3/8-inch slices and serve with some of the gravy. Garnish with rosemary sprigs.

SERVES 10 TO 12

HAM AND POTATO CASSEROLE WITH CHEESE SAUCE

This potato casserole, lightly sauced and mixed with ham and peas, is a good way to use leftovers. Simple accompaniments are Melon and Green Grape Salad (page 123) and warm French bread.

2	cups water
1 1/4	teaspoons salt
4	cups peeled and sliced potatoes
1	tablespoon butter or margarine
1/2	cup chopped yellow onion
2	tablespoons all-purpose flour
1	cup milk
	Freshly ground pepper
1 1/2	cups grated Cheddar cheese
1/2	cup sour cream
1 1/2	cups cubed ham
3/4	cup fresh or frozen peas, thawed
2	tomatoes, sliced and drained

In a large saucepan, bring water to a boil, add 1/4 teaspoon of the salt, and reduce heat to medium. Cook potatoes, covered, until tender, about 20 minutes. Cool under cold running water, drain, and set aside.

Preheat oven to 350°F. In a medium skillet over medium heat, melt butter. Add onion and sauté until tender, about 5 minutes. Add flour and stir until bubbly. Add milk, remaining 1 teaspoon salt, and pepper to taste and stir until slightly thickened, 1 to 2 minutes. Add half of the cheese and stir until melted, about 1 minute longer. Remove from heat. Stir in sour cream and set aside.

Put potatoes and ham in a 2-quart casserole lightly coated with cooking spray or oil. Add cheese sauce and toss lightly. Bake, uncovered, 25 minutes. Stir in peas, lay tomato slices on top, and sprinkle with remaining half of the cheese. Bake, uncovered, until bubbly, about 15 minutes longer. Let stand 5 to 10 minutes before serving.

SERVES 6

HAM LOAF WITH HONEY MUSTARD SAUCE

This savory ham loaf makes an excellent luncheon dish for a potluck shower. If you can't find the ground meats, you can grind them yourself in a food processor. This makes one large loaf or two small loaves. Serve it with Twenty-Four-Hour Fruit Salad (page 121). The Honey Mustard Sauce is also good on ham sandwiches and hot dogs.

1	pound ground ham
1	pound ground pork
1/2	cup diced yellow onion
1	cup milk
2	large eggs, lightly beaten
1 1/2	cups coarse dry bread crumbs
1/4	teaspoon dried thyme
1/2	teaspoon dry mustard
1/2	teaspoon salt
	Freshly ground pepper
	Honey Mustard Sauce (recipe follows)

Preheat oven to 325°F. In a large bowl, combine all ingredients, except sauce, and mix well. Spoon into a 5½-by-10-by-3-inch loaf pan lightly coated with cooking spray or oil and bake about 2 hours. Let the loaf remain in pan 10 minutes before serving. Remove from pan and slice. Serve with Honey Mustard Sauce.

SERVES 8

HONEY MUSTARD SAUCE

1	tablespoon brown sugar
1	teaspoon cider vinegar
1/2	teaspoon dried dillweed
1/4	cup Dijon mustard
1/4	cup yellow mustard
1/4	cup sour cream
1	tablespoon honey

In a small bowl, stir together sugar and vinegar until sugar is dissolved. Add remaining ingredients and whisk until smooth. Serve at room temperature.

MAKES ABOUT 3/4 CUP

HAM AND WHITE BEAN CASSEROLE

The hearty flavor and texture of this dish come from salty ham, fiber-rich beans, and a thick tomato sauce. This is a good dish to make for a potluck if you have leftover holiday ham. Serve with chilled cider and rye bread.

1	tablespoon olive oil
1	cup chopped yellow onion
1	large garlic clove, minced
2	cups cubed cooked ham
1	can (15 ounces) cannellini beans or other white beans, drained and rinsed
1	cup crushed tomatoes in thick, rich purée
1	cup grated Cheddar cheese
1/4	cup chopped fresh parsley
1/2	teaspoon dried basil
1/4	teaspoon salt
	Freshly ground pepper
1/2	cup freshly grated Parmesan cheese

Preheat oven to 350°F. In a medium skillet over medium heat, warm oil. Add onion and garlic and sauté until tender, about 5 minutes. Stir in ham.

In a 2-quart casserole lightly coated with cooking spray or oil, combine beans, tomatoes, Cheddar cheese, parsley, basil, salt, and pepper to taste. Add ham mixture and mix well. Sprinkle with Parmesan cheese. Bake, uncovered, until bubbly, about 35 minutes.

SERVES 4

ITALIAN SAUSAGE CASSEROLE

Layers of brown rice, spicy sausage, and zucchini are topped with tomato sauce and cheese in this great potluck casserole. Serve it with Antipasto Tossed Salad (page 100).

3	cups cooked long-grain brown rice (1 cup raw)
1 to 2	tablespoons vegetable oil, as needed
1	pound bulk Italian sausage
1/2	cup chopped yellow onion
1	garlic clove, minced
1	zucchini, unpeeled, ends trimmed, and sliced
1	can (6 ounces) tomato paste
1	cup water
1/4	cup dry red wine (see Note)
1/2	teaspoon salt
	Freshly ground pepper
1	cup grated mozzarella cheese
1/4	cup freshly grated Parmesan cheese

Preheat oven to 350°F. Spread rice in the bottom of a 3-quart casserole lightly coated with cooking spray or oil. In a large skillet over medium heat, warm oil. Brown sausage with onion and garlic, stirring to break up sausage, until meat is no longer pink, 7 to 8 minutes. Spoon sausage over rice in casserole, leaving drippings in the skillet. Add zucchini to the skillet and sauté until tender, about 5 minutes, adding more oil if needed. Arrange zucchini on top of the sausage mixture in casserole.

In the skillet, over medium heat, stir together tomato paste, water, wine, salt, and pepper to taste and heat until warm. Pour over casserole. Do not stir. Sprinkle casserole with mozzarella and Parmesan cheeses and bake, uncovered, until bubbly, about 40 minutes.

SERVES 6 TO 8

Note: If you prefer, omit the wine and use 1 1/4 cups water.

SAUSAGE AND EGG BRUNCH DISH

Make this easy dish the night before a brunch potluck, then bake it the next day before the guests arrive. A Summer Fruit Salad (page 125) and warm scones would be good accompaniments.

1 pound bulk Italian sausage

6 slices bread, crusts trimmed, and cut into 1-inch cubes

6 large eggs

2 cups milk

1/2 teaspoon dry mustard

1 teaspoon salt

Freshly ground pepper

1 1/2 cups grated Cheddar cheese

In a medium skillet over medium heat, brown sausage, breaking up with a spoon, until meat is no longer pink, about 5 minutes. Set aside.

Place bread cubes in the bottom of an 8-by-11½-inch glass baking dish lightly coated with cooking spray or oil. In a medium bowl, whisk together eggs, milk, mustard, salt, and pepper to taste and pour over bread in the baking dish. Sprinkle with cheese and cooked sausage. Cover and chill several hours or overnight.

Preheat oven to 350°F. Bring the dish to room temperature before baking. Bake, uncovered, until set, about 50 minutes.

SERVES 4 TO 6

Variations: Fold sausage in with egg mixture, pour mixture over bread, and sprinkle with cheese.

Replace sausage with 1 cup chopped cooked ham.

BABY BACK RIBS WITH TANGY BARBECUE SAUCE

In this recipe, the ribs are given a spicy rub and baked in the oven to remove most of the fat, then brushed with a tangy sauce and finished on the grill. Allow about 1 pound of ribs per person. Serve with Easy Baked Beans (page 211) and Coleslaw with Creamy Celery Seed Dressing (page 68). The barbecue sauce tastes good on chicken as well as ribs. Furnish plenty of napkins.

RUB FOR RIBS

1   teaspoon paprika

1   teaspoon chili powder

1   teaspoon dry mustard

Coarse salt and freshly ground pepper

4   pounds baby back ribs, membrane removed (see Note)

1   yellow onion, sliced and separated into rings

Tangy Barbecue Sauce (facing page)

To make the rub: Mix together all the ingredients in a small bowl.

Preheat oven to 350°F. Put ribs in a large pan. Sprinkle rub on meaty side of ribs and rub into meat. Scatter onion rings on top. Bake, uncovered, in the oven 1 hour. Remove from oven and pour off any drippings.

While the ribs are baking, make Tangy Barbecue Sauce. Prepare a grill for cooking over medium indirect heat. Place ribs on grill, brush with sauce, and grill, basting generously with sauce and turning several times, until meat is very tender and pulling away from the bones, about 1 hour longer.

SERVES 4

Note: Removing the membrane is an important step. It allows the seasonings to penetrate the meat and the fat to drip away during cooking. On the underside (bone side) of the ribs, loosen the white membrane with the point of a knife and make a slit large enough so that you can insert your finger under the membrane and pull it up and away from the ribs. Using a towel helps grip the membrane. Care-fully peel back the membrane at an angle. You may need to start over once or twice before you are successful, but it is worth the effort.

TANGY BARBECUE SAUCE

2 tablespoons butter or margarine

1/4 cup finely chopped celery

1/4 cup finely chopped yellow onion

1 garlic clove, minced

3/4 cup ketchup

1/4 cup chili sauce

2 tablespoons fresh lemon juice

1 tablespoon honey

2 tablespoons cider vinegar

1/2 cup water

1 tablespoon Worcestershire sauce

3 or 4 drops of Tabasco sauce

1/4 teaspoon salt

Freshly ground pepper

In a medium saucepan over medium heat, melt butter. Add celery and onion and sauté until tender, about 5 minutes. Add remaining ingredients and bring to a boil. Reduce the heat to low, cover, and simmer 10 minutes.

MAKES ABOUT 2 CUPS

BEEF AND VEGETABLE KABOBS

Kabobs are fun to make and to eat. They are a complete entrée—meat and vegetables on one skewer—and will add variety to your summer potluck. Be sure to allow at least 4 hours for the beef to marinate.

MARINADE

1/2	cup soy sauce
2	tablespoons sesame oil or vegetable oil
1/4	cup dry white wine
1	garlic clove, minced
1	tablespoon sugar
1/2	teaspoon ground ginger

1 1/2	pounds top sirloin, cut into 1 1/2-inch cubes
12	whole mushrooms, stems removed
1	green or red bell pepper, seeded and cut into 1-inch pieces
1	zucchini, unpeeled and cut into 3/4-inch slices
1	yellow onion, cut into 1-inch wedges and layers separated
12	cherry tomatoes

In a nonreactive bowl large enough to hold the meat, stir together marinade ingredients. Add meat and stir to mix well. Cover and marinate 4 to 6 hours in the refrigerator, stirring once. Bring to room temperature 30 minutes before grilling.

Prepare a grill for cooking over medium indirect heat. Remove meat from marinade, and boil marinade 1 minute to kill any bacteria from raw meat. Thread meat and vegetables onto metal skewers, alternating meat cubes with vegetables. Grill, turning several times and basting with marinade, 8 to 10 minutes for medium-rare. Serve immediately.

SERVES 6

GRILLED PORK CHOPS WITH DIJON BASTE

Thick pork chops are always popular for a summer potluck picnic or barbecue. The baste keeps them tender and juicy. You might want to suggest that someone bring a side dish of Mushroom, Spinach, and Noodle Casserole (page 194), and another guest could whip up Strawberry-Rhubarb Cobbler (page 302) for dessert.

DIJON BASTE

2	tablespoons red wine vinegar
2	tablespoons Dijon mustard
2	garlic cloves, minced
1	teaspoon dried thyme
1 1/2	teaspoons vegetable oil
4 to 6	thick boneless pork chops, 1 to 1 1/4 inches thick

To make the baste: In a small bowl, mix together all the ingredients. Spread baste on both sides of the pork chops and put on a plate. Let stand for 10 minutes at room temperature.

Prepare a grill for cooking over medium indirect heat. Grill pork chops until tender and pink is barely showing when a chop is cut with a knife, 12 to 15 minutes, turning once.

SERVES 4 TO 6

MARINATED PORK TENDERLOIN

These succulent tenderloins soak in a seasoned marinade with a Mexican twist for several hours or overnight before grilling. Ask two guests to bring Gazpacho Salad in Avocados (page 76) and Green Onion, Chile, and Rice Casserole (page 203) for a great meal.

3 pork tenderloins
(about 3 1/2 pounds total)

MARINADE

1/2 cup flat beer

Juice of 1 lime

2 tablespoons vegetable oil

1 tablespoon white wine vinegar

1 garlic clove, minced

1 teaspoon chili powder

1 teaspoon dried oregano

1 teaspoon paprika

1/2 teaspoon ground cumin

1/2 teaspoon salt

Freshly ground pepper

1/4 teaspoon grated lime zest

Lime wedges for garnish

Place tenderloins in a shallow glass dish. In a small bowl, stir together all the marinade ingredients. Pour over pork and turn to coat. Cover and marinate 4 to 5 hours or over-night in the refrigerator, turning several times. Remove from refrigerator 30 minutes before grilling.

Prepare a grill for cooking over medium indirect heat. Remove pork from marinade, and boil marinade for 1 minute to kill any bacteria from raw meat. Grill the pork, turning several times and basting with marinade, until an instant-read thermometer registers 160° to 170°F, 25 to 30 minutes.

Let stand 10 minutes before carving, then slice across the grain and arrange on a warmed platter. Garnish with lime wedges and serve immediately.

SERVES 8

Chicken dishes are popular contributions to potlucks because they are economical, healthful, and appeal to most people. In this chapter, you will find many old favorites, along with new contemporary recipes and a few grilled chicken recipes for summer potlucks. Among the tempting dishes featured are Crispy Oven-Fried Chicken (page 266), Baked Almond-Coated Chicken Breasts (page 264), Chicken Enchiladas with Creamy Salsa Sauce (page 254), Greek Chicken Pilaf (page 251), and Chicken-Sausage Stew (page 262).

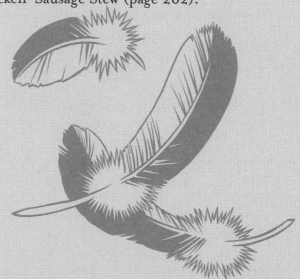

CHICKEN, ASPARAGUS, AND MUSHROOM CASSEROLE

For a taste of spring, tender young asparagus and chicken breasts are baked in a mushroom-cheese sauce and served on rice. Strawberry-Rhubarb Cobbler (page 302) would be the perfect finale.

1 1/4   pounds asparagus, tough ends snapped off

5   tablespoons butter or margarine

5   boned and skinned chicken breast halves (about 2 1/4 pounds), cut into large pieces

8   ounces mushrooms, sliced

3   tablespoons all-purpose flour

1 1/4   cups chicken broth

1   cup milk (not skim)

2   tablespoons dry white wine

1/2   cup grated Swiss cheese

1/2   teaspoon salt

  Freshly ground pepper

1/4   cup grated Parmesan cheese for sprinkling on top

1/2   cup sliced almonds for topping

Preheat oven to 350°F. Place asparagus in a 9-by-13-inch glass baking dish lightly coated with cooking spray or oil. In a medium skillet over medium heat, melt 2 tablespoons of the butter. Add chicken and sauté until lightly browned, about 5 minutes. Place chicken on top of asparagus in the dish. To the skillet, add another 2 tablespoons of butter and sauté mushrooms until tender, about 5 minutes. Put mushrooms on top of chicken in the dish. Melt remaining 1 tablespoon butter in skillet, add flour, and stir until bubbly. Add broth and milk and stir until thickened, about 2 minutes. Add wine, Swiss cheese, salt, and pepper to taste and stir until cheese is melted and flavors are blended, about 5 minutes.

Pour the hot sauce over all and sprinkle with Parmesan cheese and almonds. Bake, covered, until bubbly and heated through, about 20 minutes. Uncover and bake about 10 minutes longer to toast almonds.

SERVES 6

GREEK CHICKEN PILAF

This savory casserole of chicken and rice in a tomato sauce will take center stage at a potluck. Crisp, sliced cucumbers go well with this dish, and for an easy dessert, serve purchased baklava.

1	tablespoon olive oil
1	cup chopped yellow onion
2	garlic cloves, minced
3/4	cup long-grain white rice
1	can (8 ounces) tomato sauce
	Juice of 1 lemon (about 3 tablespoons)
1/4	teaspoon dried oregano
1/4	teaspoon sugar
1/4	teaspoon salt
	Freshly ground pepper
2 1/2	cups cubed cooked chicken breast (see Note on page 150)
1 1/2	cups chicken broth
1/4	cup crumbled feta cheese for sprinkling on top
1/4	cup pitted kalamata olives for topping

Preheat oven to 350°F. In a medium skillet over medium heat, warm oil. Add onion and garlic and sauté until tender, about 5 minutes. Stir in rice and cook 1 minute longer. Add tomato sauce, lemon juice, oregano, sugar, salt, and pepper to taste.

Transfer to a 2-quart casserole lightly coated with cooking spray or oil. Add chicken and broth and mix well. Cover and bake until liquid is absorbed, about 1 hour. Sprinkle with feta cheese and olives. Let stand 5 to 10 minutes before serving.

SERVES 6 TO 8

CHICKEN AND VEGETABLES WITH PENNE AND QUICK TOMATO SAUCE

For a satisfying main course, serve this baked pasta dish with chicken, zucchini, mushrooms, and penne. It is healthful as well as delicious. A good dish to make when zucchini are abundant.

2   small zucchini, unpeeled, halved lengthwise, and cut into 1/2-inch slices

8   ounces mushrooms, quartered

1/2 red bell pepper, seeded and cut into large bite-sized pieces

2   cups cubed cooked chicken breast (see Note on page 150)

2   cups Quick Tomato Sauce (recipe follows)

8   ounces penne, cooked as directed on package and drained

1   cup grated mozzarella cheese

Preheat oven to 350°F. In a medium saucepan over medium heat, cook zucchini, mushrooms, and bell pepper in an inch or so of gently boiling salted water, covered, until tender-crisp, 3 to 4 minutes. Drain and return to pan. Add chicken and tomato sauce and stir to combine.

Put pasta in a 2-quart casserole lightly coated with cooking spray or oil. Add vegetable and chicken mixture and mix well. Bake, covered, until bubbly, about 25 minutes. Sprinkle with cheese and bake, uncovered, 10 minutes longer.

SERVES 6 TO 8

QUICK TOMATO SAUCE

1   large can (15 ounces) tomato sauce

1   garlic clove, minced

1/2 teaspoon dried oregano

1/2 teaspoon dried basil

1/2 teaspoon salt

Freshly ground pepper

In a small saucepan over medium heat, combine all ingredients. Simmer, uncovered, stirring occasionally, until flavors are well blended, 5 to 10 minutes.

MAKES ABOUT 2 CUPS

CHICKEN, ARTICHOKE, AND BROCCOLI CASSEROLE

Layers of tender chicken breasts, artichokes, and crisp broccoli meld together in a flavorful cheese sauce. This casserole takes time and several steps to prepare, but once the casserole is made, your potluck dish will delight your guests.

4	cups broccoli florets
4	tablespoons butter or margarine
8	ounces mushrooms, sliced
1/4	cup all-purpose flour
2 1/2	cups chicken broth
1	teaspoon Dijon mustard
1/2	teaspoon dried thyme
1/2	teaspoon salt
	Freshly ground pepper
1	cup grated Cheddar cheese
4	boned and skinned chicken breast halves, cooked (see Note on page 150) and cut into large pieces
1	can (13 3/4 ounces) quartered artichoke hearts, drained
	Freshly grated Parmesan cheese for sprinkling on top

Preheat oven to 350°F. In a medium saucepan over medium-high heat, cook broccoli in gently boiling water to cover until tender-crisp, about 4 minutes. Cool under cold running water, drain, and set aside.

In a medium skillet over medium heat, melt 2 table-spoons of the butter. Add mushrooms and sauté until almost tender, about 5 minutes. Transfer to a plate with a slotted spoon. Add remaining 2 tablespoons butter and the flour to the skillet and stir until bubbly. Add broth, mustard, and seasonings and whisk until sauce thickens, 2 to 3 minutes. Add Cheddar cheese and stir until smooth.

In a 4-quart casserole lightly coated with cooking spray or oil, layer chicken, broccoli, mushrooms, and artichokes. Pour sauce over all. Cover and bake until bubbly, about 40 minutes. Stir, and sprinkle Parmesan cheese on top. Bake, uncovered, until cheese melts, 5 to 10 minutes longer.

SERVES 8

CHICKEN ENCHILADAS WITH CREAMY SALSA SAUCE

Everyone likes Mexican dishes, and this casserole with chicken and tortillas in a creamy sauce is a potluck favorite. Serve with Sunburst Salad (page 132), and ask someone to bring Chocolate Pudding Cake (page 314) for dessert. Make the Fresh Tomato Salsa, if using, about 1 hour before you begin the enchiladas.

3	tablespoons butter or margarine
1/2	cup diced yellow onion
3	tablespoons all-purpose flour
1 1/2	cups chicken broth
1/4	teaspoon salt
	Freshly ground pepper
1/2	cup Fresh Tomato Salsa (facing page) or purchased salsa, plus extra for topping
1	cup sour cream, plus extra for topping
8	large corn tortillas, softened (see Note on page 214)
3	cups diced cooked chicken (see Note on page 150)
6	green onions, including some tender green tops, sliced
3	cups grated Monterey Jack cheese
	Pitted black olives for garnish

Preheat oven to 350°F. In a medium saucepan over medium heat, melt butter. Add onion and sauté until tender, about 5 minutes. Add flour and stir until bubbly. Add broth, salt, and pepper to taste and stir until mixture boils and thickens, about 2 minutes. Stir in the 1/2 cup salsa. Remove from heat, slowly stir in the 1 cup sour cream, and mix well.

Cover the bottom of a 9-by-13-inch baking dish with one third of the sauce. Lay a tortilla on a flat surface. Add about 2 tablespoons chicken, 1 tablespoon sauce, and a few green onions down the center of the tortilla. Sprinkle with about 1 tablespoon cheese. Roll up and place, seam-side down, in the baking dish on top of the sauce. Repeat with remaining tortillas. Pour remaining sauce over all. Sprinkle with remaining cheese. Cover and bake 30 minutes. Uncover and bake until bubbly, about 10 minutes longer. Let stand 10 minutes before serving. Garnish with olives and pass additional salsa and sour cream in separate bowls.

SERVES 6 TO 8

FRESH TOMATO SALSA

4 tomatoes, seeded, chopped, and drained

1/2 cup diced green bell pepper (optional)

1/2 cup chopped yellow onion

1 tablespoon seeded and minced jalapeño pepper or 1 tablespoon diced canned chiles, drained

2 garlic cloves, minced

Juice of 1 small lime

1 tablespoon olive oil

1/4 cup chopped fresh cilantro or parsley

1 tablespoon chopped fresh oregano or 3/4 teaspoon dried oregano

1/2 teaspoon salt

Freshly ground pepper

In a medium bowl, stir together all ingredients. Cover and let stand at room temperature at least 1 hour, then store in refrigerator up to 3 days. Drain, if necessary, before using.

MAKES ABOUT 3 CUPS

CHICKEN, OLIVES, AND ORZO

Chicken is combined with tomatoes and orzo for this Greek-inspired dish served with Toasted Pita Wedges. Pita, also called pocket bread, is a Middle Eastern flatbread. When split, it forms a pocket and can be used for sandwiches.

1 teaspoon paprika

1 teaspoon curry powder

1/2 teaspoon salt

Freshly ground pepper

4 pounds boned and skinned chicken breast halves, cut into bite-sized pieces

2 tablespoons olive oil

1 cup chopped yellow onion

2 garlic cloves, minced

1 can (14 1/2 ounces) whole tomatoes, with their juices, chopped

1 1/4 cups chicken broth

1/2 cup pitted green olives

1/2 cup pitted kalamata olives

1 cup orzo

Toasted Pita Wedges (page 20)

Preheat oven to 350°F. In a medium bowl, mix paprika, curry powder, salt, and pepper to taste. Add chicken and toss to coat.

In a large skillet over medium-high heat, warm 1 tablespoon of the oil. Add chicken and sauté until lightly browned, 6 to 7 minutes. Transfer to a plate. Add remaining 1 tablespoon oil, reduce heat to medium, and sauté onion and garlic until tender, about 5 minutes. Stir in tomatoes and juice, broth, olives, and orzo. Return chicken to skillet and simmer 2 minutes. Transfer to a 3-quart casserole lightly coated with cooking spray or oil. Bake, covered, until orzo is tender and liquid is absorbed, about 35 minutes. Serve with Toasted Pita Wedges.

SERVES 6

FESTIVE CHICKEN, BLACK BEAN, AND TORTILLA CASSEROLE

This one-dish entrée is popular for potlucks and tailgates. The toppings are fun and add extra flavor. Serve the casserole with guacamole and chips, and don't forget the cold beer.

1	tablespoon vegetable oil
1	cup chopped yellow onion
1/2	red bell pepper, seeded and chopped
2	garlic cloves, minced
1	can (14 1/2 ounces) crushed tomatoes in rich purée
1/2	cup Fresh Tomato Salsa (page 255) or purchased salsa
1	teaspoon chili powder
1/2	teaspoon dried oregano
3/4	teaspoon salt
	Freshly ground pepper
2	cans (15 ounces each) black beans, drained and rinsed
2 to 3	cups cubed cooked chicken breast (see Note on page 150)
6	corn tortillas
2	cups (about 12 ounces) grated Cheddar cheese

Preheat oven to 350°F. In a large skillet over medium heat, warm oil. Add onion, bell pepper, and garlic and sauté until tender, about 5 minutes. Add tomatoes, salsa, chili powder, oregano, salt, and pepper to taste and mix well. Stir in beans and chicken.

In a 3-quart casserole or a large oval baking dish lightly coated with cooking spray or oil, spread one third of the bean and chicken mixture over the bottom of the dish. Top with 3 tortillas and sprinkle with 1 cup of the cheese. Repeat the layers once more. Add remaining bean and chicken mixture and remaining 1 cup cheese. Cover and bake until bubbly, about 40 minutes. Uncover and bake 10 minutes longer. Let stand 5 minutes before serving. Serve with toppings.

SERVES 6 TO 8

TOPPINGS

Sour cream

Avocado slices

Sliced green onions

Chopped black olives

CHICKEN AND CORN ENCHILADA DISH

This Mexican-inspired dish with chicken, corn, and a creamy enchilada sauce goes together quickly and is outstanding. Add Gazpacho Salad in Avocados (page 76) to the menu and Walnut Brownies with Caramel Sauce and Ice Cream (page 317) for dessert.

2 cans (10 ounces each) medium enchilada sauce

9 corn tortillas

1 cup sour cream

2 cups grated Cheddar cheese

1 1/2 cups freshly cooked corn kernels, scraped off the cob (about 2 ears), or frozen corn, thawed

1/2 cup sliced green onions, including some tender green tops

1 1/2 cups cubed cooked chicken breast (see Note on page 150)

1 can (7 ounces) diced chiles, drained

Preheat oven to 350°F. In a medium saucepan over medium heat, warm sauce. Dip 3 tortillas in sauce and lay so they are slightly overlapping on the bottom of a 9-by-13-inch glass baking dish lightly coated with cooking spray or oil.

In a large bowl, mix together 1 cup of the sauce, the sour cream, 1 cup of the Cheddar cheese, the corn, green onions, chicken, and chiles. Spread half of this filling mixture over the tortillas. Dip 3 more tortillas in sauce and lay on top. Cover with remaining filling mixture. Dip remaining 3 tortillas in sauce and lay on top of filling mixture. Pour remaining sauce over all. Sprinkle with remaining Cheddar cheese. Bake, uncovered, until bubbly, 35 to 40 minutes. Let stand 5 to 10 minutes before serving.

SERVES 8

CHICKEN, MUSHROOM, AND NOODLE CASSEROLE

Between office parties and church socials, this creamy combination of favorite ingredients, topped with almonds, is always in demand. It goes with almost any dish someone might bring to a potluck.

2	cups egg noodles, cooked as directed on package and drained
4	tablespoons butter or margarine
1/2	cup chopped green bell pepper
1/2	cup chopped yellow onion
6	ounces mushrooms, sliced
2	tablespoons all-purpose flour
1 1/2	cups milk
1	teaspoon dried thyme
1/2	teaspoon salt
1/8	teaspoon white pepper
1/4	cup chopped fresh parsley
1/2	cup sour cream
2	cups cubed cooked chicken breast (see Note on page 150)
1/4	cup sliced almonds

Preheat oven to 350°F. Put noodles in a 3-quart casserole lightly coated with cooking spray or oil. In a medium skillet over medium heat, melt 2 tablespoons of the butter. Add bell pepper, onion, and mushrooms and sauté until tender, about 5 minutes. Transfer to the casserole. Add remaining 2 tablespoons butter to the skillet, add flour, and stir until bubbly. Add milk and stir until thickened, 1 to 2 minutes. Add thyme, salt, pepper, and parsley. Remove from heat and slowly stir in sour cream and chicken. Transfer to the casserole and mix well. Sprinkle almonds on top. Bake, uncovered, until bubbly and almonds are toasted, about 30 minutes.

SERVES 6

CHICKEN LASAGNA

This lasagna variation of chicken and cheeses layered with noodles and a mushroom-tomato sauce is popular for a potluck any time of the year. Serve with Caesar Salad (page 78).

1	tablespoon vegetable oil
1/2	cup chopped yellow onion
6	ounces mushrooms, coarsely chopped
1	large can (14 1/2 ounces) crushed tomatoes in thick purée
1	large can (15 ounces) tomato sauce
1/2	teaspoon dried basil
1/2	teaspoon dried oregano
1/4	teaspoon sugar
1/4	teaspoon salt
	Freshly ground pepper
2	cups cottage cheese
2	cups grated mozzarella cheese
1/2	cup sour cream
3/4	cup freshly grated Parmesan cheese
1/4	cup chopped fresh parsley
9	lasagna noodles, cooked as directed on package and drained
3	cups packed shredded cooked chicken breast (see Note on page 150)

In a medium skillet over medium heat, warm oil. Add onion and mushrooms and sauté until tender, about 5 minutes. Stir in tomatoes, tomato sauce, basil, oregano, sugar, salt, and pepper to taste. Bring to a boil, reduce temperature to low, and simmer, uncovered, until flavors are blended, about 10 minutes.

In a medium bowl, mix together the cottage cheese, 1 cup of the mozzarella, the sour cream, 1/2 cup of the Parmesan, and the parsley.

In the bottom of a 9-by-13-inch glass baking dish lightly coated with cooking spray or oil, spread a little of the mushroom-tomato sauce. Layer with 3 noodles, one third of the cheese mixture (it will not completely cover), one third of the chicken, and one third of the mushroom-tomato sauce. Repeat layers two more times, ending with sauce. Sprinkle remaining 1 cup mozzarella and 1/4 cup Parmesan on top. Bake at 350°F, uncovered, until bubbly, about 50 minutes. Let stand 10 minutes before serving. Cut the lasagna into squares.

SERVES 8

CLUB CHICKEN

Enjoy this casserole with tender pieces of chicken breast and rice baked in a creamy sauce. Take it to your potluck dinner party. Try a complementary salad of Spinach and Strawberries with Candied Pecans and Raspberry–Poppy Seed Vinaigrette (page 84).

2 1/4	cups chicken broth
1	cup long-grain white rice
2	tablespoons butter or margarine
8	ounces mushrooms, sliced
1/2	cup chopped red bell pepper
1/2	cup sliced almonds
3	cups cubed cooked chicken breast (see Note on page 150)
1/4	cup chopped fresh parsley
	Sour Cream Sauce (recipe follows)

In a large saucepan over high heat, bring broth to a boil and stir in rice. Reduce heat to medium-low and cook, covered, until liquid is absorbed, about 20 minutes. Transfer to a 3-quart casserole lightly coated with cooking spray or oil.

Preheat oven to 350°F. In a medium skillet over medium heat, melt butter. Add mushrooms and bell pepper and sauté until tender, about 5 minutes. Remove from heat, stir in almonds, and combine with rice in casserole. Add chicken, parsley, and sauce and toss lightly. Bake, covered, until heated through and bubbly, about 35 minutes.

SERVES 10

SOUR CREAM SAUCE

2	tablespoons butter or margarine
2	tablespoons all-purpose flour
1/2	cup chicken broth
1	cup milk
1/2	teaspoon dried thyme
3/4	teaspoon salt
	Dash of white pepper
1/2	cup sour cream

In a medium saucepan over medium heat, melt butter. Add flour and stir until bubbly. Add broth, milk, thyme, salt, and pepper and stir until thickened, about 2 minutes. Remove from heat and whisk in sour cream.

MAKES ABOUT 2 CUPS

CHICKEN-SAUSAGE STEW

My husband, Reed, goes for any dish that includes sausage. This stew with chicken, spicy sausage, and vegetables, slowly simmered together, is his favorite. I serve it with a tossed green salad with French Dressing (page 76), also a favorite, and crusty bread. It would be good at any winter potluck.

4	Italian sausages
4	boned and skinned chicken breast halves (about 2 pounds), cut into large bite-sized pieces
2 1/2	cups chicken broth
3	carrots, sliced into 1/2-inch slices
3	potatoes, peeled and quartered
1	large yellow onion, sliced
2	garlic cloves, minced
1	bay leaf
2 or 3	drops of Tabasco sauce
2	teaspoons Worcestershire sauce
1	teaspoon soy sauce
1/2	teaspoon salt
	Freshly ground pepper
3/4	cup fresh or frozen peas
1/4	cup all-purpose flour
1/2	cup water

Put sausage on a paper plate lined with a paper towel. Prick in several places with a sharp fork. Lay a paper towel on top and microwave on high for 2 minutes. Cool slightly and cut into 3/4-inch pieces.

In a large soup pot over medium-high heat, combine the sausages, chicken, broth, carrots, potatoes, onion, garlic, bay leaf, Tabasco, Worcestershire, soy sauce, salt, and pepper to taste. Bring to a boil, reduce heat to medium-low, and simmer, covered, until chicken is no longer pink in the center and vegetables are tender, about 20 minutes. Add peas and cook, uncovered, 5 minutes longer.

In a small bowl, blend flour and water. Increase heat to medium-high and slowly add flour mixture to stew, stirring constantly, until stew bubbles and is slightly thickened, 2 to 3 minutes. Discard bay leaf. Reduce heat and simmer, uncovered, until ready to eat. Serve in bowls.

SERVES 8

CHICKEN BREASTS STUFFED WITH CHILES AND CHEESE

This is a great main course that can be assembled ahead and baked later. Serve with Baked Black Beans with Toppings (page 210) and Summer Fruit Salad (page 125).

4	boned and skinned chicken breast halves (about 2 pounds)
	Salt and freshly ground pepper
1	cup grated Monterey Jack cheese
1/2	can (2 ounces) diced chiles, drained
1/4	cup finely chopped red bell pepper
6	green onions, including some tender green tops, chopped
1/3	cup milk or buttermilk
3/4	cup fine dry bread crumbs
2 or 3	tablespoons butter or margarine, melted

Preheat oven to 400°F. Place chicken breasts between 2 pieces of plastic wrap and pound with a meat mallet until 1/4 inch thick. Remove top piece of plastic and season chicken with salt and pepper to taste. On each breast half, put 2 tablespoons cheese, 1 teaspoon chiles, 1 tablespoon bell pepper, and 1 tablespoon green onions. Roll up each breast half from narrow end and secure in place with a toothpick. Pour milk into a shallow dish. Put bread crumbs on a piece of waxed paper. Dip chicken breasts in milk and then roll in crumbs to coat. Place in an 8-inch-square glass baking dish lightly coated with cooking spray or oil. Drizzle with butter. Bake, uncovered, until chicken is no longer pink in the center, about 1 hour.

SERVES 4

BAKED ALMOND-COATED CHICKEN BREASTS

In this easy recipe, a seasoned coating of nuts, flour, and cheese keeps the chicken breasts tender and moist while they bake. Ask your guests to bring Barley and Mushroom Casserole (page 209) and Spinach-Mushroom Salad with Creamy Balsamic Vinaigrette and Toasted Hazelnuts (page 81) for a relaxed, casual potluck. This recipe can be doubled.

1/4 cup chopped almonds

1/4 cup all-purpose flour

3 tablespoons freshly grated Parmesan cheese

1/2 teaspoon crushed dried rosemary

1/2 teaspoon salt

Freshly ground pepper

1/3 cup buttermilk

6 boned and skinned chicken breast halves (2 1/2 to 3 pounds)

4 tablespoons butter or margarine, melted

Preheat oven to 350°F. On a piece of waxed paper, mix almonds, flour, cheese, rosemary, salt, and pepper to taste. Pour buttermilk into a shallow dish. Dip chicken in buttermilk, then roll in nut and flour mixture to coat.

Place chicken breasts in an 8-by-10-inch glass baking dish lightly coated with cooking spray or oil and drizzle with butter. Bake, uncovered, until chicken is no longer pink in the center, 35 to 40 minutes.

SERVES 4 TO 6

CHICKEN-ALMOND CASSEROLE WITH PEACHES

The spicy peaches atop the chicken breasts introduce a pleasing, fruity flavor and add eye appeal to this casserole. Serve with Confetti Rice (page 202) and Avocado and Mushroom Salad (page 47).

3/4 cup all-purpose flour

1 teaspoon salt

Freshly ground pepper

1 teaspoon paprika

8 large boned and skinned chicken breast halves (about 3 1/2 pounds)

6 tablespoons butter or margarine

1/2 cup sliced almonds

2 cups chicken broth

1 cup sour cream

2 cans (15 1/4 ounces each) peach halves, drained

1 teaspoon ground cinnamon

1/4 teaspoon ground nutmeg

Preheat oven to 350°F. On a piece of waxed paper, mix flour, salt, pepper to taste, and paprika. Dredge chicken in mixture and reserve leftover flour mixture.

In a large skillet over medium-high heat, melt 4 tablespoons of the butter. Brown chicken in batches, about 5 minutes on each side. Transfer to a 9-by-13-inch glass baking dish lightly coated with cooking spray or oil. Add remaining 2 tablespoons butter and the almonds to skillet and sauté 1 minute. Stir in reserved flour, add broth, and stir until slightly thickened, about 2 minutes. Remove from heat and slowly whisk in sour cream.

Pour broth and sour cream mixture over chicken and bake, uncovered, 30 minutes. Arrange peach halves, cut-side up, on top of the chicken. Sprinkle peaches with cinnamon and nutmeg and bake the casserole until peaches are warm and chicken is no longer pink in the center, 5 to 10 minutes longer.

SERVES 8

CRISPY OVEN-FRIED CHICKEN

This chicken has the same good, old-fashioned taste as fried chicken, but it is baked in the oven, saving time and work. The chicken is dipped in buttermilk and rolled in a seasoned coating for a crisp finish. This is an easy way to prepare chicken for a crowd.

1/2   cup all-purpose flour

1/2   cup fine dry bread crumbs

1   teaspoon dried thyme

1   teaspoon dried basil

1   teaspoon salt

Freshly ground pepper

1/4   cup grated Parmesan cheese

1   cup buttermilk

1/2   cup (1 stick) butter or margarine

2   chickens (3 1/2 to 4 pounds each), cut into serving pieces and excess skin and fat trimmed

Preheat oven to 375°F. In a paper bag, combine flour, bread crumbs, thyme, basil, salt, pepper to taste, and cheese. Pour buttermilk into a shallow dish. Melt the butter in a jelly-roll pan in the oven.

Dip a few pieces of chicken in buttermilk, shake off excess, put in bag with flour and crumb mixture, close bag, and shake. Remove chicken, coat in butter in the jelly-roll pan, and leave in the pan. Repeat with remaining chicken. Bake, uncovered, until chicken is no longer pink in the center, about 1 1/4 hours. If chicken is not brown enough, increase heat to 400°F and bake 5 to 10 minutes longer.

SERVES 6 TO 8

CHICKEN, HAWAIIAN STYLE

This dish requires little effort and yields great results. Keep it in mind for the next time you need a festive casserole for a potluck. Tropical Fruit Salad (page 124) is a good choice for a salad.

1/2	cup all-purpose flour
1	teaspoon ground ginger
1/2	teaspoon paprika
1/4	teaspoon ground cloves
1	teaspoon salt
	Freshly ground pepper
1	chicken (3 to 3 1/2 pounds), cut into serving pieces and excess skin and fat trimmed
1	tablespoon butter
1 to 2	tablespoons vegetable oil
1	can (8 ounces) crushed pineapple, with its juice
2	tablespoons soy sauce

Preheat oven to 350°F. On a piece of waxed paper, mix flour, ginger, paprika, cloves, salt, and pepper to taste. Dredge chicken in flour mixture.

In a large skillet over medium-high heat, melt butter with oil. Add chicken and brown, about 5 minutes on each side. Transfer to a 9-by-13-inch glass baking dish lightly coated with cooking spray or oil. Remove skillet from the heat, add pineapple with juice and soy sauce, and stir to mix. Pour over the chicken.

Cover and bake until chicken is no longer pink in the center, about 1 hour. Uncover last 10 minutes of cooking time.

SERVES 4 TO 6

LEMON CHICKEN

This flavorful chicken dish with a sweet-tart sauce will be a potluck favorite. It is easy to make and will serve an appreciative crowd.

6   tablespoons butter

2   chickens (3 1/2 to 4 pounds each), cut into serving pieces and excess skin and fat trimmed

3/4   teaspoon dried thyme

1   teaspoon salt

Freshly ground pepper

Juice of 1 lemon (about 3 tablespoons)

1   cup chicken broth

2   tablespoons dry sherry or dry white wine

1/4   cup brown sugar

1/4   teaspoon ground cloves

2   tablespoons cornstarch

Preheat oven to 350°F. Melt butter in a large baking dish or jelly-roll pan in the oven. Add the chicken pieces and turn in butter to coat. Sprinkle with thyme, salt, and pepper to taste. Bake, uncovered, 45 minutes.

In a medium saucepan over medium heat, combine lemon juice, broth, sherry, sugar, cloves, and cornstarch. Stir constantly until thickened, 1 to 2 minutes. Spoon sauce over chicken and bake, uncovered, until chicken is no longer pink in the center, about 20 minutes longer.

SERVES 6 TO 8

ROASTED MOROCCAN CHICKEN WITH DATES AND APRICOTS

This zesty dish will add a new dimension to a potluck. Chicken pieces are soaked in a spicy marinade overnight and then roasted. The dates and apricots added in the last half hour of cooking time sweeten the savory pan juices.

1 cup chopped yellow onion

4 large garlic cloves, chopped

1 cup chicken broth

1/4 cup orange juice

1/2 teaspoon salt

Freshly ground pepper

1 teaspoon ground coriander

1/2 teaspoon ground cinnamon

1/2 teaspoon ground cumin

1/4 teaspoon ground cloves

1 large chicken (4 to 4 1/2 pounds), cut into serving pieces and excess skin and fat trimmed

1 cup pitted dates

1 cup pitted dried apricots

Couscous with Pine Nuts (page 212)

1/2 cup slivered almonds

In a medium bowl, mix together onion, garlic, broth, orange juice, salt, pepper to taste, coriander, cinnamon, cumin, and cloves. Place chicken in a large resealable plastic bag and add marinade. Seal bag and place in a baking dish in the refrigerator. Marinate overnight, turning several times to redistribute marinade.

Preheat oven to 350°F. Remove chicken from plastic bag and place in a 9-by-13-inch glass baking dish lightly coated with cooking spray or oil. Pour marinade over chicken. Bake, uncovered, 1 hour, spooning marinade over chicken several times. Add dates and apricots to the pan. Bake, covered, until chicken is very tender, 30 minutes longer. Let stand 10 minutes before serving. While chicken is resting, make the couscous and transfer to a bowl. Spoon some marinade on top of couscous and sprinkle with almonds. Serve the chicken alongside the couscous.

SERVES 6

TANGY BAKED COATED CHICKEN

Here is a recipe most people like to make because it is so easy and tastes so good. The chicken is spread with a tangy, yogurt-based sauce and baked in the oven. In about an hour you have a delicious entrée. This recipe can easily be doubled for a large potluck.

1/4 cup mayonnaise

1 cup plain nonfat yogurt

1 tablespoon fresh lemon juice

1 tablespoon Dijon mustard

2 drops of Tabasco sauce

1 teaspoon Worcestershire sauce

1/4 teaspoon dried thyme

1/4 teaspoon salt

Freshly ground pepper

1/4 cup grated Parmesan cheese

1 chicken (3 1/2 to 4 pounds), cut into serving pieces and excess skin and fat trimmed

4 green onions, including some tender green tops, sliced

Preheat oven to 350°F. Mix all ingredients in a bowl, except chicken and onions, stirring to blend well. Place chicken in a 9-by-13-inch glass baking dish lightly coated with cooking spray or oil. Spread sauce mixture over the chicken, covering it completely. Bake, uncovered, until chicken is lightly browned and bubbly, about 1 hour. Sprinkle with green onions before serving.

SERVES 4

MEXICAN CHICKEN

This entrée of chicken and chiles in a spicy tomato sauce is great for a Mexican-theme potluck. Include Jicama, Red Bell Pepper, and Avocado Salad (page 55), fluffy rice, and Reunion Chocolate Cake (page 313) for a complete potluck menu.

1 to 2	tablespoons vegetable oil, as needed
4	pounds choice chicken pieces, such as drumsticks, thighs, and breasts
	Salt and freshly ground pepper
1/2	cup chopped yellow onion
1	garlic clove, minced
1 1/2	tablespoons all-purpose flour
1	teaspoon dried oregano
2	teaspoons chili powder
1/4	teaspoon ground cumin
1	can (15 ounces) whole tomatoes, with their juices, chopped
1	can (8 ounces) tomato sauce
1	cup pitted black olives
1	can (8 ounces) whole green chiles, drained, split, seeded, and cut into large pieces

Preheat oven to 350°F. In a large skillet over medium-high heat, warm 1 tablespoon of the oil. Add chicken and brown in batches, about 15 minutes. Season with salt and pepper to taste and transfer to a 9-by-13-inch glass baking dish lightly coated with cooking spray or oil. If needed, add remaining 1 tablespoon oil to the skillet, reduce heat to medium, and sauté onion and garlic until tender, about 5 minutes. Add flour and stir until bubbly. Stir in oregano, chili powder, and cumin. Add tomatoes and juice and tomato sauce and stir until thickened, about 2 minutes.

Pour sauce over chicken. Cover and bake 45 minutes. Uncover, add olives, and lay chile pieces on top of the chicken. Spoon some of the sauce over all. Bake, uncovered, until chicken is no longer pink in the center, about 20 minutes longer. Let stand 5 to 10 minutes before serving.

SERVES 8 TO 10

CHICKEN THIGHS, RICE, AND TOMATOES

Plump chicken thighs, chiles, and tomatoes are the dominant flavors in this lively rice casserole inspired by Southwestern cuisine. Cucumbers in Sour Cream (page 54) and warm flour tortillas are good accompaniments.

2   tablespoons vegetable oil

8   chicken thighs (about 2 1/2 pounds)

1   cup chopped yellow onion

2   garlic cloves, minced

1   cup long-grain white rice

1   can (15 ounces) whole tomatoes, with their juices, chopped

1   cup chicken broth

1   can (4 ounces) chopped green chiles, drained

1/2   teaspoon ground cumin

1/2   teaspoon chili powder

1/2   teaspoon dried oregano

1/4   cup chopped fresh cilantro or parsley

1/2   teaspoon salt

Freshly ground pepper

Preheat oven to 350°F. In a large skillet over medium-high heat, warm 1 tablespoon of the oil. Brown chicken in batches, about 5 minutes on each side. Transfer to a plate. Add remaining 1 tablespoon oil. Reduce heat to medium, add onion and garlic, and sauté until tender, about 5 minutes. Add rice and stir. Add tomatoes and juice, broth, chiles, cumin, chili powder, oregano, cilantro, salt, and pepper to taste, stirring until well combined.

Pour mixture into a 9-by-13-inch glass baking dish lightly coated with cooking spray or oil. Arrange chicken, skin-side up, on top of rice mixture. Cover and bake until liquid is absorbed and chicken is no longer pink in the center, about 45 minutes.

SERVES 4 TO 6

ROASTED CHICKEN THIGHS AND BELL PEPPERS

Roasting adds an intense, smoky flavor to the chicken and vegetables in this easily assembled, one-dish meal. It goes well with Coleslaw with Creamy Celery Seed Dressing (page 68) and Apple-Berry Crisp (page 307).

8 boneless and skinless chicken thighs (about 2 1/2 pounds)

4 to 6 garlic cloves, halved

3 new potatoes, unpeeled and quartered

1 small red bell pepper, seeded and quartered

1 small green bell pepper, seeded and quartered

1 small yellow onion, quartered and cut into 1-inch wedges

3 tablespoons olive oil

1/2 teaspoon dried thyme

1 teaspoon salt

Freshly ground pepper

Preheat oven to 425°F. In a large bowl, mix together all ingredients. Transfer to a 9-by-13-inch glass baking dish lightly coated with cooking spray or oil. Roast, uncovered, 30 minutes. Turn chicken and vegetables and cook until chicken is no longer pink in the center and vegetables are tender-crisp, 15 to 20 minutes longer. Arrange on a heated platter and serve immediately.

SERVES 8

GRILLED CHICKEN WITH HONEY-MUSTARD GLAZE

For a patio party, grill this wine-marinated chicken finished with a honey-mustard glaze. Serve it with Marinated Tomatoes with Fresh Herb Dressing (page 51).

HERB AND WINE MARINADE

- 1 cup dry white wine
- 1 tablespoon vegetable oil
- 1 tablespoon fresh rosemary or 1 teaspoon dried rosemary
- 1/4 teaspoon dried thyme
- 1/2 teaspoon dried oregano
- 1/2 teaspoon salt

  Freshly ground pepper

- 1 chicken (3 1/2 to 4 pounds), cut into serving pieces, excess skin and fat trimmed

  Honey-Mustard Glaze (recipe follows)

In a large glass dish, combine all marinade ingredients. Reserve 1/4 cup and set aside for the glaze. Add the chicken to the marinade and turn to coat. Cover and marinate in the refrigerator several hours, turning once.

Prepare a grill for cooking over medium indirect heat. Place chicken and its marinade in a foil pan and grill for 45 to 50 minutes, turning several times. Remove chicken from marinade and place directly on grill. Brush with Honey-Mustard Glaze and cook, turning once, about 10 minutes longer, or until chicken is no longer pink in the center.

SERVES 4 TO 6

HONEY-MUSTARD GLAZE

- 2 tablespoons Dijon mustard
- 2 tablespoons honey
- 1/4 cup Herb and Wine Marinade, reserved from Grilled Chicken with Honey-Mustard Glaze

In a small bowl, whisk together all glaze ingredients.

MAKES ABOUT 1/2 CUP

GRILLED CHICKEN WITH ZESTY BARBECUE SAUCE

Grilled chicken is always a popular and easy main course for summer potlucks, and you won't have to slave away in the kitchen. The thick, zesty barbecue sauce adds color and flavor. Ask a couple of guests to bring Light Dilled New Potato Salad (page 60) and Blueberry Pie (page 303) for a fine meal.

1 chicken (3 1/2 to 4 pounds), cut into serving pieces, excess skin and fat trimmed

Zesty Barbecue Sauce (recipe follows)

Prepare the grill for cooking over medium indirect heat. Place chicken in a foil pan and coat with barbecue sauce. Place the pan on the grill and cook, turning and brushing chicken with barbecue sauce several times, until no longer pink in the center, about 50 minutes. For a crispy finish, remove chicken from pan and place directly on the grill for 10 minutes, turning several times.

SERVES 4

ZESTY BARBECUE SAUCE

1/4 cup ketchup

1/4 cup chili sauce

1 tablespoon vegetable oil

Juice of 1 lemon (about 3 tablespoons)

1 tablespoon prepared horseradish

2 tablespoons white wine vinegar

2 tablespoons soy sauce

1 teaspoon prepared mustard

1/2 teaspoon Worcestershire sauce

1/2 teaspoon salt

1/8 teaspoon freshly ground pepper

In a medium bowl, whisk together all ingredients.

MAKES ABOUT 2/3 CUP

GRILLED BEER CHICKEN

For a bang-up Fourth of July potluck featuring grilled chicken, suggest lots of side dishes: Picnic Potato Salad (page 61), Easy Baked Beans (page 211), Marinated Tomatoes with Fresh Herb Dressing (page 51), corn on the cob, and, for dessert, Banana-Citrus Ice Cream (page 329). If you are traveling to a picnic site, grill the chicken the day before and thoroughly chill, or grill at the picnic site. It's good hot or cold. Grill two chickens for a crowd, and increase the marinade by half.

1	chicken (3 1/2 to 4 pounds), cut into serving pieces, excess skin and fat trimmed
1/4	cup honey
1	cup flat beer
1/2	cup ketchup
1	teaspoon salt
2	garlic cloves, minced
2	tablespoons diced yellow onion
1	tablespoon prepared mustard
1	teaspoon Worcestershire sauce
2 or 3	drops of Tabasco sauce

Place chicken in a large glass bowl. In a medium bowl, mix together remaining ingredients and pour over chicken. Cover and marinate in the refrigerator 2 to 3 hours.

Prepare the grill for cooking over medium indirect heat. Remove chicken from marinade and place in a foil pan. Place pan on the grill and cook the chicken, turning and brushing it with marinade several times, until no longer pink in the center, about 50 minutes. For a crispy finish, remove chicken from pan and place directly on the grill for 10 minutes, turning several times.

SERVES 4

This chapter offers a variety of seafood dishes, from the simple, but classic, Tuna-Noodle Casserole (page 289) to the elegant Shrimp Florentine Gratin (page 278). The Crab and Spinach Manicotti with Parmesan Cheese Sauce (page 286) and the Mixed Seafood Casserole (page 287) will be welcome at any potluck occasion. Seafood Stew (page 290) is a seafood lover's delight, while Scallops, Vegetables, Pancetta, and Linguini evokes the flavors of Italy (page 291).

Seafood dishes can be made any time of the year with fresh or frozen seafood. We are lucky in the Northwest, where I live, to have a supply of very fresh seafood and fish available year-round. In most parts of the country, however, supermarkets and specialty fish markets receive fresh deliveries at least several times a week.

Most seafood dishes do not store well.

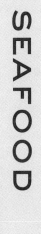

SEAFOOD DISHES

SHRIMP FLORENTINE GRATIN

For a gourmet-club potluck, serve this elegant combination of layered spinach, mushrooms, and shrimp topped with a cheese sauce and buttery bread crumbs. Serve it with fluffy rice and Citrus and Avocado Toss-Up (page 97).

5 tablespoons butter or margarine

1 pound mushrooms, sliced

Two-Cheese Sauce (facing page)

1 bag (10 ounces) fresh spinach, stems removed, cooked, drained, squeezed dry, and chopped

1 pound large shrimp (about 24), peeled and deveined

1 cup coarse dry bread crumbs

In a large skillet over medium heat, melt 3 tablespoons of the butter. Add mushrooms and sauté until tender, about 5 minutes. Transfer mushrooms to a plate. In the same skillet, make the cheese sauce.

Preheat oven to 350°F. In a 9-by-13-inch glass baking dish lightly coated with cooking spray or oil, layer the spinach, then the mushrooms. Arrange uncooked shrimp on top. Pour cheese sauce over all. In a small bowl, mix bread crumbs with remaining 2 tablespoons of melted butter and sprinkle on top of sauce. Bake, uncovered, until bubbly, 30 to 40 minutes.

SERVES 6

TWO-CHEESE SAUCE

3	tablespoons butter or margarine
1/4	cup diced yellow onion
3	tablespoons all-purpose flour
2	cups half-and-half or milk
3	tablespoons dry white wine
1/2	teaspoon Worcestershire sauce
1/4	teaspoon dried thyme
1/4	teaspoon paprika
	Dash of ground nutmeg
1/2	teaspoon salt
1/4	teaspoon white pepper
1/2	cup grated Cheddar cheese
1/4	cup grated Parmesan cheese

In a medium saucepan over medium heat, melt butter. Add onion and sauté until tender, about 5 minutes. Stir in flour, add half-and-half, and stir until thickened, about 2 minutes. Add wine, Worcestershire, thyme, paprika, nutmeg, salt, pepper, and cheeses and stir until smooth.

MAKES ABOUT 3 CUPS

SHRIMP AND CHICKEN CASSEROLE

Bay shrimp, chicken, Swiss cheese, and rice are a winning combination in this easily portable dish. For a complementary salad, serve Mixed Greens with Avocado, Blue Cheese, and Hazelnuts (page 89).

3 cups cooked long-grain white rice (1 cup raw)

2 tablespoons butter or margarine

4 ounces mushrooms, sliced

6 green onions, including some tender green tops, sliced

1¼ cups milk

3 large eggs, lightly beaten

½ teaspoon salt

⅛ teaspoon white pepper

½ teaspoon dried dillweed

¼ teaspoon dried marjoram

2 cups cubed cooked chicken breast (see Note on page 150)

8 ounces small bay shrimp

⅓ cup sliced almonds

2 cups grated Swiss cheese

Preheat oven to 350°F. Put rice in a 3-quart casserole lightly coated with cooking spray or oil.

In a medium skillet over medium heat, melt butter. Sauté mushrooms and green onions until tender, about 5 minutes, and stir into rice. In a medium bowl, whisk together milk, eggs, and seasonings. Stir into rice and mushroom mixture, add chicken, shrimp, almonds, and cheese, and mix well. Cover and bake until bubbly, 45 to 50 minutes. Let stand 5 minutes before serving.

SERVES 6 TO 8

CREOLE BAKED SHRIMP IN RICE

Creole cooking reflects the best of French, Spanish, and African cuisine. It relies on the "holy trinity" of chopped green peppers, onions, and celery. In this combination, which includes these three vegetables, large shrimp are tucked into rice flavored with a savory sauce.

2 tablespoons vegetable oil

1/2 cup chopped yellow onion

1/2 cup chopped green bell pepper

1/2 cup chopped celery

1 garlic clove, chopped

1 cup seeded, chopped, and drained tomatoes

1 can (8 ounces) tomato sauce

1/4 teaspoon Tabasco sauce, or to taste

1/2 cup chicken broth

1/2 teaspoon dried oregano

1/2 teaspoon salt

Freshly ground pepper

3 cups cooked long-grain white rice (1 cup raw)

12 ounces large shrimp (16 to 18), peeled and deveined

Preheat oven to 350°F. In a medium skillet over medium heat, warm oil. Add onion, bell pepper, celery, and garlic and sauté until tender, 6 to 7 minutes. Add tomatoes, tomato sauce, Tabasco, broth, oregano, salt, and pepper to taste and cook 1 minute.

Put rice in a 2½-quart casserole lightly coated with cooking spray or oil. Add the sauce and mix well. Cover and bake 25 minutes. Tuck shrimp into the rice and bake, covered, until shrimp turn pink, about 5 minutes longer.

SERVES 4

CRAB, SHRIMP, AND RICE CASSEROLE

This was made by a friend of ours, who was entertaining his lady friend with a potluck dinner at his home. It worked, and they got married! I think he bought a dessert, but Pound Cake (page 316) and fresh fruit would be nice.

5	tablespoons butter or margarine
3	tablespoons all-purpose flour
1 1/2	cups milk
1	teaspoon Worcestershire sauce
1/2	teaspoon salt
	Freshly ground pepper
1	cup chopped celery
4	ounces mushrooms, sliced
1	cup chopped yellow onion
1	cup chopped green bell pepper
3	cups cooked long-grain white rice (1 cup raw)
1	cup mayonnaise
1	pound small bay shrimp
1	pound crabmeat, flaked
1 1/2	cups grated Cheddar cheese

Preheat oven to 350°F. In a medium saucepan over medium heat, melt 3 tablespoons of the butter. Add flour and stir until bubbly. Add milk, Worcestershire, salt, and pepper to taste and stir until thickened, 2 to 3 minutes. Set aside.

In a medium skillet over medium heat, melt remaining 2 tablespoons of butter. Add celery, mushrooms, onion, and bell pepper and sauté until tender, about 5 minutes. Add to cream sauce in saucepan.

Put rice in a 3-quart casserole lightly coated with cooking spray or oil. Add mayonnaise, shrimp, crab, and the cream sauce and gently mix. Top with cheese and bake, uncovered, until bubbly, about 35 minutes.

SERVES 8

CRAB, SPINACH, AND NOODLE CASSEROLE

Layers of noodles, crab, spinach, and cheese meld into one terrific potluck casserole. "New" Waldorf Salad (page 120) and Lemon Flip with Fresh Raspberries (page 308) would be fine additions to the menu.

2 tablespoons butter or margarine

1/4 cup chopped onion

1 garlic clove, minced

2 tablespoons all-purpose flour

1 cup chicken broth

1 cup milk

1 tablespoon fresh lemon juice

1/2 teaspoon dried thyme

1/2 teaspoon salt

Freshly ground pepper

8 ounces egg noodles, cooked as directed on package and drained

1 package (10 ounces) frozen spinach, thawed and squeezed dry

2 cups small curd cottage cheese

8 ounces crabmeat, flaked

2 cups grated Monterey Jack cheese

Preheat oven to 350°F. In a medium skillet over medium heat, melt butter. Add onion and garlic and sauté until tender, about 5 minutes. Add flour and stir until bubbly. Add broth, milk, lemon juice, thyme, salt, and pepper to taste and stir until thickened, about 2 minutes.

In a 9-by-13-inch glass baking dish lightly coated with cooking spray or oil, layer half of the noodles, half of the spinach, 1 cup of the cottage cheese, half of the crab, half of the sauce from the skillet, and half of the Monterey Jack cheese. Repeat the layers, ending with Monterey Jack cheese. Bake, uncovered, until bubbly, about 35 minutes.

SERVES 6

SPRING CASSEROLE OF CRAB, ASPARAGUS, AND SPAGHETTI

Dungeness crab, the pride of the Northwest, is known for its sweet, succulent meat and delicate flavor. Make this elegant casserole in the spring, when fresh crab and asparagus are in season. Spinach and Strawberries with Candied Pecans and Raspberry–Poppy Seed Vinaigrette (page 84) would be a timely accompaniment for a delicious gourmet potluck.

1 cup spaghetti, broken into 2-inch pieces, cooked as directed on package, and drained

2 pounds asparagus, tough ends snapped off, and cut into 1-inch pieces (about 2 cups)

12 ounces crabmeat, flaked

Cheddar Cheese Sauce (facing page)

1/3 cup slivered almonds

Preheat oven to 350°F. In an 8-by-11½-inch glass baking dish lightly coated with cooking spray or oil, combine spaghetti, raw asparagus, and crab. Pour sauce over all and sprinkle with almonds. Bake, uncovered, until bubbly, about 30 minutes.

SERVES 4 TO 6

CHEDDAR CHEESE SAUCE

3	tablespoons butter or margarine
3	tablespoons all-purpose flour
1½	cups milk
½	teaspoon dry mustard
½	teaspoon paprika
¼	teaspoon salt
	Freshly ground pepper
¼	cup dry white wine
1	cup grated Cheddar cheese

In a medium saucepan over medium heat, melt butter. Add flour and stir until bubbly. Add milk, mustard, paprika, salt, and pepper to taste and stir until thickened, about 2 minutes. Add wine and cheese and stir until smooth, about 1 minute.

MAKES ABOUT 2 CUPS

CRAB AND SPINACH MANICOTTI WITH PARMESAN CHEESE SAUCE

In this version of manicotti, the shells are filled with a tasty mixture of crab, spinach, and cheese and topped with a Parmesan cheese sauce. This potluck dish goes well with Fruit Salad with Honey-Cream-Mint Dressing (page 127).

8 ounces crabmeat, flaked

1 package (10 ounces) frozen chopped spinach, thawed and squeezed dry

1 1/2 cups ricotta cheese or drained cottage cheese

1/4 cup freshly grated Parmesan cheese

1/2 cup chopped green onions, including some tender green tops

1 large egg, lightly beaten

3/4 teaspoon salt

Freshly ground pepper

12 manicotti shells, cooked as directed on package and drained

Parmesan Cheese Sauce (recipe follows)

Preheat oven to 350°F. In a medium bowl, combine crabmeat, spinach, cheeses, green onions, egg, salt, and pepper to taste and mix well.

With a spoon or with your fingers, fill shells and place in a 9-by-13-inch glass baking dish lightly coated with cooking spray or oil. Top with Parmesan Cheese Sauce. Bake, uncovered, until bubbly, about 40 minutes.

SERVES 8

PARMESAN CHEESE SAUCE

4 tablespoons butter or margarine

1/4 cup all-purpose flour

2 1/2 cups milk

1/4 cup dry white wine

1 cup grated Parmesan cheese

1/4 teaspoon salt

1/8 teaspoon white pepper

In a saucepan over medium heat, melt butter. Add flour and stir until bubbly. Add milk and wine and stir until thickened, about 2 minutes. Add cheese, salt, and pepper and whisk until sauce is smooth, about 2 minutes.

MAKES ABOUT 3 CUPS

MIXED SEAFOOD CASSEROLE

Seafood lovers will enjoy this casserole of brown rice and mushrooms with assorted seafoods and just a hint of curry. Start the potluck with Fresh Herbs and Walnut Dip (page 27) and end with Lemon Mousse with Blueberries (page 315) for a refreshing dessert.

3	tablespoons butter or margarine
1	cup chopped yellow onion
1	pound mushrooms, sliced
1	cup chopped celery
1	teaspoon curry powder
1	cup mayonnaise
1/2	cup sour cream
1/4	cup chopped fresh parsley
1	teaspoon Worcestershire sauce
1/2	teaspoon salt
	Freshly ground pepper
3	cups cooked long-grain brown rice (1 cup raw)
2	pounds assorted seafood and fish, such as scallops, crab, bay shrimp, and white-fleshed fish, cut into bite-sized pieces

Preheat oven to 350°F. In a large skillet over medium heat, melt butter. Add onion, mushrooms, and celery and sauté until tender, 6 to 7 minutes. Stir in curry.

In a small bowl, mix together mayonnaise, sour cream, parsley, Worcestershire, salt, and pepper to taste. Combine rice and seafood in a 3-quart casserole lightly coated with cooking spray or oil. Add vegetables and mayonnaise mixture and mix well. Bake, covered, until bubbly, 45 to 50 minutes. Stir before serving.

SERVES 6 TO 8

BAKED SEAFOOD AND ORZO CASSEROLE

Halibut and shrimp pair well in this Mediterranean-inspired dish, which also includes orzo and tomatoes. A sprinkling of blue cheese on top adds a tangy flavor. Serve this for a potluck dinner party along with Spinach Salad with Bacon, Avocados, and Warm Dressing (page 83).

1	tablespoon vegetable oil
1	cup chopped yellow onion
3	garlic cloves, minced
1	can (28 ounces) chopped tomatoes, with their juices
1/4	cup dry white wine
1	teaspoon sugar
1/2	teaspoon dried oregano
3/4	teaspoon salt
	Freshly ground pepper
1/2	cup orzo
1	pound halibut or other white-fleshed fish, cut into bite-sized pieces
12	ounces large shrimp (16 to 18), peeled and deveined
3	tablespoons chopped fresh parsley
4	ounces crumbled blue cheese

In a Dutch oven over medium heat, warm oil. Add onion and garlic and sauté until tender, about 5 minutes. Add tomatoes and juice, wine, sugar, oregano, salt, pepper to taste, and orzo. Simmer, uncovered, 10 minutes.

Preheat oven to 400°F. Fold fish, shrimp, and parsley into tomato and orzo mixture and bake, covered, until fish is white and shrimp are pink, about 10 minutes. Sprinkle with blue cheese and bake, uncovered, until bubbly, about 10 minutes longer.

SERVES 6 TO 8

TUNA-NOODLE CASSEROLE

This all-time favorite potluck casserole gets a simple white sauce instead of canned soup—better tasting and better for you. Water chestnuts are added for extra crunch. Oatmeal Cake (page 311) is a homey dessert to serve with this classic dish.

3	cups egg noodles, cooked as directed on package and drained
2	cans (6 ounces each) tuna in water, drained
1	can (6 ounces) sliced water chestnuts, drained
1	cup White Sauce (recipe follows)
3/4	cup grated Cheddar cheese

Preheat oven to 375°F. In a 2-quart casserole lightly coated with cooking spray or oil, mix together all ingredients, except cheese. Sprinkle cheese on top.

Bake, uncovered, until hot and bubbly, about 25 minutes.

SERVES 4

WHITE SAUCE

2	tablespoons butter or margarine
2	tablespoons all-purpose flour
1	cup milk
1/4	teaspoon salt
1/8	teaspoon white pepper

In a small saucepan over medium heat, melt butter. Add flour and stir until bubbly. Add milk, salt, and pepper and whisk constantly until thickened, 1 to 2 minutes.

MAKES ABOUT 1 CUP

SEAFOOD STEW

This stew, with its combination of four kinds of seafood, is one of the best. The full-flavored broth should be made a day ahead to develop the flavors. Add the seafood just before serving. For a great meal, include Citrus and Avocado Toss-Up (page 97) and baguette slices for dipping in the flavorful sauce.

6 slices bacon, diced

2 cups chopped yellow onion

1/2 cup chopped celery

2 garlic cloves, minced

3 cans (14 1/2 ounces each) whole tomatoes, with their juices, chopped

2 cups chicken broth

3/4 teaspoon salt

Freshly ground pepper

1 bay leaf

1 teaspoon dried basil

1/2 teaspoon dried thyme

1/2 teaspoon dried marjoram

1/8 teaspoon crushed saffron

1 cup dry white wine

1/4 cup chopped fresh parsley

1 pound snapper or other white-fleshed fish, cut into bite-sized pieces

1 1/2 pounds large shrimp (about 36), peeled and deveined

12 ounces shucked oysters, drained

1 can (6 1/2 ounces) chopped clams and juice

In a large Dutch oven over medium-high heat, cook bacon until crisp, about 5 minutes. Remove to a plate, leaving the drippings in the pan. Add onion, celery, and garlic and sauté until tender, about 5 minutes. Add tomatoes and juice, broth, salt, pepper to taste, bay leaf, basil, thyme, marjoram, saffron, and the bacon. Reduce heat to medium-low, cover, and simmer 20 minutes. Stir in wine and parsley and simmer, uncovered, 15 minutes longer. Discard bay leaf. (Recipe can be made up to this point several hours or 1 day ahead of time.) Add fish and seafood to hot broth and simmer, uncovered, until shrimp turn pink and fish flakes, about 10 minutes. Serve in large bowls.

SERVES 8

SCALLOPS, VEGETABLES, PANCETTA, AND LINGUINI

Tomatoes and pea pods combined with scallops make this a tricolor, showy dish. Serve it with Tossed Green Salad with Berries and Poppy Seed Dressing (page 92) and a good Chardonnay.

4 ounces pancetta or bacon, diced

4 green onions, including some tender green tops, sliced

2 garlic cloves, minced

4 ounces mushrooms, sliced

2 plum tomatoes, chopped

1/2 cup dry white wine

1/2 teaspoon salt

Freshly ground pepper

1 pound large scallops, rinsed and halved

8 ounces linguini, broken in half, cooked as directed on package, and drained

4 ounces sugar snap peas, trimmed and halved crosswise

1/2 cup grated Parmesan cheese

Preheat oven to 375°F. In a medium skillet over medium heat, cook pancetta until crisp, about 5 minutes. Transfer to a plate, leaving 1 tablespoon of drippings in the pan. Add onions, garlic, and mushrooms and sauté about 5 minutes. Stir in tomatoes and return pancetta to the skillet. Add wine, salt, and pepper to taste, stirring to blend well. Add scallops and bring mixture to a boil, stirring until scallops turn opaque, 3 to 4 minutes.

In a 3-quart casserole lightly coated with cooking spray or oil, combine scallop mixture with linguini and peas and mix well. Sprinkle with Parmesan cheese. Bake, uncovered, until heated through and flavors are blended, about 20 minutes.

SERVES 4

BAKED SALMON WITH CITRUS TOPPING

Present this classy dish of salmon topped with orange, lemon, and lime slices to the gourmet club. Serve with Romaine Salad with Marinated Tomatoes, Bacon, Green Onions, and Parmesan Cheese (page 80). For dessert, serve Pound Cake (page 316).

4 salmon fillets (about 1 pound each)

1 orange, peeled, white pith removed, and sliced

1 lemon, peeled, white pith removed, and sliced

1 lime, peeled, white pith removed, and sliced

1/2 cup (1 stick) butter

1 sweet white onion, sliced

1/2 cup brown sugar

2 cups orange juice

2 tablespoons cornstarch

1/4 cup soy sauce

1/4 cup white vinegar

Preheat oven to 400°F. Place salmon fillets, skin-side down, in a glass baking dish lightly coated with cooking spray or oil. Arrange orange, lemon, and lime slices on top of the salmon.

In a large skillet over medium heat, melt butter. Add onions and sauté until soft, about 5 minutes. Add brown sugar and cook 1 minute longer, stirring occasionally.

Add orange juice, cornstarch, soy sauce, and vinegar and stir constantly until thickened, about 2 minutes. Pour over the salmon and fruit. Bake, uncovered, until salmon is flaky, 15 to 18 minutes, or until salmon registers 145°F on an instant-read thermometer. To serve, remove salmon from skin with a spatula and cut into serving pieces.

SERVES 8

BAKED SALMON FILLETS
WITH CRUNCHY CASHEW COATING

Fresh salmon with a crunchy coating makes an appealing entrée for a potluck dinner party. Serve it with Cheese-Stuffed Zucchini (page 190) and Chocolate, Cranberry, and Ginger Trifle (page 318).

3	tablespoons butter or margarine, melted
1	tablespoon Dijon mustard
1	tablespoon honey
1/4	cup fine dry bread crumbs
1/4	cup finely chopped cashews
1/4	teaspoon dried thyme
3	salmon fillets (about 1 pound each)
	Salt and freshly ground pepper
	Lemon wedges for garnish

Preheat oven to 400°F. In a small bowl, mix together butter, mustard, and honey. On a piece of waxed paper, combine bread crumbs, cashews, and thyme. Place salmon in a 9-by-13-inch glass baking dish lightly coated with cooking spray or oil. Brush with butter mixture and season with salt and pepper to taste. Sprinkle the crumb mixture evenly over each fillet and pat down. Bake until fish flakes when tested with a fork, 15 to 18 minutes. Garnish with lemon wedges.

SERVES 6

CRAB AND SHRIMP CROISSANTS

These flaky croissants filled with a tasty combination of crab, shrimp, and cheese travel well to a tailgate or picnic. Make the filling ahead and keep it cold. The sandwiches are a favorite of my husband, Reed, who can eat several, so better double the recipe for the men in your party.

8 ounces crabmeat, flaked

4 ounces small cooked bay shrimp

1/2 cup grated Monterey Jack cheese

6 green onions, including some tender green tops, finely chopped

1 celery stalk, finely chopped

Dash of salt

1 teaspoon fresh lemon juice

2 drops of Tabasco sauce

1 tablespoon drained and chopped pimiento

1/2 cup mayonnaise, or more to your taste

6 croissants, split

In a medium bowl, mix together all ingredients, except croissants. Cover and refrigerate. Just before serving, fill croissants generously with filling.

SERVES 6

SEAFOOD QUICHE

A brunch potluck wouldn't be complete without a quiche. This one, made with a combination of crabmeat, shrimp, and mushrooms, is especially tasty. If you are short of time, you can use a purchased pie shell.

3	large eggs
1	cup cottage cheese
3/4	cup sour cream
1/2	cup freshly grated Parmesan cheese
3	green onions, including some tender green tops, cut up
2	tablespoons all-purpose flour
3 to 4	drops of Tabasco sauce
1 1/2	cups grated Monterey Jack cheese
3	ounces crabmeat, flaked
3	ounces small bay shrimp
4	ounces mushrooms, sliced
One	10-inch Flaky Pie Shell (page 301), baked for 8 minutes and cooled slightly

Preheat oven to 350°F. In a food processor, process eggs, cottage cheese, sour cream, Parmesan cheese, green onions, flour, and Tabasco until blended. Transfer to a medium bowl. Fold in half of the Monterey Jack cheese and all of the crab, shrimp, and mushrooms. Spoon mixture into pie shell and sprinkle with remaining Monterey Jack cheese. Bake until quiche is puffed and golden on top, 40 to 45 minutes. Let stand 5 minutes and cut into wedges to serve.

SERVES 6 TO 8

GRILLED MARINATED HALIBUT STEAKS
WITH SAUTÉED BELL PEPPERS

A summer potluck calls for an easy, carefree main dish. Halibut is so sweet and delicate, all it needs is a light marinade. Serve it on a bed of colorful sautéed peppers along with crusty bread and Fruit Bowl with Strawberry-Yogurt Dressing (page 129).

MARINADE

1/3	cup olive oil
2	tablespoons fresh lemon juice
1	teaspoon grated lemon zest
1	large garlic clove, minced
1	tablespoon chopped fresh thyme or 1 teaspoon dried thyme
1	tablespoon finely chopped fresh parsley
1	teaspoon salt
	Freshly ground pepper
6	halibut steaks (about 5 ounces each)
	Sautéed Bell Peppers (facing page)

In a shallow bowl, mix together marinade ingredients. Dip steaks in marinade and turn to coat. Put on a plate and let stand 10 minutes.

Prepare the grill for cooking over medium indirect heat. Grill halibut until it begins to flake, about 4 minutes on each side. Serve on a bed of Sautéed Bell Peppers.

SERVES 6

SAUTÉED BELL PEPPERS

2 tablespoons butter or margarine

2 tablespoons olive oil

2 red bell peppers, seeded and cut into 1/2-inch strips

1 green bell pepper, seeded and cut into 1/2-inch strips

1 yellow bell pepper, seeded and cut into 1/2-inch strips

1 large yellow onion, sliced and separated into rings

1/4 cup dry white wine

1 teaspoon dried thyme

1/2 teaspoon salt

Freshly ground pepper

In a large skillet over medium heat, melt butter with oil. Add bell peppers and onion, reduce heat to low, and cook, uncovered, until tender, about 15 minutes, stirring occasionally. Stir in wine, thyme, salt, and pepper to taste and cook, uncovered, about 5 minutes longer.

SERVES 6

OVERNIGHT SHRIMP AND CHEESE STRATA

For a festive brunch, feature this delicious entrée, which is assembled ahead of time. Serve it with Orange, Grapefruit, and Avocado Salad with Citrus Dressing (page 130) and warm scones.

6   slices day-old white bread, crusts trimmed, cut into 1-inch cubes (about 4 cups)

8   ounces small bay shrimp

2   cups packed grated Cheddar cheese

3   large eggs

2   tablespoons butter or margarine, melted

2   cups milk

1/2   teaspoon dry mustard

1/2   teaspoon salt

      Freshly ground pepper

In an 8-inch-square glass baking dish lightly coated with cooking spray or oil, layer half of the bread cubes, half of the shrimp, and half of the cheese. Repeat the layers. In a bowl, whisk together eggs, butter, milk, mustard, salt, and pepper to taste. Pour over bread, shrimp, and cheese mixture. Cover and refrigerate several hours or overnight.

Preheat oven to 350°F. Bring strata to room temperature before baking. Bake, uncovered, until firm and golden on top, about 50 minutes. Let stand 10 minutes, cut into squares, and serve.

SERVES 6

Variations: For a more savory dish, substitute 1 cup chopped ham or 1 1/2 cups cooked sausage for the shrimp.

Desserts are among the most popular potluck dishes, and they always disappear fast. If your name is at the end of the alphabet (like mine), you have probably been assigned to bring a dessert to just about every potluck. Some of my favorites are Best Strawberry Pie (page 300), Sour Cream Pumpkin Pie with Pecan Topping (page 304), Chocolate-Apple-Spice Cake (page 310), Walnut Brownies with Caramel Sauce and Ice Cream (page 317), and Apple-Berry Crisp (page 307).

In this chapter you will also find a selection of favorite cookies, like Snickerdoodles (page 323), the Ultimate Peanut Butter–Chocolate Chip Cookies (page 325), and Crispy Hazelnut Cookies (page 322). Serve one of these treats with homemade Banana-Citrus Ice Cream (page 329).

BEST STRAWBERRY PIE

Local berries in season are the juiciest, deliver the most flavor, and are well worth the wait. This wonderful pie will be the hit of the potluck.

2	tablespoons confectioners' sugar
One	9-inch Flaky Pie Shell (facing page), baked and cooled
4	cups fresh strawberries, hulled
1	cup granulated sugar
3	tablespoons cornstarch
1	tablespoon lemon juice
	Whipped Cream (facing page)

Sprinkle confectioners' sugar on pie crust and fill with 2 cups of the largest berries.

In a saucepan, crush remaining berries, then stir in granulated sugar and cornstarch. Cook over medium heat until mixture is thickened and clear, 8 to 10 minutes, stirring constantly. Add lemon juice, remove from heat, and cool slightly.

Pour berry mixture over berries in the pie shell. Cover and refrigerate 4 hours. Serve with Whipped Cream.

SERVES 6 TO 8

FLAKY PIE SHELL

This is a "no-guess" way to make a pie crust in a food processor. It is fast and easy and always a success. It will make a crust for a 9- or 10-inch pie.

1 1/2 cups all-purpose flour

1 tablespoon cold shortening, cut into small pieces

1/2 cup (1 stick) butter, frozen and cut into small pieces

1/4 teaspoon salt

1/4 cup cold water

Place all ingredients in a food processor and process until dough holds together and starts to form a ball, about 25 seconds. Do not overmix. Gather into a ball and shape into a 6-inch disk. Wrap in plastic wrap and chill in the refrigerator 1 hour or longer.

Preheat oven to 450°F. Place dough on a lightly floured surface and with a lightly floured rolling pin, roll dough from the center out to the edges, changing the direction with each roll, until the circle is 1/8 inch thick and about 1 inch larger than the pie plate. Fold the dough loosely in half and transfer to pie plate. Unfold and press gently against pie plate to remove air bubbles. Fold edge under and flute. Prick the bottom with a fork 5 or 6 times and bake until lightly browned, 12 to 15 minutes. Cool on a rack.

Note: If using pie shell for a quiche, do not prick. Bake 8 minutes at 450°F and cool slightly before adding the filling.

WHIPPED CREAM

2 cups whipping cream

2 tablespoons sugar

In a small bowl, with an electric mixer, whip cream until peaks form. Fold in sugar.

MAKES ABOUT 4 CUPS

STRAWBERRY-RHUBARB COBBLER

Rhubarb has a tart, tangy bite with a fruity aftertaste. It is too sour to eat raw and needs to be cooked with sugar. The season is short, so don't wait too long to make this dessert. Serve warm with ice cream for one of spring's special occasions.

4	cups strawberries, hulled and sliced
4	cups 3/4-inch chunks of rhubarb (about 1 3/4 pounds, see Note)
1	cup sugar
2	tablespoons quick-cooking tapioca or 1 tablespoon cornstarch
1/4	teaspoon ground cinnamon
1/4	teaspoon ground ginger
1/8	teaspoon ground nutmeg

TOPPING

1 1/2	cups all-purpose flour
1/4	cup sugar, plus extra for sprinkling on top
1 1/2	teaspoons baking powder
1/2	teaspoon baking soda
1/2	teaspoon salt
1/4	teaspoon ground cinnamon
2	tablespoons butter or margarine, cut into pieces
1	cup buttermilk

Preheat oven to 400°F. In a 10-inch pie plate 2 inches deep, stir together strawberries, rhubarb, sugar, tapioca, cinnamon, ginger, and nutmeg. Let stand 30 minutes.

To make the topping: In a medium bowl, stir together dry ingredients. With a pastry blender, cut in butter until mixture is crumbly. Stir in buttermilk and mix well.

Drop the topping by heaping tablespoonfuls in 8 portions over the filling and sprinkle with sugar.

Bake the pie 25 minutes. Reduce temperature to 350°F and bake until bubbly and lightly browned, about 20 minutes longer. If the topping becomes too brown, cover loosely with foil. Cool on a wire rack.

SERVES 6 TO 8

Note: If rhubarb is from the garden, discard the leaves; they are poisonous.

BLUEBERRY PIE

A combination of fresh and cooked blueberries is the secret to this delicious pie. Better make two for a Fourth of July potluck picnic. Include Grilled Chicken with Zesty Barbecue Sauce (page 275) and Picnic Potato Salad (page 61).

One   9-inch Flaky Pie Shell (page 301), baked and cooled

4   cups fresh blueberries or frozen blueberries, thawed and drained

1   cup sugar

3   tablespoons cornstarch

1/4   cup water

1/4   teaspoon salt

Dash of nutmeg

1   tablespoon fresh lemon juice

1   tablespoon butter

Whipped Cream (page 301; optional)

Vanilla ice cream for serving (optional)

Fill pie shell with 2 cups of the berries. In a saucepan over medium heat, combine remaining 2 cups berries, sugar, cornstarch, water, salt, nutmeg, and lemon juice. Bring to a boil over medium heat and cook, stirring constantly, until mixture thickens slightly and turns clear, 5 to 6 minutes. Remove from heat and stir in butter. Cool about 10 minutes, then pour mixture over the berries in the shell. Refrigerate several hours and serve chilled with Whipped Cream or vanilla ice cream, if desired.

SERVES 6

SOUR CREAM PUMPKIN PIE
WITH PECAN TOPPING

The addition of a crunchy pecan topping makes this pumpkin pie special. Bring it to a Thanksgiving potluck or any other fall or winter get-together.

1	cup packed brown sugar
1	tablespoon all-purpose flour
1	teaspoon ground cinnamon
1/2	teaspoon ground ginger
1/4	teaspoon ground nutmeg
1/4	teaspoon ground cloves
1/4	teaspoon salt
2	large eggs
1	can (15 ounces) canned pumpkin purée (not pumpkin-pie filling)
1/2	cup sour cream
1	cup evaporated milk
One	9-inch Flaky Pie Shell (page 301), unbaked

TOPPING

1/4	cup chopped pecans
1/4	cup packed dark brown sugar
1	tablespoon butter at room temperature

Preheat oven to 425°F. In a medium bowl, combine brown sugar, flour, spices, and salt. In another medium bowl, whisk eggs. Add pumpkin purée, sour cream, and evaporated milk to the eggs and mix well. Add dry ingredients to pumpkin mixture and whisk until smooth. Pour filling into pie shell and bake 15 minutes.

While the pie bakes, make the topping: In a small bowl, mix topping ingredients with a pastry blender, until crumbly. Sprinkle on top of pie after it has baked 15 minutes.

Reduce oven temperature to 350°F and bake pie until firm and a knife inserted in the center comes out clean, 40 to 45 minutes. If the edge of the pie crust becomes too brown, cover with a strip of foil. Cool on a rack and serve.

SERVES 6 TO 8

CRANBERRY-NUT CRUNCH

Canned cranberry sauce is the main ingredient in this easy recipe, which can be made in minutes. With its ruby color, it is a timely choice to take to a potluck during the holidays.

1 cup quick-cooking oats

1/2 cup all-purpose flour

1 cup packed light brown sugar

1/2 cup (1 stick) butter or margarine, cut into pieces

1 can (15 ounces) whole berry cranberry sauce, with juice

1/2 cup chopped walnuts

Vanilla ice cream for serving (optional)

Whipped Cream (optional; page 301)

Preheat oven to 350°F. Put oats, flour, brown sugar, and butter in a food processor and, using on/off pulses, process until mixture is crumbly. Alternately, put dry ingredients in a bowl and cut in the butter with a pastry blender.

Cover the bottom of an 8-inch-square glass baking dish lightly coated with cooking spray or oil with half of the crumb mixture. Spread cranberry sauce evenly on top. Add remaining crumb mixture and sprinkle with nuts. Bake until golden, about 40 minutes. Cool on a rack. Cut into squares and serve with ice cream or Whipped Cream, if desired.

SERVES 8 TO 10

SPICED APPLE CRISP

A change of season calls for this fall dessert of apples and spices. Serve it warm with vanilla ice cream or a wedge of sharp Cheddar cheese.

7 or 8 large baking apples, such as Golden Delicious, peeled, cored, and sliced

2 tablespoons fresh lemon juice

1/3 cup granulated sugar

1/2 teaspoon ground cinnamon

1/4 teaspoon ground nutmeg

1/4 teaspoon ground cloves

1/4 teaspoon ground allspice

TOPPING

1/2 cup firmly packed brown sugar

3/4 cup all-purpose flour

1/4 teaspoon salt

6 tablespoons butter

1/2 cup chopped walnuts

Vanilla ice cream for serving (optional)

Sharp Cheddar cheese slices for serving (optional)

Preheat oven to 375°F. Put apples in an 8-by-11¾-inch glass baking dish lightly coated with cooking spray or oil. Stir in lemon juice. In a small bowl, combine granulated sugar with spices and sprinkle over apples.

To make the topping: In a food processor, combine brown sugar, flour, salt, and butter. Using on/off pulses, process until crumbly. Alternately, put brown sugar, flour, and salt in a bowl and, using a pastry blender, cut in butter until crumbly. Stir in nuts.

Spread topping evenly over apples. Bake until apple mixture is bubbly and topping is lightly browned, about 40 minutes. Cool on a rack. Serve warm or cold with ice cream or Cheddar cheese, if desired.

SERVES 6

APPLE-BERRY CRISP

The contrasting flavors of apples, cranberries, and blueberries combine beautifully in this fall dessert. Fresh berries are always best, but both cranberries and blueberries freeze well and can be used year-round. Serve with Grilled Pork Chops with Dijon Baste (page 247).

4 large baking apples, such as Granny Smith, peeled, cored, and sliced (about 4 cups)

1 cup fresh cranberries or frozen cranberries, thawed

1 cup fresh blueberries or frozen blueberries, thawed

2 teaspoons fresh lemon juice

1 tablespoon all-purpose flour

1/3 cup granulated sugar

CRUMB-NUT TOPPING

1/2 cup quick-cooking oats

3/4 cup all-purpose flour

1/2 teaspoon ground cinnamon

1/2 cup packed brown sugar

6 tablespoons butter or margarine

1/2 cup chopped hazelnuts or walnuts

Vanilla ice cream for serving

Preheat oven to 350°F. In a large bowl, mix together apples, cranberries, blueberries, lemon juice, flour, and sugar. Transfer to a 9-by-13-inch glass baking dish.

To make the topping: In a food processor, combine oats, flour, cinnamon, brown sugar, and butter. Process with on/off pulses until mixture is crumbly. Alternately, combine oats, flour, cinnamon, and brown sugar in a bowl and, using a pastry blender, cut in butter until crumbly. Stir in nuts.

Spread the crumb topping evenly over the fruit in the baking dish and bake until bubbly, about 50 minutes. Serve warm with ice cream.

SERVES 6 TO 8

LEMON FLIP WITH FRESH RASPBERRIES

If you are hosting a small potluck dinner party at home, serve this refreshing dessert in individual glass bowls or large wine glasses. As the flip bakes, a sponge cake layer forms on top, while a lemon pudding lies underneath. Serve warm or at room temperature, topped with fresh raspberries or other berries.

3   large eggs, separated

1   cup sugar

1/4   cup all-purpose flour

1   cup milk

1/4   cup plus 1 tablespoon fresh lemon juice (about 2 large lemons)

     Fresh raspberries or other berries for garnish

Preheat oven to 350°F. In a medium bowl, with an electric mixer, beat egg whites until stiff. Set aside. In another medium bowl, beat egg yolks until thick and lemon colored, about 2 minutes. Beat in sugar, flour, milk, and lemon juice. Fold in egg whites.

Pour the egg and lemon mixture into an 8-inch-square baking dish. Place this dish in a larger shallow pan or baking dish containing about 1 inch of water. Bake until firm and top is golden, about 30 minutes. Remove from the pan holding the water and cool on a rack. Serve in small dessert bowls, garnished with fresh raspberries.

SERVES 6 TO 8

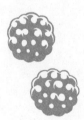

PINEAPPLE UPSIDE-DOWN CAKE

Upside-down cakes were originally baked in cast-iron skillets, but if you don't have one, an 8-inch-square glass baking dish will also work (see Note). You can make this cake any time of the year with canned pineapple.

3/4   cup (1 1/2 sticks) butter or margarine

3/4   cup packed brown sugar

6   slices fresh pineapple or canned pineapple, drained

1 1/2   cups all-purpose flour

1 1/2   teaspoons baking powder

1/2   teaspoon salt

3/4   cup granulated sugar

2   large eggs, lightly beaten

1   teaspoon vanilla extract

1/2   cup whole milk

1   cup Whipped Cream (page 301)

Preheat oven to 350°F. In a heavy 9- or 10-inch cast-iron skillet over medium heat, put ¼ cup of the butter and the brown sugar. Cook, stirring, until sugar dissolves and mixture is slightly caramelized, about 1 minute. Remove from heat. Arrange pineapple slices on top of sugar.

In a medium bowl, with an electric mixer, beat remaining ½ cup butter with flour, baking powder, salt, ¾ cup granulated sugar, eggs, vanilla, and milk for 1 minute on low. Then beat on high for 3 minutes more, scraping down bowl occasionally. Pour batter over the fruit in the skillet.

Bake the cake until a toothpick inserted in the center comes out clean, about 45 minutes. Immediately invert onto an ovenproof plate. Let skillet remain on top for a few seconds to allow cake to drop, then remove. Serve cake warm, topped with Whipped Cream.

SERVES 6 TO 8

Variation: For a different flavor, replace pineapple with fresh sliced pears, peaches, bananas, or mangos.

Note: If you are using an 8-inch-square glass baking dish, melt the butter with the sugar in the oven, stirring once. Then top with pineapple and proceed with recipe.

CHOCOLATE-APPLE-SPICE CAKE

This cake improves if it is made the day before serving. A slice of it is a taste treat bursting with different flavors. In one bite you taste the apples, in another the nuts or the chocolate chips. Top with vanilla ice cream for a heavenly dessert.

2 1/2	cups all-purpose flour
2 1/2	tablespoons unsweetened cocoa powder
1	teaspoon baking soda
1	teaspoon ground cinnamon
1/8	teaspoon ground cloves
1	teaspoon allspice
3	large eggs
2	cups sugar
1	cup (2 sticks) butter or margarine at room temperature, cut into chunks
1/2	cup water
1/2	cup chocolate chips
2	Granny Smith apples, cored, peeled, and diced
1	cup finely chopped walnuts
2	teaspoons vanilla extract

Preheat oven to 325°F. On a piece of waxed paper, combine flour, cocoa, baking soda, cinnamon, cloves, and allspice and set aside. In a medium bowl, with an electric mixer, beat together eggs and sugar until fluffy. Add butter and water and beat until well blended. Add dry ingredients to creamed mixture and mix well. Fold in chocolate chips, apples, nuts, and vanilla. The batter will be thick.

Spoon batter into a 10-inch Bundt pan lightly coated with cooking spray or oil and floured. Bake until a toothpick inserted in the center comes out clean, about 1 hour. Cool in pan on a rack about 1 hour. With a knife, loosen around the edges and invert onto a plate. When completely cooled, cover tightly or wrap in foil to store.

SERVES 10 TO 12

OATMEAL CAKE

Rediscover this moist and tender cake with a broiled, crunchy nut topping that has been a favorite for years. Take it to your next church potluck and it won't last long.

CAKE

1	cup uncooked quick-cooking oats
1 1/2	cups boiling water
1 1/2	cups all-purpose flour
1	teaspoon baking soda
1	teaspoon ground cinnamon
1/8	teaspoon ground nutmeg
1/4	teaspoon salt
1/2	cup (1 stick) butter or margarine at room temperature, cut into pieces
1/2	cup granulated sugar
1/2	cup packed brown sugar
2	large eggs
1	teaspoon vanilla extract

TOPPING

4	tablespoons butter or margarine, melted
1/3	cup packed brown sugar
2	tablespoons milk
1/2	cup chopped walnuts or pecans
1/2	cup sweetened shredded coconut
1/2	teaspoon vanilla extract

Put oats in a medium bowl. Pour boiling water over and stir. Cover and let stand 20 minutes. Uncover and let stand 10 minutes longer.

Preheat oven to 350°F. On a piece of waxed paper, combine flour, baking soda, cinnamon, nutmeg, and salt. In a large bowl, using an electric mixer, cream the butter with the granulated sugar and brown sugar. Add eggs, one at a time, beating well after each addition. Stir in oatmeal and vanilla by hand. Stir dry ingredients into the batter and blend.

Pour the batter into an 8-inch-square glass baking dish lightly coated with cooking spray or oil. Bake until a toothpick inserted in the center comes out clean, about 40 minutes.

While the cake is baking, stir together all topping ingredients. Spread topping on cake when it is done.

Preheat the broiler and broil the cake until the topping is golden and bubbly, 2 to 3 minutes. Be careful not to burn it. Cool in the pan on a rack and cut into squares.

SERVES 12

CARROT CAKE

This moist, spicy cake shows up at almost every potluck or picnic. It can be made a day ahead, and, in fact, the flavor will improve. For a fresh taste treat, use grated nutmeg. It's fun and smells great.

1½ cups sugar

3 large eggs

1 cup vegetable oil

1 teaspoon vanilla extract

2 cups all-purpose flour

1½ teaspoons ground cinnamon

1 teaspoon baking soda

¼ teaspoon salt

¼ teaspoon freshly grated or ground nutmeg

3 cups grated carrots (5 to 6 medium carrots)

½ cup chopped walnuts

Cream Cheese Frosting (recipe follows)

Preheat oven to 350°F. In a large bowl, with an electric mixer, beat sugar, eggs, and oil for 1 minute. Add vanilla, flour, cinnamon, baking soda, salt, and nutmeg and beat 1 minute longer. Fold in carrots and nuts.

Pour batter into a 9-by-13-inch baking pan lightly coated with cooking spray or oil. Bake until a toothpick inserted in the center comes out clean, 40 to 45 minutes. Cool cake in the baking pan on a rack. Spread with frosting.

SERVES ABOUT 18

CREAM CHEESE FROSTING

1 package (8 ounces) cream cheese at room temperature

1 tablespoon milk

1 tablespoon orange juice

1 teaspoon vanilla extract

4 cups confectioners' sugar

In a medium bowl, combine cream cheese, milk, orange juice, and vanilla. With an electric mixer, beat on low speed until smooth. Gradually beat in sugar, 1 cup at a time, until smooth and spreadable.

MAKES ENOUGH FOR ONE 9-BY-13-INCH CAKE OR ONE 2-LAYER CAKE

REUNION CHOCOLATE CAKE

This is an all-time favorite chocolate cake that goes to the Vollstedt family reunion every year. It is easy to transport, easy to serve, and will accommodate a large crowd.

1	cup water
1	cup (2 sticks) butter, cut into pieces
1/4	cup unsweetened cocoa
2	cups all-purpose flour
2	cups sugar
1	teaspoon baking soda
1	teaspoon baking powder
1/2	teaspoon ground cinnamon
2	large eggs
1/2	cup buttermilk
1	teaspoon vanilla extract
	Cocoa Frosting (recipe follows)
1	cup chopped walnuts (optional)

Preheat oven to 350°F. In a small saucepan over medium heat, bring water, butter, and cocoa to a boil. Stir until blended and set aside to cool.

In a large bowl, stir together flour, sugar, baking soda, baking powder, and cinnamon. Stir cocoa mixture into flour mixture and, with an electric mixer, beat until smooth. Add eggs, buttermilk, and vanilla and beat 1 minute longer.

Pour batter into a lightly buttered 12-by-15½-by-1½-inch jelly-roll pan. Bake until a toothpick inserted into the center of cake comes out clean, about 30 minutes. Cool cake in the pan on a rack. Ice with Cocoa Frosting and sprinkle with nuts, if desired.

SERVES 36

COCOA FROSTING

1/2	cup (1 stick) butter, cut into pieces
1/4	cup unsweetened cocoa
1/4	cup milk
1	teaspoon vanilla extract
4	cups confectioners' sugar

In a medium saucepan over medium heat, stir together butter, cocoa, milk, and vanilla until butter is melted and ingredients are well blended. Do not boil. Remove from heat and, with an electric mixer, beat in confectioners' sugar, 1 cup at a time, until smooth and spreadable.

MAKES ENOUGH FOR 1 SHEET CAKE

CHOCOLATE PUDDING CAKE

As this irresistible dessert bakes, like magic, a pudding forms on the bottom, beneath the cake layer. Serve in bowls topped with Whipped Cream. Kids love this dessert.

3/4   **cup all-purpose flour**

3/4   **cup granulated sugar**

1 1/2   **teaspoons baking powder**

1/2   **teaspoon baking soda**

1/4   **teaspoon salt**

3/4   **cup unsweetened cocoa**

1/2   **cup milk**

3   **tablespoons butter or margarine, melted**

1   **teaspoon vanilla extract**

1/2   **cup packed brown sugar**

1 3/4   **cups boiling water**

Whipped Cream (page 301) for topping

Chopped walnuts for sprinkling on top

Preheat oven to 350°F. In a medium bowl, mix together flour, granulated sugar, baking powder, baking soda, salt, and ⅓ cup of the cocoa. In a small bowl, combine milk, butter, and vanilla. Stir into dry ingredients until just blended. The batter will be thick. Turn batter into an 8-inch-square baking pan lightly coated with cooking spray or oil.

In another small bowl, combine brown sugar and remaining cocoa. Sprinkle evenly over batter and pour boiling water over all. Do not stir. Bake until the top is firm, about 30 minutes. Cool slightly. Spoon into bowls and serve warm with Whipped Cream and a sprinkling of nuts.

SERVES 8

LEMON MOUSSE WITH BLUEBERRIES

This light, creamy dessert with an intense lemon flavor is made with yogurt instead of whipped cream. Served in sherbet dishes and topped with blueberries, it makes an attractive presentation for a garden potluck party. The Lemon Curd is also delicious on scones. It needs to be made 2 or 3 hours before the dessert is assembled.

1 container (8 ounces) plain nonfat yogurt

Lemon Curd (recipe follows)

1 cup blueberries

Drain off any liquid that has accumulated on top of yogurt. In a medium bowl, mix yogurt and Lemon Curd. Spoon mixture into 6 sherbet dishes or stemmed goblets. Cover and refrigerate several hours. Sprinkle berries on top of mousse just before serving.

SERVES 6

LEMON CURD

2 large eggs

1/2 cup sugar

3 tablespoons fresh lemon juice, strained

1 teaspoon grated lemon zest

4 tablespoons butter (no substitutes) at room temperature, cut into small pieces

In a medium stainless-steel saucepan, whisk eggs, sugar, and lemon juice until light in color. Stir in lemon zest and butter. Cook over medium-low or low heat, whisking constantly, until mixture thickens to a pudding consistency, about 8 minutes. Transfer to a small bowl. Cover with plastic wrap and chill 2 or 3 hours. If you are using as a spread, serve cold.

MAKES ABOUT 1 2/3 CUPS

POUND CAKE

This pound cake has a light, firm texture that makes a perfect base for fresh fruit or ice cream and toppings. Serve with Four-Peppercorn Pork Loin Roast (page 238) and Spinach, Arugula, Mushroom, and Red Onion Salad with Anchovy-Garlic Dressing (page 86) at a couples' dinner-club potluck.

3	cups all-purpose flour
1	teaspoon baking powder
1/4	teaspoon salt
2 3/4	cups sugar
1 1/2	cups (3 sticks) butter at room temperature, cut into pieces
5	large eggs
1	teaspoon vanilla extract
1	cup whole milk
1	tablespoon orange juice
	Fresh seasonal berries of your choice for serving
	Cream Cheese Topping (recipe follows; optional)
	Caramel Sauce (facing page; optional)
	Vanilla ice cream for serving (optional)

Preheat oven to 325°F. On a piece of waxed paper, combine flour, baking powder, and salt. In a large bowl, with an electric mixer, beat sugar, butter, eggs, and vanilla on low speed for 30 seconds, scraping down sides of the bowl. Beat on high speed until creamy, about 5 minutes more. Beat flour mixture into butter and egg mixture on low speed, alternating with milk, until blended, scraping down sides of the bowl several times. Add orange juice and mix well. Turn into a well-oiled and floured Bundt pan.

Bake the cake until the top is golden and a toothpick inserted in the center comes out clean, about 1 hour and 15 minutes. Remove cake from oven and cool in the pan for 20 minutes. Remove from pan and serve with desired toppings

SERVES 8 TO 10

CREAM CHEESE TOPPING

1	package (8 ounces) cream cheese at room temperature, cut into chunks
1/4	cup chopped walnuts
2	tablespoons milk
1	tablespoon honey

In a food processor, blend all ingredients until smooth.

MAKES ABOUT 1/2 CUP

WALNUT BROWNIES WITH CARAMEL SAUCE AND ICE CREAM

No need to use a mix when you can make these delicious, light, chewy brownies just about as fast. Cocoa packs a lot of flavor but has less fat than solid chocolate. Serve this warm with vanilla ice cream and Caramel Sauce.

1	cup (2 sticks) butter
1/3	cup unsweetened cocoa
2	cups sugar
4	large eggs
1	cup all-purpose flour
1/2	teaspoon baking powder
1	teaspoon vanilla extract
1/2	cup coarsely chopped walnuts
	Vanilla ice cream for serving
	Caramel Sauce (recipe follows)

Preheat oven to 350°F. In a small saucepan over medium heat, melt butter. Add cocoa and mix well. Add sugar and stir until dissolved and mixture is well blended. Transfer to a bowl. Add eggs, one at a time, and with an electric mixer, beat well after each addition. Beat in flour, baking powder, and vanilla. Fold in nuts and pour into a 9-by-13-inch baking pan lightly coated with cooking spray or oil. Bake until a toothpick inserted in the center comes out clean, 35 to 40 minutes.

Remove from oven and let stand on a wire rack 10 minutes. Cut into 2-inch squares and remove brownies from pan while warm. Place on a rack to cool. Serve, topped with ice cream and Caramel Sauce.

MAKES ABOUT 15 SQUARES

Variation: To give brownies a Mexican flavor, add 1 teaspoon ground cinnamon to the batter.

CARAMEL SAUCE

1 1/4	cup packed brown sugar
1/2	cup (1 stick) butter
1/2	cup whipping cream

In a heavy saucepan over medium heat, whisk brown sugar and butter until butter melts, about 3 minutes. Add cream and whisk until sugar dissolves and sauce is smooth, about 2 minutes longer. Reheat before serving.

MAKES ABOUT 2 CUPS

CHOCOLATE, CRANBERRY, AND GINGER TRIFLE

This party dessert takes time but is well worth the effort, and your guests will be impressed. Make the fillings ahead and refrigerate before assembling. Then refrigerate the finished trifle for at least 4 hours before serving.

1 1/2   cups whipping cream

1   tablespoon sugar

One   10 3/4-ounce frozen pound cake, thawed

3   tablespoons Grand Marnier liqueur

Cranberry Filling (facing page)

Chocolate Pudding (facing page)

1   tablespoon grated orange zest

In a small bowl, whip cream with sugar until it holds soft peaks. To assemble the trifle: Cut cake into 16 slices and quarter each slice. Cover the bottom of a 3-quart trifle bowl with a single layer of cake pieces, turning crusts away from sides of bowl. Sprinkle cake with 1 tablespoon Grand Marnier. With a slotted spoon, spread about 1 cup cold Cranberry Filling over cake, extending it to the sides. Spread 2/3 cup cold Chocolate Pudding over Cranberry Filling, all the way to the sides of bowl. Layer cake, Grand Marnier, Cranberry Filling, and Chocolate Pudding two more times. Spread whipped cream over top of the trifle, building up the edges and leaving an indentation in the middle. Fill the middle with remaining Cranberry Filling (there will be some juice left), and sprinkle with orange zest.

Cover and chill at least 4 hours. Serve in glass bowls.

SERVES 8

CRANBERRY FILLING

- **2** packages (12 ounces each) fresh cranberries (8 cups) or frozen cranberries, thawed, rinsed, and drained
- **1 3/4** cups granulated sugar
- **1 3/4** cups orange juice
- **1** teaspoon grated orange zest
- **1/2** cup chopped crystallized ginger (see Note)

In a saucepan over high heat, combine all ingredients, except crystallized ginger, and bring to a boil. Reduce heat to medium and cook until cranberries begin to pop, about 5 minutes, stirring occasionally. Stir in ginger and mix well. Cover and refrigerate until cold and slightly thickened, about 3 hours.

MAKES ABOUT 4 CUPS

Note: Crystallized ginger has been cooked in a sugar syrup and coated with sugar. It can be purchased in most supermarkets.

CHOCOLATE PUDDING

- **2** large egg yolks
- **1/2** cup sugar
- **1/3** cup unsweetened cocoa
- **2** tablespoons cornstarch
- **1/4** teaspoon salt
- **2** cups half-and-half or milk
- **2** tablespoons butter at room temperature
- **1** tablespoon Grand Marnier liqueur

In a medium bowl, beat egg yolks lightly and set aside.

In a medium saucepan over medium-high heat, mix sugar, cocoa, cornstarch, and salt. Slowly stir in half-and-half. Cook, stirring constantly, until mixture boils and thickens, about 5 minutes. Then boil, continuing to stir, 1 minute longer. Slowly stir one third of the hot mixture into the egg yolks, then return this mixture to the pan. Reduce heat to medium and continue to boil, stirring constantly, 1 minute. Remove from heat and stir in butter and Grand Marnier. Cover with a piece of plastic wrap and refrigerate until cold, about 4 hours.

MAKES ABOUT 2 CUPS

CHEESECAKE BARS

These bars impart the same flavor as a cheesecake but are easier to make. Remember them when you need a dessert in a hurry for an impromptu potluck or for unexpected guests.

1/3 cup packed brown sugar

1 cup all-purpose flour

1/2 cup walnut halves

6 tablespoons butter, cut into pieces

12 ounces cream cheese, cut into pieces

1/3 cup granulated sugar

1 large egg

2 tablespoons fresh lemon juice

1 teaspoon grated lemon zest

1 teaspoon vanilla extract

Preheat oven to 350°F. In a food processor, combine brown sugar, flour, nuts, and butter. Process with on/off pulses until crumbly. Alternately, combine brown sugar and flour in a bowl and, using a pastry blender, cut in butter until crumbly. Stir in nuts. Set aside 1 cup for topping. Press remaining crumb mixture into a buttered 8-inch-square baking pan. Bake until set, about 10 minutes.

Meanwhile, in a medium bowl, with an electric mixer, beat cream cheese, granulated sugar, egg, lemon juice, zest, and vanilla until fluffy, about 1 minute. Pour on top of crust and spread filling with a spatula to the edges of the baking pan. Sprinkle the reserved crumb mixture on top and gently pat down with the back of a spoon. Bake until top is golden, about 30 minutes. Cool on a rack and cut into bars. Store, covered, in the refrigerator. Do not freeze.

MAKES ABOUT 16 BARS

BUTTERSCOTCH–CHOCOLATE CHIP BARS

In an updated version of an old favorite, these "blondies" are studded with chocolate and butterscotch chips. Just the right treat for a business meeting or some hungry children.

4	tablespoons butter or margarine
1	cup packed brown sugar
1	teaspoon vanilla extract
1	large egg
3/4	cup all-purpose flour
1	teaspoon baking powder
1/4	teaspoon salt
1/2	cup semisweet chocolate chips
1/2	cup butterscotch chips

Preheat oven to 350°F. In a medium saucepan over medium-low heat, melt butter and remove from heat. Add brown sugar, vanilla, and egg and mix well. Stir in flour, baking powder, and salt. Cool slightly, then stir in chocolate and butterscotch chips. Spread into an 8-inch-square baking pan lightly coated with cooking spray or oil. Bake until a toothpick inserted in the center comes out clean, about 30 minutes. Cool slightly on a rack and cut into squares while still warm.

MAKES 16 ABOUT BARS

CRISPY HAZELNUT COOKIES

These cookies are by far the most delicate and delicious I've ever eaten. I have a friend who can eat the whole batch at one sitting. I doubled the recipe so that it will make enough for a potluck.

1	cup all-purpose flour
1/4	teaspoon ground cinnamon
	Dash of salt
1	cup (2 sticks) butter or margarine at room temperature
1/2	cup sugar
1	teaspoon vanilla extract
1	cup coarsely chopped toasted hazelnuts (see Note on page 89)

On a piece of waxed paper, mix flour, cinnamon, and salt. In a medium bowl, with an electric mixer, beat butter, sugar, and vanilla until fluffy, about 3 minutes. By hand, stir in the flour mixture and then the nuts. The dough will be stiff. Form the dough into two 9-inch-long logs and wrap in plastic wrap. Chill several hours or overnight. (The logs can be frozen for up to 4 weeks.)

Preheat oven to 350°F. Unwrap dough and cut into ⅜-inch slices. Arrange slices about 1 inch apart on ungreased or parchment-lined baking sheets. Bake until lightly browned, about 20 minutes. Cool on the baking sheet 5 minutes, then transfer to wire racks to cool completely. Store in an airtight container.

MAKES ABOUT 4 DOZEN COOKIES

SNICKERDOODLES

These crinkly cookies originated in England in the nineteenth century. The name doesn't have any special meaning—it's just whimsical and fun. Kids love these, and so do adults.

2 1/2   cups all-purpose flour

2   teaspoons cream of tartar

1   teaspoon baking soda

1/4   teaspoon salt

1   cup (2 sticks) butter or margarine or 1 cup shortening

1 3/4   cups sugar

2   large eggs

1   tablespoon ground cinnamon

Preheat oven to 400°F. On a piece of waxed paper, combine flour, cream of tartar, baking soda, and salt. In a large bowl, with an electric mixer, beat butter and 1 1/2 cups of the sugar. Add eggs, one at a time, and beat until fluffy. Stir dry ingredients on waxed paper into butter mixture by hand and mix well. Dough will be stiff.

Shape dough into 1-inch balls by rolling it between the palms of your hands. In a small dish, combine remaining 1/4 cup sugar and the cinnamon. Roll balls in sugar mixture and place 2 1/2 inches apart on an ungreased or parchment-lined baking sheet. Bake until golden, 8 to 10 minutes. Let cookies remain on baking sheet until firm, about 1 minute. Transfer to a rack to cool. Store in an airtight container.

MAKES ABOUT 3 1/2 DOZEN COOKIES

CHOCOLATE-GINGER COOKIES

These spicy cookies with the subtle flavor of molasses are just right for a fall potluck gathering. They are so good, you may want to double the recipe. Serve with cider for a Halloween party.

3/4 cup (1 1/2 sticks) butter or margarine

1 cup, plus 3 tablespoons sugar

1 large egg

1/4 cup light molasses

2 cups all-purpose flour

1/4 cup unsweetened cocoa

1 1/2 teaspoons baking soda

2 teaspoons ground ginger

1/4 teaspoon salt

Preheat oven to 350°F. In a medium bowl, with an electric mixer, cream butter. Gradually add 1 cup of the sugar and beat until light and fluffy. Add the egg and beat well. Stir in molasses, flour, cocoa, baking soda, ginger, and salt by hand and mix well. Refrigerate 30 minutes for easier handling.

Place remaining 3 tablespoons sugar on a plate. Shape dough into 1-inch balls by rolling it between the palms of your hands, and roll the balls in sugar. Place 2 inches apart on an ungreased or parchment-lined cookie sheet. Bake until cookies are light brown, about 12 minutes, and transfer to a rack to cool. Store in an airtight container.

MAKES ABOUT 3 DOZEN COOKIES

THE ULTIMATE PEANUT BUTTER–CHOCOLATE CHIP COOKIES

Cookies are so portable, they are great to take to a potluck meeting. Here is a favorite cookie recipe with chocolate chips added to make them twice as good.

1 1/2	cups all-purpose flour
1/2	teaspoon baking soda
1/4	teaspoon salt
1/2	cup (1 stick) butter or margarine, cut into pieces
1/2	cup peanut butter (crunchy or smooth)
1	cup packed brown sugar
1	large egg
1/2	teaspoon vanilla extract
3/4	cup semisweet chocolate chips
	Granulated sugar for topping cookies

On a piece of waxed paper, mix flour, soda, and salt. In a medium bowl, with an electric mixer, beat butter, peanut butter, brown sugar, egg, and vanilla until well blended. Stir dry ingredients into butter mixture by hand and mix thoroughly. Stir in the chocolate chips. Cover the dough and refrigerate 30 minutes for easier handling.

Preheat oven to 375°F. Form dough into 1 1/4-inch balls by rolling it between the palms of your hands and place 2 inches apart on an ungreased or parchment-lined baking sheet. Flatten with the tines of a fork dipped in granulated sugar to form a crisscross pattern on top. Bake until lightly browned, 10 to 12 minutes. Store in an airtight container.

MAKES ABOUT 2 1/2 DOZEN COOKIES

LEMON DROP COOKIES

If you're in charge of refreshments for a PTA or business meeting, offer these light, elegant cookies. They also make a great finale after Seafood Stew (page 290), served with Banana-Citrus Ice Cream (page 329). Transport in a single layer on a large platter to prevent sticking.

2 2/3	cups all-purpose flour
1/2	teaspoon baking powder
1	teaspoon baking soda
1/2	teaspoon salt
1/2	cup (1 stick) butter or margarine
1 1/2	cups sugar
2	large eggs
1	cup light sour cream
1	teaspoon grated lemon zest
1	tablespoon fresh lemon juice
	Lemon Frosting (recipe follows)

Preheat oven to 375°F. On a piece of waxed paper, combine flour, baking powder, baking soda, and salt. In a large bowl, with an electric mixer, cream butter and sugar until fluffy. Beat in eggs, one at a time. Add flour mixture and sour cream to egg mixture in thirds, alternating between the two and beating well after each addition. Stir in lemon zest and lemon juice. Drop by heaping tablespoons, 1½ inches apart, onto an ungreased or parchment-lined baking sheet.

Bake the cookies until lightly browned, about 10 minutes. Remove and cool on a wire rack. Ice with Lemon Frosting.

MAKES ABOUT 4 DOZEN COOKIES

LEMON FROSTING

6	tablespoons butter
2 1/2	cups confectioners' sugar
1	tablespoon fresh lemon juice
1/2	teaspoon vanilla extract
	Water as needed

In a medium saucepan over medium heat, melt butter. Stir in sugar, lemon juice, and vanilla. Add only enough water to make frosting spreadable.

MAKES ENOUGH TO FROST 4 DOZEN COOKIES

ICEBOX COOKIES

These old-fashioned cookies, sometimes called refrigerator cookies, will bring back childhood memories. The dough needs to be made and then frozen a day in advance for easy slicing. Keep the bars frozen up to 4 weeks and use as needed. This recipe makes a lot of cookies.

1   cup (2 sticks) butter at room temperature, cut into pieces

1   cup (2 sticks) margarine at room temperature, cut into pieces

1   cup granulated sugar

1   cup packed brown sugar

3   large eggs

4   cups all-purpose flour

1/2 teaspoon salt

1   cup chopped walnuts

1   teaspoon vanilla extract

In a large bowl, with an electric mixer, cream together butter, margarine, and both sugars until fluffy. Add eggs, one at time, beating well after each addition. With a large spoon, stir in flour, salt, nuts, and vanilla and mix well (it will take a long time). The dough will be soft and sticky.

Chill dough in refrigerator 30 minutes for easier handling. Divide dough into 3 equal portions and place each one onto a 12-by-14-inch piece of waxed paper. With wet hands, form each portion into a 1½-by-12-inch log. Smooth the top of each roll with your hand, wrap in waxed paper, and freeze at least 8 hours or overnight.

Preheat oven to 400°F. Remove logs from freezer and let stand about 5 minutes before slicing. Cut into slices ¼ inch thick and arrange ½ inch apart on an ungreased or parchment-lined baking sheet. Bake until lightly browned, 10 to 12 minutes. Cool on a wire rack. Store in an airtight container.

MAKES ABOUT 9 DOZEN COOKIES

SUGAR COOKIES

Need a sugar fix? These rich, crisp cookies almost melt in your mouth, they are so good. Easy to make, too. Serve with tea or coffee for an afternoon get-together.

1/2 cup (1 stick) butter at room temperature, cut into pieces

1 cup sugar, plus extra for topping cookies

1 large egg

2 1/2 cups plus 2 tablespoons all-purpose flour

1 teaspoon baking soda

1/2 teaspoon salt

1 teaspoon cream of tartar

1/2 cup vegetable oil

1 teaspoon vanilla extract

Preheat oven to 350°F. In a large bowl, with an electric mixer, cream together butter and I cup of the sugar. Add egg and beat until fluffy. Beat in all remaining ingredients.

Form dough into I-inch balls by rolling it between the palms of your hands and arrange 2 inches apart on an ungreased or parchment-lined baking sheet. Place some sugar on a piece of waxed paper. Using a drinking glass, dip bottom of glass in sugar. Press each cookie flat and repeat, dipping the glass in the sugar each time before pressing.

Bake until golden, 12 to 15 minutes. Remove to wire rack to cool. Store in a covered container at room temperature up to I week.

MAKES ABOUT 4 DOZEN COOKIES

BANANA-CITRUS ICE CREAM

Homemade ice cream is a must for a Fourth of July potluck or any picnic. This mellow ice cream has a sweet but tart flavor—forget the calories and enjoy! Serve with Snickerdoodles (page 323).

1 cup whipping cream

2 cups half-and-half

1 1/2 cups sugar

1 cup orange juice

3 tablespoons fresh lemon juice

1 ripe banana, mashed

Combine all ingredients in a bowl. Freeze in an ice-cream maker according to manufacturer's directions.

SERVES 6 TO 8

INDEX

TABLE OF EQUIVALENTS

The exact equivalents in the following tables have been rounded for convenience.

LIQUID/DRY MEASURES

U.S.	METRIC
1/4 teaspoon	1.25 milliliters
1/2 teaspoon	2.5 milliliters
1 teaspoon	5 milliliters
1 tablespoon (3 teaspoons)	15 milliliters
1 fluid ounce (2 tablespoons)	30 milliliters
1/4 cup	60 milliliters
1/3 cup	80 milliliters
1/2 cup	120 milliliters
1 cup	240 milliliters
1 pint (2 cups)	480 milliliters
1 quart (4 cups, 32 ounces)	960 milliliters
1 gallon (4 quarts)	3.84 liters
1 ounce (by weight)	28 grams
1 pound	454 grams
2.2 pounds	1 kilogram

LENGTH

U.S.	METRIC
1/8 inch	3 millimeters
1/4 inch	6 millimeters
1/2 inch	12 millimeters
1 inch	2.5 centimeters

OVEN TEMPERATURE

FAHRENHEIT	CELSIUS	GAS
250	120	1/2
275	140	1
300	150	2
325	160	3
350	180	4
375	190	5
400	200	6
425	220	7
450	230	8
475	240	9
500	260	10